Creating a Cash Cow in Kenya

Adventures in Starting a Social Business and Living in Africa

Nat Robinson

This book is dedicated to Ouida Wingerter and my parents, Jim and Dianne. Thanks for all the love and support.

Contents

Foreword

Perusing the business section in a bookstore, I noted that plenty of wonderful books exist about the social enterprise industry. However most are told by the investors, journalists or by academics. The only exception was Jessica Jackley's recent book, *Clay Water Brick*, which documents the world-changing experience of starting Kiva.org. I also found very few business self-help books published in the last five years from authors outside the tech and internet businesses. I have the utmost respect for any entrepreneur and especially those who can master complex industries, such as those in software and online retail. Perhaps the old "bricks and mortar" business story which takes ten years to reach a valuation of $100 million is not as exciting in a time when an entrepreneur can quickly create hundreds of millions of dollars in two years or less. I thought it might be more helpful to find a book about a business that was not started by a technology prodigy or an Ivy League graduate. Perhaps I was just looking in the wrong place. I know there are plenty of entrepreneurs out there with fantastic stories, but I could not find their books. This story will hopefully fill some of those gaps not covered by the numerous other business books especially in the realm of social businesses and impact investing.

I struggled regularly in starting and running a company in Kenya. I made ridiculous mistakes along the way and learned hard lessons. But an aspiring entrepreneur should not have to go through all the drama that I did in securing funding and growing a business. There must be a better way. The goal of this book and its collection of stories is to offer some semblance of advice to entrepreneurs, so they do not repeat the same mistakes when starting a business.

It tells the story of the six years I spent living in Kenya and of starting a social business to help rural smallholder farmers get themselves out of poverty. To keep readers from completely falling asleep, I have added stories about my adventures as an expat in Kenya. I want to tell the wonderful story of life in Kenya and all the exciting adventures waiting for anyone willing to take the chance. I hope to dispel some of the myths of Nairobi's dangers. Like any major city, crime happens. Those who can do their best to avoid trouble generally do. Airport fires, terrorist attacks, muggings, carjackings, Ebola outbreaks and rhino tramplings can happen anywhere. People also get hurt from slipping and falling in their bathtubs. The benefits of living a life outside the comfort zone far outweigh the risks (which are usually exaggerated in the media). As the old saying goes: "A ship in harbor is safe, but that is not what ships are built for." I was fortunate in my six years in Nairobi not to have any personal problems with security or violence. However, my heart goes out to my friends and their families who have lost someone in the Westgate terrorist attacks or other senseless acts of violence in Kenya.

I like to think our work at Juhudi Kilimo has helped the larger security problem in some very small way by investing in the unemployed rural youth and allowing them to focus their energy on running a productive agribusiness, instead of turning to a future of violent crime. Kenya may not have the oil, diamonds or other natural resources of some of its neighboring countries, but the vast potential locked away in the Kenyan young entrepreneurs I met along the way vastly outstrips the value of anything the earth can provide. If this book can help a single entrepreneur to think differently about their endeavor, inspire one person to start a social enterprise or even simply encourage a traveler to visit a magnificent country like Kenya, then I have succeeded. Some of the names in this book have been changed to respect the privacy of individuals.

"Twenty years from now you will be more disappointed by the things that you didn't do than by the ones you did so throw off the bowlines. Sail away from the safe harbor. Catch the trade winds in your sails. Explore. Dream. Discover." – Mark Twain

Chapter 1 | How I Got Here

The Emirates Flight 719 banked over the land that was to be my new home for the next eight months.

Bleary-eyed, I blinked and tried to make out several tall trees standing together. For a moment they looked surprisingly like giraffes.

The Kenyan woman sitting next to me was an executive at Toyota and quite pleasant company. She was also looking past me through the window. I pointed to the trees. "Don't those look a lot like giraffes?"

She smiled. "Honey, those are giraffes. That is Nairobi National Park we are flying over. Karibu Kenya. Which means welcome to Kenya. I know you will enjoy your time here." We laughed and I realized how naïve I must have appeared. I tried to compose myself and responded: "Asante sana," which in Kiswahili means "thank you."

"You must think this is my first time to Africa. But it isn't. I have done a bit of traveling all over the world."

Several years earlier I had spent ninety days sailing on board the Institute for Shipboard Education with the Semester at Sea program. The trip had profoundly changed my life despite the program's reputation for being a party cruise for 600 college kids. While I did meet some of my most wonderful friends with that program, I was also exposed for the first time to extreme poverty in Vietnam, India, South Africa and Cuba.

The combination of the country visits and the residential academic environment on board allowed for close examination of the similarities and differences between each country. As an economics major, I tracked the pricing and distribution of several common goods such as bottled water and gasoline. I was also enrolled in a World Religions class with an outlandish professor who clearly had a deep passion for the subject. During this time I noticed two very powerful and influential forces in society and human behavior. One was the drive of commerce through daily business activity and the other was the persuasion of faith through organized religion. Both were capable of reaching millions of people and responsible for ninety percent of the daily activity I saw in each country.

As my thinking began to develop I was influenced by one of the 'senior passengers', a retired businessman named Tucker Murray. He had traveled on several voyages with Semester at Sea, along with his wife Gail. Each senior couple had the option of 'adopting' a group of students to become a temporary family while away from home. The families would meet each week, have dinner together and talk about the countries and our plans.

When I spoke privately with Tucker about my dilemma about whether to focus my remaining academic time on divinity or business, he talked to me about his life and outlined some of the benefits of focusing a career on business. I remember thinking that by learning to manage money and other resources efficiently you can achieve great outcomes. This was the nudge I needed to finish my degree in economics and pursue a career in business.

My first job out of college had me supporting the grant-making and investing work of a mid-sized private Colorado Springs foundation called El Pomar. I discovered that the corporate and business network was always missing from most community grant-making programs and activities. This bothered me for some reason. It eventually became the premise for me going to business school at Vanderbilt in Nashville, Tennessee, where I connected with like-minded people through the Net Impact network. This was my first major exposure to microfinance. Alongside nine of my classmates, we founded an organization at Vanderbilt called Project Pyramid, which was inspired from CK Prahalad's book, *The Fortune at the Bottom of the Pyramid*.

We managed to raise nearly $300,000 through the Dollar General mogul, Cal Turner. I remember pitching the concept of starting an integrated social business program with the Divinity school that used business solutions to address poverty and other social problems. Cal said to us: "I have absolutely no idea what you all are talking about but I love the passion and energy with this group. You seem to be addressing several of the areas I have been trying to support at Vanderbilt through the Cal Turner Center for Moral Leadership. I would like to see where you can take this idea."

Several months later we had our new class course and speaker series, along with an international trip to visit existing social businesses.

Jessica Jackley, one of the founders of Kiva.org, which is an online peer-to-peer website that was just getting some major publicity through Oprah Winfrey and the Wall Street Journal in 2006, came to speak to our new class as the first speaker. She was high-energy and full of magnetic optimism about her work at Kiva and the potential it had to change lives around the world. That evening, over drinks with Jessica, I opened my personal Kiva account and made my first loan to an entrepreneur in Vietnam in September of 2006.

The Project Pyramid course then brought us to India, where I somehow became the de facto tour guide and India expert because I was the only student who had been to India before. We were able to set up a visit and meeting with SKS Microfinance in Hyderabad, run by the celebrity and business icon, Vikram Akula. The class had studied a few of the microfinance models and spent time learning about one of the fathers of microfinance, Muhammad Yunus and the Grameen Bank. We tried to get in touch with Yunus, but as he had recently won the Nobel Peace Prize, he was a little too busy for a group of MBA and Divinity students. However, Vanderbilt did manage to invite Yunus to Vanderbilt to be our graduation speaker. I was able to shake hands with one of the world changers at my graduation in 2007.

Vikram Akula's approach at SKS was different to Yunus in that he wanted to build his microfinance non-profit organization into an efficient for-profit business where he could then access the global capital markets to fund the business's growth instead of relying on donations. Yunus, on the other hand, preferred to keep the ownership local. Of course, the pure capitalistic approach struck home with my MBA classmates who were all former bankers and consultants from large corporations in the US.

In 2006, SKS had just transformed from a non-profit entity into a for-profit entity and was one of the fastest growing microfinance institutions in the country. I visited several of their client groups in India and noticed the high-level of organization and the respect that the clients had for the loan officers. At each meeting, the clients would repeat a phrase on their commitments to repay the loan, almost as a religious chant, before the loan officer started handing out cash loans of $50-100 to each woman at the meeting. It was changing lives all across India by creating access to finance for extremely low-income communities. I loved it.

Then graduation came. Like everyone else in my class I was under tremendous pressure from the business school to take a high-paying job with a big name company. The career counselor told me that if I wanted a career in international business, I needed to get some names on my resumé that were recognized outside of Colorado. So I took a consulting job with Accenture in Washington DC.

Of the nine 'experienced-hires' in my start group I was the only one remaining after six months, the rest had either left the company or been fired. My first two projects were staffed by executives who were over-committed with other projects and never had much time for me. I was constantly told to wait until the project was fully 'staffed-up' and then there would be more action. I tried to be as pro-active as could by learning new skills through the company's impressive online learning portal or by signing up for outside research projects. The general inactivity drove me crazy.

I had read Muhammad Yunus' book about social businesses that were using business structures to reduce poverty, improve child nutrition and provide low-cost housing. I quickly realized that my heart was in international social business and I had to find a way to work abroad. I discovered that there was a new and exciting program that sent consultants to work in developing countries at half salary. To my disappointment, these overseas assignments were only available to top employees with a minimum of two years at the company, so I did not qualify.

There had to be another way.

I networked all over DC and connected with a Colorado College alum, who had been in the Peace Corps and was now managing the corporate social responsibility program at Disney. His advice was, "just go abroad. Just go even if it means volunteering and not taking a salary. The experience will be worth it."

I came across a program based in Washington DC called the MBA Enterprise Corps. The MBA Enterprise Corps functions like Doctors Without Borders but sends business experts to work in developing countries for eight to fourteen months. I discovered that some of the clients who used the MBA Enterprise Corps were also Accenture clients such as the International Finance Corporation (IFC), Department of Defense and USAID.

It occurred to me that I might be able to take a leave of absence from Accenture and enroll in the MBA Enterprise Corps, then help sell the Accenture services to the MBA Enterprise Corps clients. It was a long shot, but in my nine months at Accenture, I'd done well, winning a performance bonus and a high performance award. These accolades must have shown up on my file someplace because my application for an eight-month leave of absence to work independently on business development abroad was granted. The MBA Enterprise Corp then placed me on a program in Nairobi, Kenya. It sounded good to me. To get ready for life in Kenya, I bought a Kenya guidebook and re-watched the classic movie *Ghost and the Darkness*, starring Michael Douglas and Val Kilmer. The film is about the British railroad project in Tsavo, Kenya where over 160 rail workers were killed by lions. In the summer of 2008, I was 27 and about to embark on a life-changing trip to Africa.

Chapter 2 | Harold and the GBF

The Starbucks in DuPont Circle in Washington DC teemed with activity as young professionals, students and tourists crowded in line to get their morning caffeine fix. I noticed that two of the coffee blends for the day came from Kenya. Standing next to me was C.D. Glin from the MBA Enterprise Corps.

"There's Harold," said C.D., pointing to the front of the line.

"Harold Rosen?" I said. "The famous guy from the Harvard Business School? Big shot at the IFC?"

Harold Rosen had graduated from Harvard Business School and then spent nearly thirty years with the World Bank and IFC. He was a legend in development finance.

C.D. nodded as Rosen walked towards them.

"Hi Harold, this is Nat, the new MBA who is headed to Kenya," he said.

Harold smiled. "We will see you upstairs in a few minutes." He continued towards the stairs.

"He seems like a nice guy," I said.

C.D. chuckled. "Well, he's one of the smartest guys I know and he's been all over the world. Great to work with."

We headed upstairs for a meeting with Jaime Ramirez, originally from Colombia, now one of the portfolio managers. I recognized his South American accent immediately from the phone interview. He was one of the friendliest individuals I had met, yet possessed a clearly sharp wit about him that took me off guard at times. The other person in the room was a younger guy named Vinay Bachireddy, who was the portfolio analyst. I knew he had gone to Yale, then worked for several years on Wall Street before coming to the Grassroots Business Fund – GBF. They were an intimidating duo.

Harold finally came into the room for a conference call with Aleke Dondo, the Managing Director of the K-Rep Development Agency or KDA, which was a business incubator that used microfinance to address social problems such as low-cost housing in slums, rural agriculture development and youth unemployment.

I jumped when Harold shouted: "Hi Aleke, how is Nairobi?" into the conference call speaker on the table. Aleke answered back with a deep booming voice that reminded me of James Earl Jones from *Coming to America*.

I flashed back to what I knew of Aleke Dondo and K-Rep. I knew K-Rep had started in the early 80s as part of a USAID grant to stimulate rural enterprise development in Kenya. As part of the program, USAID sent some Kenyan executives to India and Bangladesh to learn about the emerging microfinance business model with Grameen Bank and BASIX India. These executives brought the microfinance model back to Kenya and adjusted it to fit the needs of the Kenyan market.

With the microfinance model in hand, the K-Rep founders started microlending and by 1999 had become so successful that it transformed from an NGO (non-governmental organization or non-profit) into a for-profit and regulated bank called K-Rep Bank. This bank spurred the growth of microfinance in Kenya by supporting the growth of institutions like Kenya Women Finance Trust (KWFT) that today is one of the largest microfinance institutions in Kenya, with hundreds of thousands of clients. In 2008 the bank took heavy losses as a result of the post-election violence. While many of the other banks and microfinance institutions seemed to recover more quickly, K-Rep soon became overshadowed by a much faster growing bank called Equity Bank, which had been declared insolvent in 1993 but returned to have more than seven million customers by 2011.

I wondered how K-Rep was doing now.

Harold and Aleke talked for a while about politics and the recent election in Kenya, which resulted in countrywide upheaval and ethnic violence, but from Aleke's tone it sounded like things had settled down and the country was getting back to rebuilding.

"Aleke, we have Nat here from the MBA Enterprise Corp, who is flying out to Kenya tomorrow."

Aleke responded with a jubilant "Hi Nat! We are looking forward to you joining us. Have you ever been to Africa before?"

I moved close to the speaker. "No, not to Kenya, but I have been to South Africa."

Aleke boomed out a laugh. "South Africa is not Africa. That does not count. You come to Kenya. This is the real Africa."

We worked out a few of the logistics. My general role would be to help GBF gather more data about the financial performance of some of the pilot programs in KDA and to assess if any of them showed enough promise for an investment by GBF to become a company in the future. Then select one of the programs to build a business plan and spin off from KDA. Sounded easy enough.

Thirty minutes later I was back out in the street by the Starbucks with C.D.

"Well, have a good trip. Make sure to go to Mombasa and have some fun on the beach while you're out there," said C.D.

"Thanks," I shouted back as he started towards the busy intersection at DuPont Circle.

Eight months in Kenya seemed like a very long time to be away from all of this in America. I had never been out of the country for that long. My parents were of course very supportive but anxious at the same time, given how much negative publicity that Kenya, and Africa as a whole, was getting in the media. Nairobi or "Nairobbery" as it was called in the guidebooks, still had a very high crime rate and armed carjacking was a growing problem. I imagined that I probably would not be working in any of the slums or dangerous areas. Besides, by that time I had traveled to over thirty countries and been in dangerous cities before. How bad could it really be?

Chapter 3 | My First Day with K-Rep

It was a bright blue and clear cloudless sky which I later discovered to be typical weather in Nairobi. The city sits at 5,500 feet above sea level and 88 miles south of the equator. This combination produces a temperature of 75 degrees Fahrenheit (24C), with no humidity and few insects nearly 365 days a year. The taxi dropped me off at a quaint hotel called the Gracia Gardens House, situated in a quiet residential neighborhood called Kilimani. The hotel was right behind an old and run-down shopping mall, called the Yaya Centre.

The hotel, like nearly every building in Kenya, had ten-foot high fences with razor wire and a security guard at each entrance. The Gracia Gardens was also a popular spot for foreign missionaries, who flooded out of minivans in the parking lot from their daily activities in the city. I could smell some kind of grilling meat in the kitchen that reminded me that I had not eaten since the previous day. I strolled down to the mall next door in search of a nice Kenyan dinner.

The Yaya Centre was a giant yellow building flanked by two thirteen-story yellow apartment towers. They were the only major high-rises in the area, save for a strange lime-yellow building with an oversized flat roof about two blocks away that had to be eleven floors. Inside the Yaya Centre, I found a grocery store, hardware store, bank and a basic food court with Indian, Italian and Chinese restaurants, all serving decent food. I could not find a Kenyan restaurant or even an African restaurant in the mall. Surprised and disappointed, I walked out of the mall and back into the street.

I noticed a dark building lit by a neon light over a sign that read, Trackers Bar. Maybe they would have something local? I pushed aside the hanging beads, which served as a door, and walked into the dimly-lit room that smelled of stale beer. There were three large-sized women sitting at the bar, all very well dressed. Two older men were sitting in the corner at another table with several rows of brown bottles in front of them. Every single person was staring at me. I sat down and a younger man came over to me.

"Hello," he said.

"Hello. Do you serve food here? Can I please have a menu?"

He looked at me confused but turned around to go back to the bar and speak with an older woman. The men in the bar had gone back to their conversation but the women were still looking at me. The young man returned from the bar to tell me the "food is not ready yet" but "how about a Tusker?" I had seen big signs at the airport so I knew that Tusker was the local beer. I said sure. He brought me a tall brown bottle of warm beer that did not taste too bad.

Just as I was getting settled, one of the women yelled to me, "Hey mzungu! Where do you come from? England?"

This is the question I always hate answering when abroad. At the time, most of the world hated America and I had inadvertently created tension with total strangers in India, Singapore and even Brazil by saying I was American.

Smiling apologetically, I told them I was from America, which brought some nods from around the room. I explained that I was coming here to work for a few months.

"One of the presidential candidates in the US has a father who is from Kenya," I said, trying to find some common ground.

One of the older men turned to me. "Yes. The Senator. He has a beer named after him in Kenya."

"Obama?" I said.

"No. Senator. The beer is called Senator."

The women started to move a little closer and one of them said: "Obama is Kenyan and he is her uncle." She pointed to one of her friends. "If he becomes president then we can all move to America."

The three women started to sit down all around me. I thought I had really charmed them with that Obama connection. Then it dawned on me that maybe these women were not just three harmless patrons of a bar drinking on a Sunday afternoon but perhaps had some other motives. I had been harassed many times in Southeast Asia and China by commercial sex workers, so I knew how to manage them politely. But I had never been out-numbered like this before. Panicking, I stammered, "I need to get going" and quickly pulled out a 1,000-shilling note (worth about $10) since that was the only denomination the ATMs produced. My beer was only 90 shillings but I did not want to wait for my change so left a huge tip.

"Come back again, mzungu!" The women shouted and laughed as I bolted out the door into the streets. I had Chinese food for dinner that night at the mall.

The next morning I threw on my button-down shirt and dress pants and headed out. It had rained during the night. The unexpected water had flushed out termites that were over one inch long and had four dragonfly-like wings. They were swarming around the entrance to the hotel. Wings and dead termites were littered all over the floor. Once outside the security barrier, I merged with the flood of pedestrians coming from the famous Kibera slums on their way to offices around Kilimani.

It was a beautiful day with minimal humidity, even after the rains from the night before. I later realized that the weather in Kenya rarely fluctuates more than 15 degrees all year from its normal 75 and sunny forecasts. The sidewalk abruptly entered a long stretch of thick brown soil and grass nearly

200 yards from the office. I trudged along and sank into nearly three inches of mud. When I lifted my foot it carried a few extra pounds of clinging dirt. This was the fertile 'cotton soil' of Kenya, I later learned.

When I arrived at the office I could not find a grate, rug or anything useful to clean the mud off my shoes. So I tracked mud all over the nice tile floors and headed into the elevator to go to the 11th floor on the top of the building where K-Rep Bank and KDA had their offices. I was directed to Catherine, Aleke Dondo's personal assistant, and strolled down the hall admiring the panoramic views of Nairobi and the green Ngong Hills in the distance. I stood there in my business-casual clothes, a trail of mud leading to my shoes as three of the K-Rep directors stepped out of Aleke's office.

All were dressed in immaculate dark suits as if they were directors of any corporate investment bank in New York or London. I'm not sure what I was expecting, but for some reason, the formality of business in Kenya surprised me. Aleke Dondo was a college wrestler and still kept a heavy build. At over 6ft he had quite an intimidating presence. His deep booming voice, which seemed to rattle the windows could command a room. I would discover soon that Aleke is one in a million. He cares deeply about the development of his country and about helping the rural poor. He has a big heart and was someone I learned tremendously from over my six years in Kenya.

All of the directors greeted me warmly, with a typical firm Kenyan handshake. Aleke invited me into his office for tea. I did not drink tea or coffee at the time so I politely declined. The directors looked up in shock.

"You really do not take tea?" one asked.
"No. He is American," replied Aleke. "Mid-morning tea is an English thing. But in Kenya we have some of the best tea and coffee in the world."

I looked down at the jar of instant coffee and wondered about that.

Aleke went into a speech about the exports and how tea and coffee represented thirty percent of the export market and was a major source of income for some of the rural farmers in Kenya. The other directors took a kettle of boiled milk and poured it in with tea bags into their cups. Then I watched as each dumped three or four heaped spoonsful of sugar into the tea. It may not be the healthiest of daily drinks, especially with whole milk, but I later found out that it tastes great and is solely responsible for fueling the growing local dairy, sugar and tea markets in Kenya.

After the directors left, Aleke asked me, "So, what do you think of Nairobi?"

"Well, the weather is fantastic and there seems to be a lot of activity. I think I will like it here."

Aleke went on to outline the various pilot programs under KDA that I was to evaluate in the coming months. They had pilot programs in urban microlending for at-risk youth, adolescent girls savings, low-cost housing finance, rural honey production, a village banking model and one in an agricultural asset financing.

The village banking model interested me the most, since it used existing community infrastructure and networks to provide credit to very remote towns and villages, yet all the profits stayed within the communities. KDA would help a community mobilize a certain threshold of capital, between $2,000 and $10,000, to build a village bank. These banks were creatively called Financial Services Associations or FSAs. Those who contributed money to the project would become shareholders. Then one of the donors working with KDA would finance the rest of the startup costs and train the local leaders on how to be good board members of the village bank. KDA would supply professional management services (bank manager, tellers, IT, etc.) to the village bank at a service fee. This way the village bank could access high-quality technical skills that might be difficult to find from the local community, yet all the ownership and profits would remain local with the community.

The village banks could then lend to the community members at a fraction of the cost of a bank. The model was similar to that of a Savings and Credit Cooperative (SACCO) but the outsourced management service was an interesting twist. I made plans with Aleke to help him at the opening ceremonies of two of these village banks in Western Kenya and Eastern Kenya. Aleke suggested that I spend the next two weeks meeting with his staff and then visit the programs around Nairobi to build my understanding of what exactly KDA does in Kenya.

I spent the next couple of days looking at other projects. One of these was in Nairobi's largest slum, called Kibera. It houses somewhere between 200,000 and one million people, depending on which politician or NGO you talk to or census report you read. It is also home to between 6,000 and 15,000 charitable organizations working in the slum, yet the poverty and abysmal living conditions seem to be getting worse over time.[i]

KDA was one of the many NGOs providing micro loans to the urban, slum-dwelling youth. My assignment was to meet with one of the KDA loan officers who worked in Kibera and follow her around for the day, visiting young entrepreneurs in the program. I was anticipating seeing loan groups full of hopeful young business people similar to those in Bangladesh and India. The weekend before, I had ventured out into the Central Business District and taken a bus to the heart of downtown Nairobi, so I had a little understanding of the organized chaos of the public transportation system. Kibera was probably not too much more difficult to navigate than downtown. I followed my instructions to get on the Number Eight matatu outside the

---

[i]   Muchiri Karanja, "Myth shattered: Kibera numbers fail to add up," *Nation Media Newspaper*, September. 3 2010.

Yaya Centre and take it to the Olympic stop in Kibera where the KDA loan officer named Dora "would find me." I imagined it would not be too difficult for her to spot a tall mzungu getting out of the matatu in Kibera.

The Olympic stop reminded me of stepping into the ocean surf but with a sea of people, carts, stray dogs, motorcycles and more matatus assaulting my senses from every angle. Fortunately, Dora came right up to me and grabbed my arm before I could wander off and get into too much trouble.

Dora was well-dressed and very quiet but certainly knew her job well. I had been told she was the best performing loan officer at KDA. We journeyed deep into the slum and the farther away from the road I got the more attention I seemed to attract.

The first client we met was selling fresh water. This is big business. Nearly twenty percent of household income is spent on water, since most families do not have access to clean water and sanitation.[ii] By this stage, I had gathered about seven small children, all saying "mzungu" and "how are you" in repetition like a flock of little birds.

A grizzled man looked out of his corrugated roofed home. He smiled when he saw me and called me over, offering a drink of a strong local brew called Changaa. Given that it was 8:30 in the morning I politely declined. The local authorities have a difficult time regulating the home brew in the urban areas, which has been known to cause blindness or death and is the root cause of many social or health problems in the slums.

We moved farther in, stepping over mounds of trash, and crossed a river that seemed to be flowing with more human excrement than water. Kibera was not all that different from some of the slums I had seen in India and South Africa. Nevertheless, it was still hard to take in the deplorable living conditions. We visited several other entrepreneurs including a metalworker,

---

ii   Kevin Watkins, "Beyond scarcity: Power, poverty and the global water crisis," *UNDP Summary Human Development Report*, 2006: 16.

a music and DVD salesman, a clothing store and even an entrepreneur who had started his own private school.

Dora showed me through a place called Toi, a market that was a great place to buy second hand clothes from the US and Europe. We ran into the first group of mzungus I had seen all day who were shopping for clothes. Dora could not understand why these foreigners would donate their clothes and then fly all the way to Kenya to buy them back again. I did not have any good answers for her. We stopped for lunch at a place called Kenyatta Market where I finally found some Kenyan food called Nyama Choma, which literally translates into burned meat. Usually goat meat, Nyama Choma is a favorite dish in Kenya. We sampled pieces of meat from several stalls before selecting our favorite. The butcher brought a leg of well-seasoned and grilled goat over to our table, and then hacked it into small pieces. With our hands we dug into the meat and dipped each piece into a pile of salt. The soft and flavorful goat meat melted in our mouths. The accompaniments included Skuma Wiki (chopped kale), Kachumbari (chopped tomatoes and onions) and the Kenyan staple, Ugali, which is like a thick polenta corn meal with less taste. I loved all of it.

In the afternoon we met with a client who sold clothing and I asked about men's suits so I could keep up with the K-Rep directors. He put me in touch with a guy named Tom, who makes great tailored suits. It was a fantastic day and I would visit Kibera a dozen or so more times during my evaluation.

When I arrived in Kenya I knew only two people outside of my work colleagues. They were an American couple named Greg and Krysten. Greg worked at the US Embassy and Krysten with an NGO called TechnoServe, which works with rural smallholder farmers. I had met Greg at a mutual friend's party in Washington DC months earlier.

They were impressive people. Greg had a Master's in Public Policy from Columbia and Krysten had an MBA from Harvard.

My first weekend in Nairobi they invited me out to a party at the US Embassy, which was a solid hour's drive from my hotel. The compound was massive and the security was not very happy to let me inside with my Washington DC driver's license. The security took my phone and I had to be escorted by Krysten who came to meet me at the gate. The US Embassy in Nairobi is one of the largest in Africa and under tight security ever since the previous location was bombed in 1998, killing 213 people and wounding an estimated 4,000 more.[iii]

The US Marines assigned to protecting the Embassy had organized the party and it reminded me of a typical Friday night at a college fraternity house. The Marines had Jack Daniels, Bud Light and an ongoing beer pong tournament that required teams of two to throw ping-pong balls into cups of beer across a table. It was popular in US college campuses and apparently at the Nairobi US Embassy. I felt at home.

During the drinking that followed I got talking about my desire to see more of the African wildlife and in the late hours of the night Greg, Krysten and I made some plans to go for a safari in Nairobi National Park.

The next day we rented a safari van. It had a roof that opened up so the passengers could stand up and view the scenery. The park was just fifteen minutes from my hotel and downtown Nairobi. Nairobi's two airports border the park to the East and North.

As it was so close to the city, I thought it might be more like a zoo than a national park. I could not have been more wrong. Nairobi National Park

---

iii   US Department of Justice "Bombings of the Embassies of the United States at Nairobi, Kenya, and Dar Es Salaam, Tanzania," FBI Executive Summary, November 18, 1998.

opens up into a breathtaking valley full of green ravines that run like smoke tendrils to the south and east. The park is home to a healthy population of giraffe, zebra, water buffalo, hippos, lions and a protected population of black rhino.

This was my first safari so we acted like little kids in a theme park when we came across our first herd of giraffe. I took a great picture of a giraffe eating from an acacia tree with the downtown Nairobi skyline in the background. Apparently, the two airports and urban city do not bother the animals too much. The roads were soaked from earlier rain, causing our van occasionally to slide in the tracks.

Our driver announced: "This is where we find the lions," and all three of us peered out of the van in search of the big cat. The van lurched as it entered a particularly long patch of mud and slowed to a stop. We were stuck. No other vehicles were in sight and we were in a valley that limited our mobile phone connectivity. The driver got out to inspect the situation and sank past his ankles in mud. Greg and I found a machete (or panga as they call it in Kenya) in the van and jumped out with the driver. We instructed Krysten to be on the watch for lions as Greg and I pushed the van. I could just imagine how my family would take the news if they found out I was eaten by a lion during my first weekend in Kenya.

The driver revved the engine and we both heaved the van through the mud. It made it through, but the driver needed to keep the momentum going, so he continued driving down the road until he disappeared over a hill, leaving both of us standing in the road. We glanced at each other and then looked around. No animals in sight, but I doubt we would really see a lion before it pounced on us. We jogged down the road finally to find the van on a dry section of road, with Krysten reprimanding the driver for abandoning her husband and friend.

Chapter 4 | Western Kenya

Aleke and I boarded the small prop-plane headed for Kisumu. We were on our way to open a new FSA in a remote town called Mabera, which is on the border with Tanzania. The plane glided over lush green hills and I glimpsed the shimmering Lake Victoria in the distance as we came in for a landing in the bustling town of Kisumu.

A driver named Isika picked us up and I recognized him from the office in Nairobi. He had driven from Nairobi to Kisumu to pick us up at the airport and drive us around for the week. Aleke would fly back but I opted to return by road with Isika. The logistics seemed a little elaborate to me but in a place where it is difficult (and expensive) to rent a 4x4, and public transportation would take days to reach the rural towns we were visiting, this was the most affordable option.

We drove for several hours through the rolling hills of Kisii, in the Nyanza region of Kenya. Small plots of land were scattered the countryside where smallholder farmers grew maize, bananas, sugar or tea and raised goats, cows and chickens. Along the roadside older women were selling bananas and papayas. We stopped a few times to buy fruit or pick up various KDA staff on their way to meetings with clients.

It was Wednesday November 5th, 2008, and Barak Obama had just won the election in the US. Kenya announced a two-day holiday (Wednesday and Thursday). We had to go back to work on Friday. Overnight I had become a celebrity as an American in Kenya, especially in Western Kenya, where Obama's grandmother still lives. The morning after the election results were announced, the US Embassy had a record turnout for Kenyans applying for

US visas, many of them claiming to be Obama's relative. I think many of them went home disappointed. We were not sure how the US election and holidays would affect the launch of the FSA that day.

The truck finally arrived in Mabera, where the infrastructure had clearly been neglected, probably for a hundred years. Aleke and I stepped out and were greeted by a junior government official who led us into the largest structure in the small town. It was a two-room house that apparently was being used by the District Officer as a personal office. A small young man sat behind an enormous desk that made him look even smaller. I was surprised to see Aleke giving this man so much deference but I followed his lead and greeted the officer respectfully. The guy could not have been any older than thirty.

We spoke politely about Obama, K-Rep and the village bank we were launching. He seemed to be very pleased with the program and told us all about the challenges of youth unemployment in his district. He seemed to have a solid command of the statistics in his area and told us how he was working on improving the social conditions. The community had raised all the required money and the village bank had been recently built in a new building near the District Office.

We met with the treasurer who was collecting payments for shares in the bank and I asked Aleke if I could purchase some shares. "Of course!" he said. I bought $20 worth of shares and still have my share certificate.

Close to two hundred people turned up for the launch of the village bank that afternoon. We were treated as the guests of honor and dancers dressed in animal skins and beautiful beads danced all around us. The village elders came to greet us and a very old general from the Kenyan Army, dressed in his fatigues, walked over to shake our hands.

Then started the speeches…

The Kenyans love giving speeches at formal gatherings and everyone seems to be very good at public speaking. When it was his turn, Aleke stood up and gave an elegant forty-five minute speech, changing between at least three languages. I did not understand anything that was said since it was primarily in Kiswahili with a good mix of the local dialects. An old lady from the crowd shouted something and it sparked more shouts. Did Aleke say something to upset them?

Aleke turned to me. "They are calling to hear from you. The mzungu. Just say a few words to them."

I stood up and greeted them all in English and started to tell them I was from the US and worked for the Grassroots Business Fund. The blank stares told me that the crowd didn't understand what I was saying. I only knew about two or three words in Kiswahili at the time but I did read a banner that day, which said, Obama Ameshinda! (Obama has won). At the end of my brief speech I said "Obama ameshinda!" and received a standing ovation. Women brought me small stone carvings as gifts and men bought me beer. It was great to be an American in Kenya that day.

Isika and I took two days to drive back to Nairobi. This drive will always be embedded fondly in my memory since Isika turned out to be the most honest, loyal and hard-working Kenyan I ever came across in my entire time in the country. He took his job very seriously and was extremely good at navigating the treacherous rural roads of Kenya.

Isika had already been working with KDA for five years and had likely clocked more than a million kilometers driving to the organization's various projects around the country. KDA had FSAs in remote parts of Northern Turkana and Marsabit, but also operations in the South, in small towns like Wundanyi on the way to the coast off Mombasa road.

Isika visited all of them and as a result could speak in many of the local dialects. This turned out to be quite helpful for me if I were to expand my vocabulary beyond a few words. Isika taught me important phrases in Kiswahili such as "msichana mrembo sana" meaning "very beautiful women" and "ninataka tuskers mbili" meaning "bring me two more Tuskers."

We passed a farm that had a large wooden structure resting on the upper branches of a large tree.

"Come. Take a picture of this crazy guy who lives in the tree," Isika instructed.

The owner of this treehouse had had an argument with his father-in-law about borrowing land. I guess the father-in-law did not approve of the marriage and refused to support the newly wedded couple by handing over some of his farmland. So the entrepreneurial son-in-law built his home in a tree above the land and did not take up any additional real estate. I could now see a young woman (perhaps his wife) cooking the midday meal over an open flame in the treehouse. I snapped the picture and Isika and I headed down the road again.

Isika also made it a point to educate me more about the tribes of Kenya, or at least helped me understand the commonly held stereotypes. The Kikuyu tribe, around Mt. Kenya, was one of the largest and its people, he told me, were known to be very good in business and with managing money. He then warned me against dating a Kikuyu because she would probably try to find a way to take all of my money. The Luo tribe was the second largest and inhabited the regions in the West around Lake Victoria. He said this tribe makes up a lot of the professors and academics in the country and can sometimes come across as aloof or extravagant. The Kalenjin was the third largest and populated the Rift Valley region that ran north to south in the western part of the country. This was where the Olympic runners lived. The Kalenjin also loved their cows. They were particularly violent during the post-election period.

I asked Isika what his tribe was and he smiled.

"Me, I am a Kamba, from the areas past Machakos and Kasikeu, East of Nairobi."

"And what are they known for?" I asked.

"They are known for their honesty," he smiled. "Also, if you marry a Kamba lady she will make you very happy, especially at the nighttime." Isika started laughing out loud, which happened to be an incredibly contagious and jolly laugh.

One of the final KDA pilot programs I reviewed was experimenting with financing milk-chilling plants, coffee washing stations and other mechanized rural enterprises. It showed tremendous potential to lift larger rural communities out of poverty. Aleke and I had pitched to a group of partners from the East African Dairy Development Program (EADD) to help manage a $2 million fund from the Gates Foundation to finance about twenty rural milk-chilling plants around the country. The program required us to collaborate with several other large NGOs. I found myself meeting regularly with the cow experts from Heifer International and the International Livestock Research Institute, as well as the farming experts from TechnoServe.

I embarked on another rural Kenya tour to learn all about these milk-chilling plants in random places like Lelan, Metkei and Longisa. Put those in a Google search over Kenya and you can see how truly rural they are. The cooling plants basically purchased milk from local farmers during the day and then had a truck from a larger milk processing company pick up the milk in the afternoon. The cooling plant would pay the farmers slightly less per liter for the milk and the processor would pay slightly more for the milk and make its money on the margins. This helped the farmers, since over seventy-five percent could not sell directly to the processors anyway. I also learned that a cow can be milked two or three times per day and if it is not milked it can get infections such as mastitis, resulting in even less milk production.

On average, fresh milk needs to be cooled within six hours of leaving the cow. This is not easy for the rural farmer with no electricity. The brokers who buy the milk only come by the farm in the day. The result is that most of the farmers would have to throw away the milk from the evening milking, since they could not sell it or consume it in their homes. With the local cooling plant in place, the farmers could sell their evening milk to the plant and dramatically improve their incomes.

The cooling plants that KDA was setting up with the rest of the Gates Foundation's "cow coalition" had a complicated financing structure. The local farming communities would put down ten percent of the equity, then the Gates Foundation would give a zero percent repayable loan that converted to another twenty percent more of the farmers' equity when paid. Then KDA would provide a seven percent 'soft' loan repayable over three to five years, worth thirty percent of the plant; and finally, a commercial bank would finance the balancing forty percent with a one hundred percent guarantee from Gates. Now try to explain that to a room of rural smallholder farmers with limited project finance experience, through a translator.

That was my job.

My small team sat with a group of fifteen elders from the rural cooperative in a dark and musty shed to discuss the program. The elders were all farmers themselves and dressed in rubber gumboots, faded sports coats and button-down shirts. I had a translator who moved between Kiswahili and two other local dialects I could not follow very well. We started the meeting with introductions and a long speech by the Chairman of the local co-operative. Then it was my turn.

"We are here to help you invest in building a new milk cooling plant so you can sell more milk." I then paused to let the translator rattle off the line in his multiple dialects.

"Our group, KDA, will provide a loan alongside a fund supported by the Gates Foundation in the US. We are working with many partners to also improve milk production of your individual farmers. The partners will help source high-yield cows and provide veterinary services such as artificial insemination."

The farmers looked at me with blank and tired stares. Then the translator hit the part about the high-yield cows and the group woke up. A few of them smiled. Several of the men asked questions. I caught the occasional "Bill Gates" and "interest rate" in the mixed Kiswahili questions.

"They want to know why Bill Gates does not just give them the money to buy cows instead of charging them interest on a loan."

I was battling a long-held culture of hand-outs from foreigners who had visited these farmers and given away money. The idea of charging interest and repaying an investment was new. Some farmers understood our plan was more sustainable than the hand-outs. Many others dismissed us as selling an elaborate loan scam or Ponsi scheme. Unfortunately, other financing projects in the areas had led to disastrous results, with farmers losing money and the program managers being left with the big cars and allowances provided by the donors.

One of the more successful groups of farmers was in Lelan, which became my favorite area of Kenya. The breathtaking Cherangani Hills, in the northwest part of the country, open out to a vast plain that gradually becomes arid desert towards Lake Turkana. It took a two-hour ride on a rough road from civilization to reach the mountain community in Lelan.

On one of the drives up to the community, Isika and I had witnessed an enormous truck carrying tanks towards the Northern border with Sudan.

We came to a bridge where one of the tanks had accidentally slipped off the truck and was on the side of the road behind a bridge with its turret pointed in the air. A few of the Kenyan military were staring, dumbfounded, at the tank. At the time, Sudan was nearing the end of its Darfur crisis and Kenya was forbidden by the UN to provide any arms in support of the conflict. I called up Greg at the embassy to report the tanks but he never heard anything more about the incident.

The remote region of Lelan reminded me of parts of my hometown in Colorado with the undulating, stream-filled valleys and cooler temperatures. The farming community were a tough lot and not used to receiving any support from the government or aid agencies. Lelan was on the border of two warring tribes, which had seen decades of violence and cattle rustling – where individuals steal the life-sustaining cows of the other tribe. The towns were mostly cut off from electricity, health services and banks. The mobile phone networks had difficulty penetrating the hills in the area. I visited Lelan several times to help set up the cooling plant and, several years later, a branch office for Juhudi Kilimo. The men and women farmers traveled for miles with bright yellow plastic milk cans strapped to the backs of donkeys or attached to the sides of rusting motorcycles. The families milked their cows early in the morning, before the long journey could be made to the Lelan plant. Young boys skipped alongside their parents helping carry the gallons of creamy white liquid to the steel collection container in the plant. Milk technicians dressed in white lab coats and black gumboots would test each canister for fat content and bacteria count. Small test tubes were filled with a sample of milk and swirled with alcohol. The technicians would then smell the samples to estimate the bacteria content. I had no idea how affective this was since the entire plant smelled strongly of stale milk.

A single strand of electrical wire provided power to the plant from below the mountains. If the plant had electricity for more than three days in a week we were lucky. A loud diesel generator ran the plant during the outages. Many times the plant would lose an entire 10,000-liter batch in a day when the generator ran out of diesel and the roads were too muddy to buy more fuel. Once a day, the large milk tankers from the processing plants in the larger towns drove up to the Lelan plant to collect the batch of milk. The processors paid the Lelan plant at the end of month and then the Lelan plant would pay the farmers their share. I do not remember many months that the farmers were actually paid on time, but most of the money found its way back to the farmers. Even with all of these hardships, the plant transformed the Lelan economy. Before the plant, the Lelan farmers could only sell their morning milk locally for perhaps KShs 30 ($0.33) per liter to milk brokers and earn around KShs 160 ($1.76) per day depending on the amount of milk produced by the cow. Now, the farmers could sell both their morning and evening milk (the cows need to be milked twice each day) earning KShs 320 ($3.50) per day. The brokers did not come by the farms every day either, so farmers were forced to travel for many hours to find someone to buy their milk before it went bad. For the farmer's family, which actually depends on milk sales to have enough to eat each month, this can be incredibly stressful. The tight family economics do not leave much room for financial shocks such as a doctor's visit or school fees for children. The regular and predictable income provided by the cooling plant made life a little easier for thousands of rural farmers in Lelan.

On one of my trips with Isika, we were generously ordained as elders and provided with a colorful hat, indicating our status to the communities. Lelan was a story of true rural finance working to improve the lives of thousands. It was something I thought Juhudi Kilimo should always strive for in its expansion to reach remote communities similar to Lelan. Unfortunately, due to its remoteness, it was also vulnerable to fraud by government officials and predatory lenders. However, as of March 2015, the area had rebounded and was one of the leading offices in the country in terms of portfolio quality and growth for Juhudi.

By February of 2009 I had finally evaluated all of KDA's pilot programs and focused my attention on one particular program that had the best financial performance. K-Rep had noticed that nearly seventy-five percent of the Kenyan workforce was in agriculture but in 2008 only thirty-three percent had access to any formal financial services. The result was that Kenya was thirty percent less productive in agriculture than its peer countries. The result was rural poverty and food insecurity for the country.

None of the banks or microfinance institutions wanted to provide loans to rural smallholder farmers, because of the perceived risk in agriculture, as well as the lack of collateral to secure a loan. KDA had solved both of these problems with a simple solution that, when properly executed, showed tremendous promise.

What KDA had learned from working with farmers was that there was a demand for larger loans for productive assets. Most of the microfinance loans started at KShs 10,000 ($110) and then the clients could graduate to larger loans after first proving their credit-worthiness. This was the conventional thinking for risk management in microfinance at the time. But the asset financing program was experimenting with first-time loans of KShs 40,000 to 60,000, or over $500. These loans were to purchase assets such as high-yield dairy cows, poultry units or heavy irrigation equipment. The assets would then generate income by producing milk, eggs or more produce, which could then be sold for income. The new income could then help the farmers service their interest payments on the loans. An inbuilt bonus was that surplus milk, eggs or farm produce could be consumed by the farmer's families, thereby improving child nutrition.

The assets could also act as additional collateral on the loan if the farmers missed payments. The KDA loan officers could repossess a cow, irrigation equipment or a greenhouse to recover some of the value of the loan instead of taking savings or household items as the collateral. This prevented the clients from getting deeper into debt or poverty, which was the case with many other microfinance institutions around the world. KDA even found an insurance company to insure the cows against death and disease, which was bundled into the price of the loan and further protected the farmers against losses. And the best part was that the farmers loved it!

One of the star farmers was named David, who lived in a village near the western agricultural town of Kitale. David, like many young Kenyans living in rural villages, had inherited a small half-acre plot of land from his father and was expected to grow enough food to survive off the land. David admitted to struggling to get by as a smallholder farmer. He could make between KShs 100 and 250 per day from selling tomatoes grown on his farm but that income was never guaranteed. He was not eligible for a bank loan since it is difficult to use land as collateral. David enrolled in the KDA asset-financing program with a group of twenty-five other men and women farmers from his community. Over the next two months, David received training in financial management, the KDA loan process, the group guarantee system and the value of saving money. The group then elected a chairperson, secretary and treasurer to help the group self-govern to oversee the future loans. Each member also saved a small amount each month. The savings would be later used to provide the required ten percent down payment on the loan. This savings payment would later be returned to the farmer at the completion of the loan. A government agronomist then visited David's group to provide more technical training about irrigation and land management. David and four of his group members were selected to be the first to take the loans from KDA. The remaining twenty members would guarantee the five loans and help repay each month if needed. This is a similar system to the SKS model I had seen in India.

David applied for a small loan to purchase a water pump for KShs 17,000 ($187) to irrigate his tomato fields in the dry season. By using the information provided in training, David was able to dramatically improve the productivity of his land and take advantage of the higher tomato prices in the off-season. David quickly paid off his loan in eight months and applied for a second loan, this time for a dairy cow worth KShs 40,000. The KDA team connected David with a dairy expert who taught him how to look after his cow properly. With the milk and tomato income, David paid off his second loan and worked his way up to a much larger loan of KShs 150,000 for a greenhouse to expand his tomato business. Each Juhudi loan helped David diversify his production and stabilize his income, allowing him to expand his business. Today, David produces tomatoes, along with milk, maize and flour. He sells his produce to his community and supplies the major supermarkets in Kitale. His next priority is to expand his greenhouse.

When I spoke to David he told me: "I have hit the highway. Now the sky is the limit for my life and farm." I asked him about the loan and what he thought about the KDA project. He responded: "Joining KDA was the best decision I have ever made. I had nothing before. Nobody would provide me with a loan. Now I have these tomatoes, my cow and my beautiful wife." I was not sure if the loan from KDA helped him find his wife but I imagine the additional income generated from his farm made him a more eligible bachelor in the village. He waved his arm at to two younger men feeding his cow and said: "I am happy now that I can also provide jobs for these young boys from our village too."

This pilot program was regularly turning potential clients away because it did not have the funds to expand beyond the 1,000 farmers in the pilot. The initial donors to the project included Swiss Contact, which was an innovative international development arm of Credit Suisse, and a Dutch development NGO called Hivos.

From my point of view KDA had found a low-risk way of reducing poverty and improving food security for all of Kenya, if not East Africa. It just needed to be expanded to reach millions of farmers.

Despite my optimism for the project, it turned out to be prohibitively complex and this was one of the reasons why nobody had yet done it. One of the key challenges was that this model was quite expensive to run. It needed a lot of human resources and travel to sparsely populated rural areas was quite difficult, given the deplorable road infrastructure and transportation. But there was a massive market for this kind of loan (we estimated about nine million farmers in Kenya) and there was a strong demand already. All that needed to be done was to improve the operating efficiency to get the costs down and raise more money to fund growth. Seemed do-able to me.

I informed Harold and the GBF that my three favorite programs were the agriculture asset financing program, the youth lending program and a new rural enterprise/milk plant financing pilot, which I knew Harold liked already.

Harold was happy with all this and said GBF would put up a loan of $200,000 and another $80,000 in grant capital to help train staff and set up a system. Harold went on to say all we needed now was a business plan that explained what was 'bankable' that we could put in front of potential lenders and investors.

"Nat, since you have the most information, can you take a crack at drafting this and we will chip in where needed?"

"Sure," I said.

I had drafted a few business plans in business school and knew the gist of how they should be crafted.

I spent the next month focusing all of my energy writing a business plan for an urban youth, rural farmer and rural enterprise financing business.

In the process of finalizing the loan from GBF, we hit a snag. Harold wanted to charge an interest rate of ten percent on the loan, but since the program was still experimental Aleke was arguing for something lower. Commercial banks at the time were charging about thirteen percent for loans, so Harold's suggested rate seemed fair to me.

Aleke and Harold started to argue more and, after one particularly tense conference call had escalated to some shouting, I had the feeling that maybe GBF would not give the loan at all. What would happen then? Would I need to go crawling back to Accenture after six of the twelve months of my sabbatical? Harold finally settled on seven percent but the negotiation had left some scars on the relationship.

I finished the first draft of the elaborate fifty-page business plan, along with a shorter summary presentation. I worked with Vinay on a financial model that told us the company would need a total of $5 million in loans to farmers to break even. This meant we needed $2 million in equity and $3 million in debt to get the ratios right so we could continue to raise debt funding over the next three years. I had never raised a dime for anything outside of a garage sale in high school for a local charity, but $5 million did not seem too bad. GBF had something like $15 million in their fund at the time, so maybe they could chip in some more if needed.

*****

Greg and Krysten, who were to become dear friends, lived in a fully furnished luxurious four-bedroom house on a US Embassy staff compound, which reminded me a lot of a country club with nice tennis courts, a swimming pool and, best of all, a US commissary shop that sold US goods duty free. If I missed anything from the US, like Kraft macaroni and cheese or Oreos, which could not be purchased in Kenya in 2009, I could buy them at this store.

Each house on the compound came with a gardener, maid\cook and a nanny, if needed, to care for children. Greg was also given a great Toyota Highlander, which was a little smaller than the popular Prado. In Nairobi, the upper income communities were dominated by expatriate diplomats or NGO staff who lived a fabulous lifestyle, compared to my somewhat more meager one, limited by a $1,000 per month stipend. I met a US Embassy intern who was twenty-five and living in a five-bedroomed mansion in Nairobi for the summer. It had been purchased by the US Government. I was not quite sure what my tax dollars were paying for in Kenya but no doubt there was some logic at work.

I could not complain about it too much since, after a month in the Gracia House Hotel, I was moved to some new K-Rep-owned apartments next to the K-Rep building. I did not have hot water for the first two months and the main entrance opened up onto a dirt alley full of burning trash, car mechanic huts and the occasional fruit seller. A friend, who visited later, said the road at night looked like the post apocalypse scenes in movies like *The Matrix* or *The Terminator*, with dark figures huddled over bonfires and heaps of scrap metal and trash lining the roads. I learned to love this alley, now called Ring Road, and got to know many of the mechanics and fruit vendors.

I only once had a problem in this alley. It was 2am and I was walking home from a bar down the street called Casablanca. Nobody, especially expats, should be walking at night in Nairobi. I came to my eight-foot-high gate lined with electric fencing and banged on the door for the security guard to open. I kept pounding but no luck. He must really have been sleeping. All the noise alerted five street dogs, who came running my way to investigate. Alone in the alley and outnumbered, it was too far to make it to the other side of the street before the dogs got to me. I looked around and grabbed a rock and tensed for the strike. The dogs rushed at me and then jumped past me to land together in a heap of trash where they eagerly started digging for food.

Getting around Nairobi without a car proved to be a challenge. Most evenings I would take taxis around the neighborhood, even if it was only a few minutes' walk away. This frustrated me. However, taking taxis was not guaranteed to avoid trouble either. One evening when I was coming home from one of the best Ethiopian restaurants in Nairobi – called Habesha – I was pulled over at a police checkpoint. My taxi had just pulled out of the driveway and I was in the process of putting on my seatbelt when the police flashlights pointed our way. The officer started his standard intimidation dialog, asking where I was going, where I lived and to show my passport. I mentioned K-Rep.

"I saw you were not wearing your seatbelt. That is a 2,000 Kenyan Shilling ($24) fine."

He had me. Although I knew the fine was not that high and he most certainly would be pocketing the money, I told him I did not have that kind of money on me.

"What about that?" he said pointing at a bag on my lap.

"That's leftovers from my meal," I said.

"I am hungry."

"Seriously?" I blurted back. "This food is very spicy and I do not think you will like it."

Many Kenyans I had encountered were not into spicy food or any other food outside their home comforts.

Fortunately, I was lucky and the officer changed his mind about the food. I eventually parted with 2,000 Kenyan Schillings, which I hated to do. But he was right, technically, I was not wearing my seatbelt at the moment he stopped us.

Later that week I made a great Kenyan friend named Hillary (which in Kenya is a common name for a guy). He worked at the K-Rep Bank. In addition to being a banker, he was also a talented poet and reader of world history. Hillary was short and bald with glasses, but somehow he could produce an intense gaze that spoke of a deep intelligence. He was quick with a smile or joke, which I found unique to the accounting crowd he worked with at K-Rep. Hillary also had a car. He took it upon himself to show me around the rougher parts of Nairobi such as River Road where you can buy a fake Somali passport for $10 or even hire someone to kill anyone you like for just $25.

"These are some bad guys," Hillary told me as he pointed to a group of Kenyan men in overalls sitting by a pile of car parts.

"Like some of the rough guys in the *Godfather* movie. You know?"

I took out my camera to snap a quick picture. Hillary grabbed my arm before I could get the window down.

"I know these guys but they will not think twice about taking a camera from a mzungu like you," Hillary scolded.

Hilary had grown up on the streets with his single mother and his first job as a teenager was selling drugs. His mom married a police officer who whipped him into shape and Hillary applied his business skills to start a scrap metal company in one of the slums. Hillary went on to be a fabulous student at some of Kenya's top academic institutions and had recently completed his MBA. Some of Hillary's childhood friends had now graduated to become the slumlords, drug lords or ran the various seedy establishments in Nairobi's toughest neighborhoods.

One particular night, Hillary drove me out to a section in East Nairobi near a neighborhood called Kayole, which in 2008 and 2009 was notorious for its crime and carjacking. I cringed at what the US Embassy would say if they saw me there. Hillary's university friend had just bought a bar and he wanted me to meet him. The guy was the president of his class at the University of Nairobi and quite the smooth talker. He was well on his way to becoming a classic Kenyan politician.

I was enjoying my complimentary drinks in the two-room building which was surrounded by sheet metal, woodpiles and wire mesh. While observing the crowd coming in for the evening, I realized that all the people – and there were twenty-five or so – were men.

I turned to the young owner and told him: "I really like your bar. But there seems to be a problem."

"And what is that?" He asked.

"Why are you discriminating against women? You are not abiding to the new 'gender equality' requirements from parliament."

The owner and his friend laughed hard. The owner pointed at the door. "Here comes our female representative." In strolled a gorgeous Kenyan girl who made her way over to the owner and slipped her arm around him. She was introduced as his girlfriend but the music was so loud I did not catch her name.

A few more rounds of Tusker later the girl started dancing by herself, seemingly with nobody paying attention but me. The owner had stepped outside and was slapping hands with a large group of younger men out on the street. The guy was already running for office it seemed. His girlfriend looked out at me and waved me over.

"Come dance with me, Mzungu," she slurred and grabbed my hands.

I looked over at Hillary who just gave me the thumbs up. The next thing I knew the girl had pinned me and started kissing me. Normally I would not have minded but I was in a dangerous part of town and probably the only white American guy for miles. Now I was making out with the bar owner's girlfriend and surrounded by his thugs who could easily make me disappear forever. I broke away from the girl and grabbed Hillary who drove me home, laughing all the way.

The commute from my apartment to the office took between four and seven minutes (depending on the elevators) and I never had to leave the security compound. It was a good thing too, because the Nairobi traffic was getting worse every day and some of my colleagues would commute for several hours across town to get to work.

The K-Rep office building also had a pretty good restaurant, called Tinto's, on the first floor which served a decent breakfast and had a great happy hour deal of two burgers and a beer for KShs 400 or $4.50. As a result, I did not leave my apartment and office much during the week. Whenever I did, it was usually for work meetings. I would step out on the street and try to find a decent looking taxi, then argue about a price for five minutes before setting off on my journey.

One day I found a particularly friendly and competent driver named Benson. When I told him my last name was Robinson he got excited and thought we must be related in some way. Benson gave me a great price and drove me exactly where I wanted. I started using Benson more and more and told him that all my friends would use him if he kept his prices competitive and showed up early for his rides. It worked. I recommended Benson to five of my friends in Nairobi and they started using him. The next thing I knew, Benson had recruited three other drivers and started a company called La Playa – The Beach in Spanish. He'd learned a little Spanish from his time as a driver for one of the embassies in Nairobi and liked the word. I was not sure if Benson's early success was due to the lack of reliable taxi drivers in Nairobi or if Benson was just that much better than everyone. Maybe it was both.

The money from GBF finally hit our bank account and I got busy spending it. The company had six small rural field offices with two to three staff in each office. Only two of them had working computers and nobody used email.

Monthly, handwritten, reports were sent by mail, outlining how many loans had been disbursed, how much had been repaid, and a series of other indicators outlining the activities around gathering new clients. One of the accountants at the head office had the tedious job of receiving the paper reports and typing the data into an Excel spreadsheet. If a mistake was discovered, it took weeks to manually correct and update the reports.

The first thing I invested the grant money in was upgrading the technology. I found a great organization in the UK that refurbished computers and sold them to social organizations in Africa for a fraction of the price of a new computer. We bought eighteen (for the same price of three new computers in Kenya) so that each office could have at least two. The head office could also upgrade its equipment. I personally went around to each office and delivered the computers so that I could earn some early credibility with the teams and get to know the office staff and clients, a trick I learned at Accenture with the clients. The rest of the grant money I spent on staff training.

Client repayment rates were floating at around eighty-eight percent, which was not bad but not good for microfinance institutions, which averaged ninety-five percent and above. So I found a consultant from an organization called FrontFin and put him to work training our staff on delinquency management and business planning. The delinquency management training was a big success. Repayment rates improved to ninety-six percent in four months but the business planning training was a flop.

The training focused on teaching senior loan officers and managers how to use a very complex and slow Excel program. The staff would enter in over fifty different types of assumptions and data points for the model to then spit out a plan. I was not sure if I should blame the program or perhaps the lower level of computer literacy of my staff at the time.

We focused our attention on business process mapping and improvement (another good consulting skill). From this exercise we realized that we could improve loan processing time and repayment reconciliations if we opened bank accounts for each office instead of making them share with other branches. The maps also outlined how terribly dependent we were on paper, since a loan form would travel back and forth via courier three times between the head office and field. With quickly improving internet speeds in the rural areas through the mobile carriers, it seemed we could use technology here to speed up the loan process. However, Kenya had not adopted the digital signature as legally binding so we needed all of the paper to stand up in court if a client were to sue for whatever reason. It seemed that loan digitization was a project for a later date.

I spent a lot of time visiting offices and loan groups. I helped the managers think through their growth strategy or assisted the loan officers tag the cow assets with ear tags. This was not an easy job and took several people to hold down the cow while the tagger used a large hole-punch to put the tag in the ear. If the tagger missed on the first attempt then the cow realized it was in danger, it was much more difficult to settle it down for a second attempt. After about twenty cows I had become quite accomplished at tagging, a skill that has not really been put to use outside of Africa.

In general, I thought I would have a difficult time gaining credibility with the staff and clients as a young foreigner, but this did not seem to be the case. In fact, I quickly discovered that our clients and staff trusted me much more than any of the Kenyan management. Even the FSAs I helped to open benefitted significantly from having me at their launch ceremonies. At the time, a foreigner was seen as someone who was there to help and not interested in stealing money in a scam or some tribally motivated ploy. This just shows how deeply the history of corruption has hurt the culture of the country and business.

The Portfolio Manager at GBF, whom I had met in Washington DC, Jaime Ramirez, came to visit in February of 2009 to learn more about the KDA pilot programs and provide more help on the business strategy. He had seen the business plan and spent several days in the field visiting farmers and staff. He was surprised at how similar parts of rural Kenya looked to his hometown in Colombia, with the green hills and farms.

Jaime sat Aleke and me down to think hard about the structure and strategy of the company. He walked us through some of the activities outlined in Jim Collin's book, *Good to Great,* and focused on a story about a fox and hedgehog. Many entrepreneurs and early-stage businesses fall into the shiny penny syndrome and are constantly changing strategy and focus, similar to how a fox hunts its prey. This takes a lot of energy and can prevent a business from executing its strategy. However, the hedgehog only has one defense mechanism – deploying its spikes if it gets in trouble. It may be boring but at least it works. This session resonated with Aleke and me. We quickly saw that the business had too much complexity with the youth lending program and even the rural enterprise program. We cut out youth and put the rural enterprise in a later phase of the business plan. These activities were draining resources and we were better off sticking to the rural asset-financing program that we knew worked. Then we spent the remainder of Jaime's visit working on the first mission statement and mission for Juhudi Kilimo.

In March of 2009 I made a general presentation to the K-Rep Group board, which oversaw the operations of KDA. The board had esteemed members of Kenyan society such as Kimanthi Mutua, who was the Managing Director of the K-Rep Bank, and Bethuel Kiplagat, who was a former

Kenyan ambassador to France and currently the chancellor of Egerton University in Kenya.

I told the board that KDA had a very promising opportunity to spin off some of its pilot programs into a new company that was now being funded by GBF. To my surprise the K-Rep Group was receptive to transferring all the required assets as soon as possible to the new entity but agreed that it needed a name.

Aleke and the rest of the K-Rep Group board really liked the name Juhudi, which means 'effort' or 'hard work' in Kiswahili, but it was already the name of a specific loan product at the K-Rep Bank. I suggested that we add something about agriculture since two of the business lines were in agriculture. I had my Kiswahili dictionary in my bag and started reading off all the translations for agriculture, farmers, farming, crops and a few others. I shouted "Kilimo" and that seemed to sit well with everyone. Kilimo literally means 'agricultural' in Kiswahili. The phrase 'juhudi kilimo' does not mean anything other than 'agricultural effort' or some would later interpret it to be 'hardworking farmer'.

"Juhudi Kilimo," said Aleke. "I like that."

And the new company had a name.

In order for the asset transfer to be legal, the company needed to be registered with the government Registrar, overseen by the Kenya Revenue Authority and guided under the Companies Act. I expected the process of registering a company in Kenya to be drawn out, bureaucratic and full of corruption. We completed all the forms, had a K-Rep lawyer sign them and paid a small registration fee. In less than three weeks we heard back that the new company, Juhudi Kilimo, was officially registered with the Government of Kenya on April 1st, 2009, April Fool's day. Perhaps this should have been a sign for me of things to come.

Chapter 5 | Amboseli

Greg, Krysten and I went on another safari to Amboseli National Park, but this time brought tents and camping equipment. I am not sure how Greg convinced the embassy to let him do a trip like this since most US Embassy staff had strict travel restrictions for security purposes. It was a four-hour drive from Nairobi. Mombasa Road was under heavy construction as it was being improved to help the truck traffic flow from the port in Mombasa to Nairobi, then Kampala and beyond. It was a dry time of year and we drove into a dry lake bed in the middle of Amboseli. Mt. Kilimanjaro peaked through the clouds to present a majestic backdrop to the wispy acacia trees that were surrounded by elephants and giraffes. This was what I had pictured Africa to be. Our campsite was in the middle of the park and consisted of a small bar/guard station and several water spigots set up in various corners of the camp. The site was surrounded by an electric fence. This fence had wide holes and was designed more to keep the elephants out than anything else. Snakes, hyenas and even a small lion could easily slip under the fence. The camp was thick with underbrush and trees. We selected a clearing below a tree to park the car and set up camp for KShs 300 or $3. The cheapest lodge in the park was $240 per night. We were the only campers at the entire place. A group from a local Maasai tribe, who had been made famous in Hollywood for their traditional dress and warrior reputations, managed the camp. It made me feel better that the tribe who kills more lions than any other was standing guard. That night, after cooking our dinner, we were surrounded by the wild animal calls and terrifying whoops of the hyenas. I shone my headlamp on the perimeter of our camp and sets of eyes glowed from every dark corner. Most of them turned out to be small jackals or monkeys. I awoke just as the sun was coming up and walked outside my tent. I heard a crack and looked over to a Maasai who was walking my way. He pointed behind me and I turned to see a massive elephant not 30 feet from where I stood. The electric fence was between us but the elephant could have stepped over it. Its soft padded feet helped the elephant glide soundlessly over the ground. If the Maasai had not pointed it out I would have missed it. Just then the first rays of sun hit the peak of Kilimanjaro lifting the whole mountain up in a rose pink hue. The Maasai and I watched in silence as the elephant slowly moved to join its herd across the valley. I would go on to have hundreds more safaris and nights camping in Kenya but that first trip to Amboseli will always be remembered.

Harold's Visit, Disaster

I was technically the only GBF employee in Kenya, so the preparation for Harold's visit fell heavily on my shoulders. Harold had spent the past thirty years of his life at the IFC, where employees fly business class and stay in five-star hotels around the world. Their itineraries and local transportation were managed for them by armies of local staff from the World Bank and its affiliates in the countries they visited. Needless to say, Harold's expectations were a little higher than anything I could deliver for him.

Three of the larger events I had to organize included a breakfast with VIPs to talk about GBF, a lunch at the IFC and a dinner meeting where we were inviting the high-net-worth investors to see if any would invest in Juhudi Kilimo. After sending out volleys of emails I had twenty-five people coming to the breakfast and six coming to the dinner.

We held the breakfast at the Norfolk Hotel in downtown Nairobi and spent some decent money preparing a room and a buffet that would run from

7:30am to 9am. By 7:45am we had two people who arrived and I suspected that the rest were stuck in typical Nairobi traffic. By 8:15am our third guest came and I was getting worried. I had received solid RSVPs from twenty-two other people. What had happened? Harold started fuming. Finally we went ahead with three guests and Harold told them all about the new GBF investment facility. We fielded a few questions and then the guests left.

Harold and I got in a taxi for the next meeting. We travelled in silence for about ten minutes. Finally, Harold broke the tension.

"I know this is probably not your fault but I have nobody else to blame here. That breakfast was an absolute disaster. We wasted a lot of the fund's money only to have three junior staff show up." He continued to berate me for the next 15 minutes in the taxi. It did not bother me too much but who was this guy and why was he such a jerk? Did he realize I had left my nicely-paid job at Accenture to earn $1,000 a month working really long and hard hours for him?

The IFC lunch was not much better. I think I was the oldest person in the group at twenty-eight. I did get a few promising contacts for a potential investment with the IFC. I would meet a total of eight more times with the IFC but none of those resulted in anything valuable for KDA or the new pilot programs.

Our afternoon meeting was a follow-up talk with an extremely talented American entrepreneur named Jay Kimmelman, who had already made his millions at a young age developing educational software. Now he was trying to improve education opportunities for Kenyans.

Jay had just started a social business called Bridge International Academies that provides low-cost, high-quality schools for children living in Nairobi's slums. I had visited Jay and one of the schools earlier as part of a side project for GBF. I absolutely loved the concept of utilizing all of Jay's knowledge in education software to equip non-teachers with technology and scripts to read as lessons for the students. The result was very high quality educational content for a fraction of the cost.

Jay already had some investors lining up to fund him but he liked GBF's combination of providing capacity building grants alongside their investments. Harold's dour mood, however, spilled into the meeting. Harold got hung up on the challenge of purchasing land from slumlords, who could not (or would not) provide proof of ownership. This was a major risk since the school buildings were the primary assets of the company at the time and a slumlord could just decide to claim the school at any time. I felt Jay was still onto something big and Harold was not seeing it. GBF never made their investment but Bridge International went on to be a smashing success and set up hundreds of schools, educating over 100,000 students.

I dropped Harold off at the hotel for a few hours before getting ready for the dinner event. At least Aleke would be at the dinner and he could help deal with Harold if that also turned out to be a disaster. Fortunately we had four people out of the six show up for this one. Aleke and I delivered the business plan presentation for the new company after Harold gave his GBF summary. The guests listened politely and asked a few insightful questions. Then one person who managed a series of private Kenyan investment clubs asked: "Why would we want to invest in something that is high risk in agriculture, a long-term investment of five to seven years and a low expected return of nine to seventeen percent?"

The other investors all started to nod their heads and one added: "This looks like it might be a better project for the donors. Can't you talk to some of the development institutions instead of investors?"

We thanked them all and they left.

Harold, Aleke and I sat in the large banquet room finishing our drinks. Harold's tone and body language matched that of a gambler who had just lost big at the blackjack tables.

"This does not look good at all, guys. Just so you know, we can't keep funding this much longer, especially if we are not getting any traction from outside investors."

"Surely there are others, Harold. We just need some more time to reach them," Aleke said.

"No. What you need to do is start offering more of these rural enterprise loans. That is how every microfinance institution reached profitability sooner and started generating the returns these investors are looking for."

"But Harold, we don't even know if these loans will work. They are also not necessarily benefitting the very rural poor like the smaller loans."

Harold slammed down his drink. "Aleke, if you don't start doing this, there is not going to be a bankable company."

"Harold you can't just come in here and dictate what we are going to do. We are not investing in the rural enterprises until we can learn more about them."

Harold stood up. "Yes we can Aleke. Do you want me to give you a number of these things to invest in? I will! You will have to do it if you want us in on this. $5 million is far too much for us to invest or raise for you. You're on your own." Harold looked at me. "Oh and Nat's contract is coming to an end next month and we are not keeping him here."

My stomach dropped. I had worked absurdly hard for Harold over the last eight months, pulling late nights and trying desperately to get this company together. Now he was just going to abandon us? It took all the control I could gather to keep from throwing my beer at Harold.

Aleke stood up. "But Harold, we are partners in this. Partners hold hands and rise together. They support each other when things are down too."

Harold was not hearing any of it and walked out.

Aleke and I got into his car. We sat in silence for some time as the car meandered its way through the traffic.

"I don't ever want to talk to Harold again," I said to Aleke once my emotions were under control. "That guy is awful. My loyalties are with you and KDA. You have taken such good care of me and treated me like family."

"No, Nat," Aleke replied in his booming voice. "Do not hold grudges with people like that. Just let it go. We will set up a call with Harold in a week. He will be reasonable again. You watch."

Just like that Aleke had forgiven Harold and looked at the bigger picture. I still had a hard time doing this for Harold, what with all the anger and emotion running through me.

But Aleke was right. A week later Harold agreed to pay for me for an additional three months after my contract so I could help Aleke raise money. Harold also offered to put us in touch with anyone in his network to help with the fundraising. I would have regretted throwing my beer at Harold that night at the hotel.

It was June 2009 and I thought I could probably raise the $5 million before I went back to Accenture in September.

How hard could this fundraising game really be?

Chapter 6 | Fundraising

I will be first to admit that Aleke and I were clueless about how to raise $5 million through investors. Aleke was quite successful at raising grant money from donors, but that was quite different. Most grants require a formal proposal and perhaps a site visit to see the operations. Sometimes it was just a meeting or phone call with some donors to convince them to send money. The emphasis of the pitch or sell was also quite different. Aleke told me that most of the donors he had worked with in the past were most concerned about helping rural, poor Kenyans. Most donors had specific ideas about what they wanted to do with their money and sent out requests for proposals to see who could carry out the work. While chasing after grants in the past, KDA was constantly changing its plans and strategy to meet the needs of various donors. If a donor wanted a project to be done in a specific town, slum or area of Kenya, it was done without any consideration for the viability of the area. Many donors then required rigorous monitoring and evaluation of the funded project, which could almost cost as much as the entire project itself. KDA had several full time staff that were dedicated to monitoring the various pilot projects and preparing lengthy reports to the donors.

Investors were different. They were interested in funding businesses or ideas that closely fitted their investment focus. If an investment did not fit their criteria, instead of asking the company to change their business, they would not invest. Investors also seemed to want well- thought-through financial projections, a strong business plan and a capable management team as a minimum, even before starting a conversation.

Aleke knew someone who worked at a new private equity fund in Nairobi called the Blue Line Mirror Fund, whose base was the Netherlands. Aleke sent them our business plan and a few days later we were invited over for a meeting. Both of us put on our best suits and brought copies of the business plan.

I was expecting them to ask us to pitch our business in a formal presentation room to a panel of experts. We met with two women portfolio managers, one Kenyan and one Dutch. They were very pleasant and asked some probing questions. It was just like having a conversation about the business as opposed to a formal pitch. We thought this was going very well, then the ladies talked about their various funds and how they only invest in companies with at least two years of audited financials and a base case projection to reach a return on equity of twenty percent. We were a long way from reaching both of those and it seemed the only reason they even met with us was due to Aleke's connection. The women politely ripped apart the business, identifying our flaws on the profit margin analysis, market analysis and outlined a few operation risks related to the poultry loan business that neither Aleke nor I had ever considered.

It was embarrassing. These women seemed to know more about our business than we did. It turned out that one of the portfolio managers had been investing in microfinance institutions for the last ten years and could spot patterns in the business just from reviewing a business plan and some financial ratios. However, I found myself leaving the meeting with pages of notes. The meeting provided us with some great insights to improve the business plan for the next investor.

It was also clear that the initial financial model we had built with Vinay was becoming outmoded quickly. The model was high level and difficult to update with new data each month. I spent a few weeks looking through spreadsheets and scouring the internet for good microfinance projecting models. One of the consultants we worked with suggested that we hire a full-time analyst to build and update these models. That turned out to be a difficult skill set to find in Kenya.

We had plenty of accountants and all the finance people we interviewed were also more focused on accounting than real financial forecasting. The only financial tool I could find to help was the same massive Excel program called Microfin. It was over 100mbs and would usually crash my computer every other time I opened it. But it was quite detailed and designed specifically for microfinance. So I locked myself in my office for two weeks and learned everything I could about how to set up and run the model. By the end of it all I think I had become an expert in the clunky thing and we had some beautiful financial projections for our five-year income statement, balance sheet and cash flow statement. It also provided nice operational data on the number of loans, loan officers and key ratios, which were all built on over two years of historical data as our assumptions. I hoped it would stand up to the scrutiny of future investors.

✱✱✱✱✱

In 2009 the ratio of single women to single men in my circle of friends in Nairobi was significantly in my favor. I started dating a young photographer from the US who was addicted to adventure. We spent a weekend on Kenya's beautiful coast, which was a quick forty-five minute flight from Nairobi. Much of the northern coast is populated by Italian communities and it was rumored that many of the homes belonged to former Mafia bosses who came to Kenya to keep a low profile. Whatever the reason, it means that you can find fantastic gelato on the coast and rent beautiful villas on the beach for a fraction of the cost of a hotel. The houses come complete with a cook, maid, gardener and fishermen who sold fresh fish at your doorstep.

This particular weekend we were staying in Diani beach to the south. We rented bikes and rode for several hours until we reached a remote village called Gazi. I brought my phone and KShs 500 since I did not want to lose much if we were robbed. At some point during the ride we stumbled upon a large complex that resembled a country club. The place was deserted but the bar had cold beers in the refrigerator. We grabbed two and drank them, expecting someone to come and kick us out of the place. Nobody did and I (against my girlfriend's wishes) put KShs 500, or about $6, in the refrigerator. Then we biked a few more miles back to the road since it was getting late and we had a long ride back.

We had ridden through a field of sharp thorns without noticing and suddenly became stranded on the side of the road with four flat bike tires. Normally, this is never a problem in Kenya since every town has several mechanics and bicycle repair facilities. We found one and the man got to work identifying eighteen separate punctures. He wanted KShs 10 per puncture, which seemed reasonable. Then it dawned on me that I had nothing to pay the man. I had spent all our money on the beer a few miles away. We pleaded and begged but the man would not repair the tires for free. I even tried to offer my phone as payment but the cheapest Nokia model on the market was certainly not worth KShs 180 to him.

It was getting dark, we had no place to stay and could not even afford a local matatu to get us back. Some young children were watching the discussion with interest and suddenly all started talking and running around. They dug into their small pockets pulling out small coins while others ran home or to their friends to get more money. They somehow managed to collect KShs 150 in coins, which was a small fortune for these children. After more negotiating with the bicycle repairman he finally agreed to do the work for 150. I could not believe how he just sat and watched these very poor children, who could not even afford shoes, donate their life savings to help two complete strangers who were in dire need. I did not even know what to say to the children for this kind of generosity. I asked if I could send the money back to them over M-Pesa (which is the world-famous money transfer system in Kenya) when I got back to Nairobi. One of the children gave me the number for his older brother who had a phone and M-Pesa account. But he told me "it will not work because if you send any money to him he will never give it to me". We biked the few hours back to Diani just as the sun set without any more incidents. I sent the money to the brother but, of course, I never heard back.

******

Aleke and I continued meeting with potential funders and had several conference calls with a few of Harold's contacts. From our meetings with the more commercial funds it became clear that an investment in Juhudi was a stretch for them but they recommended meeting with a newer type of "impact investor" or "social investor". These funds invest donor money or low-cost money into businesses that can generate social as well as financial returns. In the coming two months we had set up more meetings or had calls with close to fifteen potential institutional investors.

Once the word was out that we were looking for money, some of the investors we met referred us to other investors. Aleke and I managed to get some contacts for a few big name impact investing funds like Acumen, Rockefeller Foundation and Ford Foundation. We met with someone named David Kitusa, who managed the entire partner relationships for an organization called Kiva.org which crowdsources capital for microfinance institutions around the world. David had worked with Aleke before at K-Rep and was very enthusiastic about the prospects. However, once again we did not meet the minimal criteria to be funded by Kiva, but we applied anyway and sent David our financials.

Things seemed positive that I might be able to close on the funding before my time was up at GBF but in the end, nearly all of them said no. Juhudi was in a difficult position. As we had spun off to become a for-profit entity, the traditional donors were not interested in funding us, yet we were far from being attractive to commercial investors and local banks. The social investors seemed to be our only hope, yet none of them invested in startup companies. They required three years of audited financials and profitability. We had neither and were about to complete our first year as an independent company. In emails and meetings, investors started to get more critical of the business.

We had one US foundation that was quite interested in providing a grant or low-interest loan, so we invited them out for a visit to our field operations. I personally went with the foundation officer in our company vehicle, driven by Isika for the day. My field staff and I answered his tireless questions about Juhudi and Kenya. At the end of the long and draining day, I thought things had gone well and the foundation officer seemed quite interested. As we pulled into his five-star hotel in Nairobi he said to me: "You are doing some great work here and I love the company. Although with the recent downturn in the US markets, our foundation does not have the funds at the moment to devote to any early-stage companies. Sorry!" He jumped out of the truck and I never heard from him again.

Our company driver, Isika, was much more upset with him than I was for not telling this to us before he wasted our entire day. I told Isika that this was the game we have to play. We just smile and move on to the next investor.

Later that same week Kiva rejected us for a second time that year. It was late August and I only had one more month on my GBF contract. I was getting a little desperate. Kenya had really grown on me and I did not want to leave Juhudi right in the middle of fundraising and launching the business. The work was much more fun than what I was doing at Accenture anyway.

On a rainy afternoon in September, I met with a French private equity fund called I&P, which invested in early stage companies and had a track record in Africa for investing in microfinance institutions. They were a perfect fit on paper. We sat in the lobby with a shorter, younger portfolio manager and a much bigger independent consultant. I had sent them the entire business plan earlier so we jumped right into questions.

"So, explain to me why this rural enterprise business line is so important and when do you expect to merge it with the rest of the business?" the younger man snapped at me as he sat back and fixed me with a penetrating gaze.

I stammered out an answer that clearly did not impress him.

"Your operating expense ratio is far too high for your portfolio yield. That should make it nearly impossible for you to reach profitability, especially with more commercial financing as you are planning. This really is not a very good business structure and certainly not something we will invest in anytime soon."

I left the hotel exhausted and started thinking seriously about returning to the US.

✶✶✶✶✶✶

That weekend my girlfriend and I took another adventurous trip to visit some lava caves and a supposedly beautiful volcanic crater called Mt. Suswa, a few hours from Nairobi. Information about this place was scarce and we had some sketchy directions from a random blog post, which we followed.

I rented a small sedan from my taxi friend Benson, who had now grown to ten drivers and a few safari vans.

We drove for several hours and never found the turn off or sign for Mt. Suswa. It was the dry season and the dirt roads had turned into a dust bowl with massive clouds of dust following us wherever we went. Dusty zebras and random herds of skinny goats marched past us with their heads down and eyes closed to the dust. The road took us miles from any semblance of a town, so we stopped to talk to several of the local Maasai living alongside the road. We did our best to translate "cave" into Kiswahili but only received some confused looks or a halfhearted point in a random direction. Finally, we drove past a dilapidated green sign at an intersection that said Mt. Suswa Conservancy. The sign had fallen off its hinge on one side and pointed towards the ground. We guessed the sign originally pointed to the right and followed a road that eventually led us to a Maasai village. My girlfriend was driving. We stopped to ask the Maasai about the caves and the entire town came over to see us. We could not get a straight answer out of anyone about where these caves were and the men continued to say we needed to pay them so they could show us the way. We were both frustrated with this so my girlfriend hit the gas and we started to drive out of the town and away from the crowd of people. We didn't get far.

We slammed into a two-foot ravine and crumpled the front bumper of the car. The rear wheels were off the ground. The Maasai just watched. I got out of the car and started to dig. My girlfriend got the tire jack out of the car so we could elevate the tires and perhaps put rocks under them. The Maasai slowly started to gather again and the children joined in the digging. We spent hours digging and pushing, with little success. It was getting late and I thought we might have to camp in the village, or perhaps I could call Benson to send another car to rescue us. He would not be happy with me for the damage done to his car. I was not carrying much money or anything else of value so I did not worry much about being mugged. In any case, the Maasai have different views of personal property and most of them do not derive value from the modern sense of material wealth. The cows and goats owned by an individual or family represent the only wealth and source of livelihoods. In looking at the herds of cows in the village, I realized that these animals were the savings and investment accounts of the village. Wealth was stored with each animal and accumulated interest from the milk or offspring produced each year. Unlike cash in the bank, the animals are susceptible to drought and disease, which can wipe out entire flocks, destroying years of hard-earned wealth. The Maasai have been doing this for centuries and seemed to endure each hardship after the droughts by picking up and starting again. I admired the simplicity of the life and balance with nature. Many books and movies told the stories of foreigners who leave their lives of material wealth to live with the Maasai or Samburu. I occasionally envied that type of life, away from the chaotic rush of the modern world.

A loud "clank" interrupted my daydreaming as we somehow managed to get the car out of the ravine. It took ten of the Maasai boys pushing alongside me to finally move the car. Once out, I thought we should just drive back to Nairobi. My girlfriend wanted to go on and try to find the caves. This time we took one of the Maasai guides. We got the car stuck two more times and scraped the bottom of the car badly but we made it to the top of the volcano. The views were some of the best I had ever seen in Kenya. Mt. Suswa is a bowl miles wide with lush forest inside the crater. We hiked through the extensive cave networks in tubes that were a hundred feet high in places. They were filled with bats and guano (bat droppings) several feet deep on the floor of the caves. If the Maasai wardens of Mt. Suswa would work on the signs, road and some other amenities, it could become a spectacular site for visitors. Several weeks after our visit, the BBC filmed a documentary in the caves as part of their widely popular Planet Earth series.

Then again, the Maasai also consider Mt. Suswa to be one of the most sacred places in the world. An elder must bless any non-Maasai visitor with cow's milk before entering the center of the crater. Perhaps some pristine places are better left free of tourists and development.

******

I attended a local Association of Microfinance Institutions (AMFI) event in Nairobi, where all the industry leaders met to discuss relevant regulatory issues. After all the attendants left, I noticed that someone had left a thick book that had a title in French and another in English. It was the African Microfinance Transparency (AMT) book of investor members. It outlined nearly eighty microfinance investment funds around the world by summarizing the types of investments they made and the general structure of their investments (debt, equity, long term, etc.). This was a windfall find for me. I already had a list of forty funds I had built on my own and my spreadsheet of potential investors was growing quickly. Out of so many funds there had to be one that would invest in us.

I noticed that the AMT website said they were having an investor conference in Nairobi the next week and got excited when I saw one of the organizers was a girl I had met the week earlier at another networking event. I called her up and asked if we could attend. She informed me that there was a 'speed dating' session for microfinance institutions but that the event was only open to 'regulated or rated microfinance institutions'. I was not sure what it meant to be rated but I knew we were not regulated. I talked to Aleke about it and we both decided to just crash the event anyway. We could at least get a beer in the hotel bar if the organizers turned us away.

Aleke and I put our suits on again and walked into the five-star Serena Hotel, which was hosting the conference. My friend saw me and rolled her eyes.

"You are lucky because a microfinance organization from Nigeria had their flight canceled last night and could not attend. I will put you in their spot on the speed dating schedule but please do not tell anyone you are not rated or I will get in trouble."

What proceeded was probably the most effective and valuable two hours Aleke and I had ever spent fundraising.

The banquet hall was set up with twenty booths, one for each investor. The microfinance representatives would then spend five minutes at each booth talking about their respective institutions. At the end of the five minutes, all parties would exchange contact information and decide if a follow up was necessary.

While Juhudi Kilimo was still at too early a stage for many of the investors, we made some very promising contacts with the Grameen Foundation USA, Alterfin from Brussels, Triple Jump and Triodos from the Netherlands, Agora from London, Incofin, and ResponsAbility from Switzerland. Most of the portfolio managers or portfolio associates at the conference were in their mid-to-late twenties so I connected well with many of them. This was a first trip to Nairobi for many of the junior staff working with the investors.

That evening I took them all out for drinks, dinner and then went dancing into the late hours of the night at all my favorite places. I remember looking around and thinking that none of the other microfinance institutions had any of their staff out socializing with these investors.

The time spent building these relationships with the junior staff paid off later. For these portfolio staff were the gatekeepers to the funds.

Chapter 7 | The End is Near

My contract with GBF expired in October. As Harold warned earlier, GBF stopped paying me and was not interested in continuing to support Aleke or KDA until more investors put up the funds. My options were to return to Accenture in Washington, DC, try to find another job someplace, or remain in Kenya with Aleke and KDA. The third option would likely not come with a salary until some new outside funding was secured. I had some savings I could live off, but it was a risk to jump into an early-stage organization with no clear future. I was having too much fun in Kenya and we had met so many great potential investors. One of them had to be interested in investing. I thought to myself, if I give it three months, I could gauge the probability of any of these new investors putting money into KDA. Accenture might even take me back after extending my leave of absence another three months. After some long talks with my parents and twin brother, I decided to stay in Kenya as volunteer without a salary until the end of December to try and close an investment. That seemed like an appropriate timeline to me. Accenture later agreed to extend my sabbatical a few more months but after December I had to come back if I still wanted my job.

The rejections kept coming in from investors. Triple Jump, Triodos, ResponsAbility and Incofin all told us to talk to them after we had two years of audited financials and were closer to profitability. Agora said that they decided not to make any investments in Kenya. Grameen said we were too small for their main fund but might fit their new 'pioneer fund' being launched next year. Alterfin was also launching a new 'early stage' fund called

FEFISOL but it would not be ready until the next year. I had applied to Kiva for a third and final time to be one of their partners.

We had contracted out a local auditing firm to help us separate the financial data for Juhudi Kilimo while it was a pilot program at KDA from 2006-2008. We thought this might get us another two to three years of audited financials to qualify for these investors. The process was messy and the resulting report did not exactly look like a formal financial audit but it was something.

I was not sleeping much and Aleke started to spend more and more time with the other pilot program at KDA. Out of my list of 130 investors, five said they were interested, twenty-five said to talk to them next year and the rest said no. It was not particularly encouraging.

To make things worse the new company was quickly running out of cash. We were burning through KShs 1 million ($11,000) per month and with only KShs 4.5 million ($50,000) in the bank, it was easy to do the math. We did not have many months left. We would probably run out of money just as my own timeline was up at the end of December. I hated the idea of telling all the young and hopeful Kenyan staff that we had to shut down since I could not raise any money for them. What was worse was the notion of telling the thousands of rural poor smallholder farmers that we could no longer be their way out of poverty, to better lives. The backlog of new farmers wanting to take our loans was growing every day as word spread around the rural communities in Kenya that we had a loan product that really worked to help farmers. In my desperation, I decided to reach out to my friend Jessica Jackley from Kiva, essentially to beg her to let Juhudi into their program. I had not done a very good job keeping in touch with Jessica and tried to set up a phone call with her, but I ended up writing an awkward email. I tried to appeal to her about how unique our program is and how it mirrored Kiva's original story of helping a rural goat herder with a loan in West Africa. Jessica very considerately wrote a short reply saying she "would see what she could do" but that Kiva was recovering from some bad relationships in Kenya and trying to work with more established institutions to improve Kiva's own reputation.

I never head back from Jessica again and knew that I had probably hurt our personal relationship by trying to exploit her role in Kiva with a business proposition. By now it was late November of 2009, only one month away from my personal deadline and with two months of cash in the bank left to fund operations. Kiva's next review cycle would evaluate my proposal in early December. I told myself that if Kiva did not come through then I would leave Kenya before Christmas and accept that it just was not meant to be.

On a beautiful and warm summer day in Nairobi, David Kitusa called to inform us that Kiva had agreed to move us forward as a partner and conduct its 'due diligence'. Aleke and I were elated. Maybe Jessica had come through or maybe they just felt sorry for us. This was the first good news I had had in months and Aleke and I took David to his favorite Chinese restaurant to celebrate. Little did we know that this was just the beginning and probably not much to celebrate.

First, Kiva needed to put us through their rigorous due diligence and review process, which would last approximately one month before we could start fundraising on their website. If we passed the review, then we would be allowed to raise a small amount of money each month through Kiva during their probation period of three months. This meant, in the best-case scenario, we could get a small amount of money in the coming January but nothing substantial until April. It might mean we could keep the company going until April but that would certainly require more budget tightening and perhaps letting go some of our staff. It felt like the company was someone starving, receiving only one small piece of bread to eat each month for three months.

Then after waiting, they would get a dinner roll with a slice of cheese each month. It was enough to keep hope alive but not nearly enough to survive. I was put in touch with another Kiva employee named Ben Elberger. He was from New York and employee number five at Kiva in 2004 when he joined as an intern. Ben's boundless energy literally leapt through the phone when Aleke and I first had a conference call to discuss the logistics of the visit.

The due diligence consisted of Ben and David spending two days in Nairobi meeting with the management team (which consisted of Aleke, our accountant and me) as well as some of our support staff. They then wanted to spend four days in the field visiting as many offices as they could. Before that all happened, they needed a massive Excel spreadsheet completed with our monthly financial data going back as far as possible. Then they had a laundry list of legal documents, registration files, policy documents and board minutes, which we also had to provide. It took me nearly a week to get all of this material together for them and it was still not complete.

Ben Elberger had graduated from Stanford and somehow learned the entire microfinance business inside and out in a few years. He was on another level of intelligence but also one of the happiest people I have ever come across. Both Ben and David Kitusa spent a majority of their meetings laughing together. Ben also had the uncanny ability to get the entire room laughing and at ease, only then to fire an incredibly complex and critical question my way to throw me back on my heels.

Ben and David interrogated our staff and turned the business upside down. While in the field they tracked the paper trail of several loans to make sure the loan forms reflected the reality with the clients and field staff. Both Ben and David had done dozens of these visits all over Africa and were quite skilled at recognizing patterns or asking probing questions.

Ben had unearthed all kinds of issues with the business that nobody knew about. He found everything from a fraudulent loan officer who was taking money from clients to a major mistake in our equity flows from year to year that our auditors had missed. Ben produced a fifty-page document on all of his findings at Juhudi, which he delivered in the same way a jovial game show host tells his contestant has just won a new car.

After the exhausting week with Kiva I was not sure if they were happy with us or thought we were hopeless. A week of emails with more questions followed from Ben, then a week of silence. Agonizing silence. I had no idea what I should do about staying in Kenya. It was too early to know if I should buy a plane ticket home in January since we still had a chance with Kiva. Aleke and I went for a beer one evening that week where I thanked him for all of his support and apologized for not being able to bring in more money for them.

"At least now you know Kenya. You can tell people you have now been to Africa," he reflected.

We finally got a phone call from David at Kiva that Juhudi had been tentatively approved as a partner, with the condition that the K-Rep Group act as a guarantor on the Kiva loan. Kiva would provide a long disclaimer on their website that Juhudi did not technically fit the minimum audited financial requirement and was very high risk for any Kiva lender to fund. This was it. The sign I was waiting for. I would ride out the Kiva investment and hope that it would bring in more. Finally something worth celebrating.

Kiva only allowed us to raise $9,000 per month on their website for the first three months, then we could increase that to $20,000 if they were happy with us. It was a long cry from our projected $5 million but it was our first bit of new money in the door. Kiva managed to complete its due diligence and sign a loan agreement within one month of receiving formal approval from their investment committee.

Chapter 8 | Chief Financial Officer

Even if we maximized our Kiva funding each month, the company would still run out of money. Kiva was providing a loan that had to be repaid gradually, each month. We could generate income on the interest from our own loans to our clients but it still was not enough to cover our operational expenses. Kiva only extended our deadline of doom until perhaps June of that year. We needed so much more money. I was surprised that many of our employees did not quite understand how the business worked. I did my best to explain the financial problem we were in during a question and answer session with some of our new employees who had not yet been out to see the lending operations in the field offices.

"The business of Juhudi worked by borrowing large loans of $250,000 to $1,000,000 for two to three years from large institutions or banks," I told them. "Then, Juhudi would break these amounts into smaller loans of $500 to $2,000 to provide to the farmers for twelve months." One of the employees immediately raised his hand. My Kenyan staff, while very polite, never passed up an opportunity to share their thoughts. I would discover this to be true with our farmers as well.

"What does Juhudi actually do? And why don't the large institutions just lend to the farmers directly?" The employees asked.

"Juhudi does all the groundwork of screening the farmers and training them so they can repay their loans. Juhudi then would collect the repayments from the farmers and repay the larger institutions at the end of the two or three year period. The larger institutions do not have the staff or ability to meet with the thousands of farmers we meet with every day. I also think the banks are afraid to lend to farmers because they do not understand them." The room nodded in vague approval.

"However," I continued, "Juhudi also needs longer-term funds to operate the business such as paying staff, buying vehicles and office supplies. This longer-term funding is provided by equity investors who usually did not want their money back until five to seven years." It was this kind of equity funding that we badly needed.

A young woman who recently joined our accounting team raised her hand and asked: "How will the equity investors get their money back?"

"Good question." I responded. "The equity investors become the partial owners of the company. When they invest, they buy shares in the company. They will not get their money back until usually a new investor comes by and wants to buy their shares from them. This new investor could be a local bank or another investment fund." The accountant nodded in apparent satisfaction.

"Our problem is that we are having a hard time finding these equity investors." I said.

"But don't worry. I will not sleep until I have found a few to invest." I ended the meeting but I could tell some of the staff seemed worried.

In truth, nobody wanted to provide a long-term investment into an early-stage, agriculture finance company in Kenya. I later told my parents I would give Juhudi three more months to help them get through the probationary period with Kiva and then reevaluate my personal position again in March. With the Kiva funding secured, I felt that now we needed to hire a CFO to help with the fundraising while Aleke and I continued to build the business.

Harold had introduced us to a group he worked with while at the IFC, called the African Management Services Corporation, or AMSCO. The group was formed by collaboration between the IFC, United Nations

Development Program and the African Development Bank. The idea behind the program was to help bring professional expatriate managers who have international experience and place them with growing local companies in Africa. The managers in the program would technically be employed by the United Nations as a diplomat with some of the benefits such as a work visa and tax-free status. AMSCO would occasionally subsidize the salary of the manager and provide training grants to the African companies, especially if they had a very developmental focus (as Juhudi did). Given that hiring a Kenyan CFO would be difficult and the salary far above our budget I thought AMSCO might be a great deal for Juhudi because it would help pay a manager's salary.

I jumped through all of their hoops and completed their reams of paperwork. We were accepted into their program and I worked with the AMSCO team on the candidate hunt.

Once we had put together the job description for this CFO, the AMSCO staff realized that I was already doing all of the CFO work along with the General Manager work.

"Why don't we just bring you in under AMSCO since you seem to be qualified?"

Yeah, right, I thought. A CFO? I was terrible with details and only knew about finance from what I had learned in business school. But Aleke really liked the idea and the next thing I knew I was the General Manager/CFO for Juhudi Kilimo. This was a nice promotion from Technical Assistant / glorified intern.

Mt. Kenya

That January I went on the Mt. Kenya climb with my friends, as it was now clear that I would be in Kenya a little longer. My friend Greg, in addition to being a Columbia graduate and high-ranking Foreign Service officer, had also been a decathlete in college. At well over six feet, Greg still exercised all the time and was in great shape. Greg invited another very tall and slender friend of his from college who was living in Canada as a track coach. The two could have been brothers.

Nairobi is not the safest place to run or bike for recreational purposes so I had done little physical activity in months. To train for the climb, I used the stairs every day to the 7th floor K-Rep offices. On the first day of our four-day climb to Lenana peak, I was relieved to see that our guide had to be close to 250 pounds and had a giant beer belly. He was an American, who had spent the last twenty years living in Kenya. Even better, he smoked a pack of cigarettes a day. All I had to do was keep up with this guy. So what if the two track stars left me in the dust?

Our other friend was a tough guy named Doug. He was stout and sported a crew cut that made most people mistake him for one of the Marines at the US Embassy. Doug worked at the embassy as a mechanic and drove a fantastic Land Rover. The last person to join our group was in his early thirties, much shorter than the track stars and an extremely talkative ex-investment banker named Stephen Whitt. Stephen worked for TechnoServe in Nairobi as a volunteer consultant and had already done some work on the Gates Foundation's dairy project. Stephen seemed to be quite brilliant on every topic from agriculture value chains to the underground music pirating scene in the US.

We climbed the Sirimon route in the North, which is one of the longer but more scenic trails. It was a slow ascent up the shield volcano that had fallen in on itself when it erupted a long time ago. The summit consisted of three jagged peaks that at some angles looked like the head and shoulders of a bird or ostrich. Mt. Kenya's name in the local Kikuyu language is Kirinyaga, which translates to 'God's Resting Place'. Not many Kenyans have ever climbed the 17,057 foot peak and most do not have any desire to do so.

We crested the tree line where the high altitude prevented the larger trees from growing. What existed up there were strange furry plants with long stalks and others with spiky leaves. It looked like a place out of one of Dr. Seuss's books. We were the only people on the trail for days.

My peaceful contemplation was shattered by Stephen, who shouted up to me: "Did you know that 2 Live Crew was the first artist to have an album banned by the FCC in the US?" Stephen was quickly making me an expert on the history of the US hip-hop movement.

"No, I did not. My brother and I met them once in Colorado. I should have asked them about it," I answered back.

As I walked in front of Stephen I started to truly appreciate his tireless monologues, which took my mind off the drudgery of the climb. I found out later that Stephen had applied his brilliance in an investigative book called *How Music Got Free*, all about the first person to start the music-sharing boom of the early 2000, and the rise of Napster, which threatened the entire music industry.

The clouds on the mountain would roll in during the mornings and evenings but we eventually rose above all of the weather to see spectacular views of the sprawling farmland below. At times it looked like our peak was the only island in a white cloud ocean. At one point, I glanced down to see a large Boeing 747 airplane on its way to Nairobi and realized that this was the first time I had ever stood on the ground above an airplane in flight.

The last climb towards the summit was a grueling eight-hour hike on a freezing cold night over some of the steepest terrain on the entire trip. It was on this section that the two track athletes started to slow and show signs of altitude sickness. The guide and I were strolling along behind them (the guide still smoking) with not much trouble. Fortunately we all made it to the summit just in time for a beautiful sunset. I pulled out my mobile phone and called my brother in Colorado, since it was about 5pm on a Saturday. He was at a bar and had been skiing with my cousin in some great snow that day. He was about to tell me all about it, but when he heard that I was on the top of the tallest mountain in Kenya and second highest in Africa, he told me that my news outranked his. The connection was clear and did not cost much more than a local call, thanks to Safaricom. I only wished my phone was advanced enough to also send a picture.

Free Lunch

As much as I disliked Harold at that time, he was full of great experience and perspectives. He said we should try to invite all of the potential investors we could to a lunch together. At this lunch, Aleke and I would give an update about the business and answer questions. Harold said that nobody wanted to be first "into the pool" but once that first one jumps in, nobody wants to be left standing on the side. This way, if things went bad then more than one person would be left with "egg on their face" which I think is a cooking reference for when cake batter explodes. Now that Kiva was officially on our side, I eagerly hoped their commitment would motivate some other investors to get involved.

We invited Kiva, Acumen, Rockefeller, Oikocredit and a few others such as the Financial Sector Deepening (FSD), which had provided grants to KDA in the past. In total we had around twelve people come to the lunch. I did my best to present Juhudi in a positive light by highlighting our unique model. In reality, the actual picture was dismal. We might be able to survive perhaps five more months until June with Kiva, but then we would be back to bankruptcy again. I had to put all those thoughts away since none of these investors would work with someone who sounded desperate. It made me feel like someone on a first date who is dying of a terminal illness and needed to get the formalities of getting to know each other over with quickly, so we could get married and have children.

Some in attendance were openly skeptical of our presentation, while others threw out some helpful ideas such as "why don't you collateralize your loan portfolio for cash and sell it to a bank or insurance company." But overall, it generated a buzz about Juhudi, especially when the investors could see there were a few other serious investors and Kiva, who had already given us approval. Both Acumen and Rockefeller set up meetings with us to discuss their initial due diligence a few weeks after that lunch. It was time for the second date.

Chapter 9 | Due Diligence

I was quite familiar with how to lend to the borrower profiles on the Kiva.org site by selecting the picture and story of the entrepreneur I liked, and then sending them $25. This seemed simple when looking in from the outside, but it turns out that the actual scenario behind the scenes for Kiva is quite a complicated process.

My $25 did not actually go directly to the entrepreneur, but instead went to the Kiva 'partner', usually a financial institution, who then provided the loan to that entrepreneur. Kiva had limited staff around the world and depended on these partnerships to manage the loans. I did not mind very much, as long as my $25 went to the person pictured in the profile story. Author Bob Harris, who visited Juhudi Kilimo in 2011 wrote a fantastic book about his travels around the world, visiting the Kiva entrepreneurs, called the *International Bank of Bob*.

Since inception, Kiva has provided $726,714,750 worth of loans and retained a repayment rate of 98.7%. It has also won a string of awards, such as Time magazine's top fifty websites and Oprah Winfrey's list of Ultimate Favorite Things. Getting a chance to be a part of Kiva as an institution was fascinating and represented a less known story.

Kiva operates like a wholesale lender but provides low cost (zero percent) and very high-risk tolerant capital to microfinance institutions. The Kiva partners would be required to write short profiles about what their clients intend to do with the loan and take a picture for the Kiva website. The profiles had one month to fundraise on Kiva. After they had fully fundraised, Kiva would send the total amount raised each month to the partner, either to lend to the clients in the profile, or refinance funds already provided. Either way the partner must ensure the client is funded. At the end of each month the partner would report how many of the Kiva clients repaid their loan and would send an invoice or deduct the repayments from what was raised that month.

A Kiva Fellow was sent to work with us for three months to help train our staff and ensure our profiles met Kiva's standards. The Kiva Fellow program is extremely competitive and accepts about one percent of all applicants to the three-month volunteer program. Applicants come from all walks of life and experience levels. I was told that our Kiva Fellow was someone named Rachel Brooks and she would be visiting sometime in the next few weeks.

I was expecting a young college grad with no experience and who would probably be more of a burden than anything else. Rachel Brooks turned out to be a tall blonde American with two kids who had worked at Adobe as a senior product developer for over ten years before moving to France and then South Africa with her husband, an executive at Microsoft. On top of all that, Rachel was hilarious. I don't think we talked about anything Kiva-related in the first hour of our meeting. We joked about living abroad, the latest pop TV shows and a dozen other random topics.

My entire Kenyan team loved Rachel. Even though Rachel was a volunteer, her 'boss' was another American living in Kenya, named Stephanie, who spoke fluent Kiswahili and was equally entertaining and great with the Juhudi staff. Stephanie could also be tough as nails and nearly made me cry in a few meetings when she threatened to revoke the new Kiva partnership after discovering a minor incorrect detail on one of our client profiles. Kiva had little tolerance for fraud and misrepresenting clients, since it was Kiva's reputation on the line if anything went wrong.

In our first month with Rachel, we had posted our full $9,000 worth of loans without any problems. In fact, the loans were a big hit at Kiva and funded in less than ten hours of being posted. Most loans took a few days or even weeks to fund. We even had our long disclaimer on our Kiva profiles saying how risky loans were to Juhudi Kilimo. It did not seem to matter to the Kiva lenders providing $25 from all over the world. The new Kiva money was disbursed all too quickly to our seemingly endless line of clients who were awaiting loans. Juhudi was slowly dying without new money to meet the demand of our clients. We could only provide new loans to clients after existing clients made their repayments each month. As a result, some clients had to wait four to five months for their loans from the time of application. The new Kiva money became symbolic to our staff and clients at least. It signaled we could start giving out a few more new loans each month. Everyone looked at me as the mzungu who brought in the funds.

But we needed so much more money. The little trickle from Kiva, while producing a tremendous morale boost, merely slowed our imminent financial death spiral. To reach our break-even and cover our expenses we needed another $4,991,000.

Amon Anderson and the Acumen Fund

One of the contacts GBF gave us was with the Acumen Fund in Nairobi. Acumen has been a leader in the impact investing world for over fifteen years and has generated global recognition for its work. The founder and key driver behind the organization is Jacqueline Novogratz, who was named as one of the most influential women in the world. Acumen was on Forbes' list of best global nonprofit organizations. Aleke was skeptical. He was under the impression that they only supported non-microfinance organizations, as Acumen had funded a low-cost housing program, an urban sanitation company and a network of low-cost health clinics in Kenya over the past four years.

In June of 2009, I set up a meeting with the agriculture portfolio manager, Amon Anderson. With a name like Amon I was expecting someone from the Middle East, Ethiopia or Northern Africa. Instead, I was greeted in the K-Rep lobby by a young, blond-haired, blue-eyed American from North Carolina. Amon had been living in Nairobi for about the same amount of time as me and the Acumen office was two blocks from K-Rep, yet I had never seen this guy anywhere in the last year.

Amon and I hit it off right away. He was a graduate of the University of North Carolina from the prestigious Morehead Fellowship. The Fellowship was extremely selective but provided a full-ride scholarship along with summer work experiences abroad every year. Amon had worked in Ethiopia for a few years, learning to be an expert in agriculture impact investing. For whatever reason, Amon loved the Juhudi business model and thought it would fit well into Acumen's agriculture portfolio. He felt that Juhudi "had legs". He wanted to run the concept by his local team and move forward with some initial due diligence. Since Acumen did not have many in-house experts in microfinance, they hired an outside firm to run their due diligence for them. Amon and I exchanged numbers and managed to meet up for drinks several times and attend a few ultimate frisbee games on the weekend.

Ultimate frisbee is a cross between basketball and touch American football but played with a frisbee. The sport is played all over the world and is especially popular among the embassy and international development communities. The Nairobi ultimate frisbee scene was also quite social, with between forty and fifty people coming out each weekend. Some of the players took the game a little too seriously, in my opinion, and seemed to use the game to let out job-related frustration on the field.

Another character I brought along to the ultimate games was a New Yorker named Andreas Zeller who was working for the IFC in Washington, DC and visiting East Africa on a work trip. Several months earlier Andreas had been introduced to me by a mutual friend from the MBA Enterprise Corps. Before gaining full-time employment at the IFC (which was unheard of for an American citizen only twenty-five years old), Andreas had worked as an investment banker at Credit Suisse and Citigroup after he graduated with honors from the University of Chicago. He was fluent in French, played concert level cello, was a triathlete and a talented cook. Andreas wanted to work for an investor so I did my best to help by introducing him to many of the investors on my list.

After a thorough scanning of the industry, Andreas told me that the problem with investing in Africa was not the lack of funds or businesses but the lack of any services matching the two together.

Most entrepreneurs in Africa (like me) have no idea how to contact the right kind of investors for their business or even speak their business language. Instead of working for a fund, Andreas wanted to start his own consulting company to bridge this gap between local entrepreneurs and international investors. I nodded politely but could not hide the fact that I thought it was a terrible idea.

I was having an abysmal time getting Juhudi started, even though we had all the credentials and backing from K-Rep and GBF. From my time as a consultant, I understood some of the challenges of finding clients, selling work and managing a services business in a very competitive environment. I thought it might be particularly challenging to start an independent consulting company with no name recognition or track record. I thought he was crazy to consider leaving a cushy job at the IFC to fend for himself in Kenya. I estimated that he would last about four months in Kenya before going back to the IFC or going to the US for business school. Then I realized that I was sounding like some of the negative investors I met while fundraising for Juhudi. Who was I to tell this young entrepreneur what he could or could not do? So I decided to be more supportive and not trash his dreams.

I set Andreas up with his first roommates, Jeremy, one of our Kiva Fellows, and a friend of mine named Nick, who was selling solar lights in Nairobi. Andreas had questions about registering companies, getting visas and shared a few of our general experiences at Juhudi. He turned out to be a great fit with my expat social group and quickly became a good friend. Andreas convinced one of his Chicago classmates, Annie Roberts, to leave her lucrative consulting job and an offer at Stanford Business School to join him. Another classmate named Neal, who was a Harvard lawyer, joined later. The team was stacked. Andreas named his company, Open Capital Advisors.

Four years later, with the help of his brilliant co-founders, Open Capital has grown to become one of the largest and most successful consulting businesses in East Africa. Juhudi would later hire Open Capital on a significant consulting contract through one of our investors. It turns out that I was right to keep my mouth shut about criticizing Andreas' business idea!

Steve Wardle and the Grameen Foundation

In following up from the business speed-dating event, Steve Wardle, from the Grameen Foundation emailed me to say he was interested in Juhudi for one of their first investments with their new Pioneer Fund. He emailed the first term sheet I had ever seen which was a two page document that outlined the general structure of their proposed investment with items such as the interest rate, duration and some financial ratios that needed to be met. If we agreed to the initial terms, Steve then wanted to schedule a time to talk and potentially come out for a due diligence visit.

Steve was an American from the Chicago area and had worked for an investment bank before entering the world of microfinance. While at Grameen, Steve was asked to travel to Haiti to act as the interim CFO for a year to help one of the major microfinance organizations through a rough spot in its development.

Grameen also had a plethora of documents that it required, and spreadsheets to complete. Fortunately, I had a lot of material from the Kiva due diligence so it was easy just to update them for Grameen. Kiva was very generous in sharing its entire due diligence report with potential investors. This report helped make the job of future investors a little easier and reduced the number of questions that the management received.

Several weeks later Steve flew out to Nairobi with one of his colleagues for a week long due diligence and visit to the field. They followed the same methodology as Kiva – a series of meetings with the head office management team and then a few days in the field with clients and staff. Steve visited our Murang'a office since it was just under two hours from Nairobi. Unfortunately, it was one of our worst performing offices. Clients were not repaying and our staff were having difficulties making new loans. We mostly blamed the higher level of competition from banks, other microfinance institutions and local savings cooperatives due to the proximity to Nairobi. However, many of the offices' staff felt the problems were due to the local Kikuyu tribe who "were just bad clients and refused to repay their loans".

We did have a few run-ins with the local mafia group, called the mungiki. This group was made up of the remnants of a militant political group, employed by President Kibaki during the 2008 post-election violence as a supposed hit squad to intimidate or murder people. This group was still quite influential in Kenya and occasionally our loan officers would show up to a client's farm to collect on an overdue loan, only to find ten young men armed with machetes and clubs. We did not mess with them and did our best to work through the local governments and police.

Steve's visit to Murang'a was a disaster. Nearly all of the files he carried with him to the office did not match what the loan officer had in his books. The office manager was clueless about the discrepancies and offered little assurance to this would-be investor. A heated argument ensued about some overdue loans. Steve expressed his concerns about all of this when he was back in the office.

I told Aleke that evening that we probably should not expect any funding from Grameen anytime soon. Fortunately, Oikocredit had also requested a due diligence visit and another fund, Agora, whose representatives Aleke and I met at the speed dating event, decided that they would like to invest in Kenya after all and wanted a due diligence visit.

For the next two months it felt as though all our management team did was host international investors and answer their questions. I might have been able to save some time if I had just recorded a video of my management team answering the questions since each investor essentially asked the same things. However, the investors needed to physically visit their potential investments to tell their investment committees that they had seen the operations. I also felt that the international travel was a perk for some of the junior analysts who were able to go to Kenya for a week and then spend the weekend on safaris. However, meeting and hosting investors did not mean any of them would actually provide any money. If anything, the strain on our management and extra costs of shuttling around the visitors put more strain on our cash reserves, which continued to dwindle. It looked like we might survive through June but the game was over after that. Everyone would have to go home. The investor visits did have one unseen benefit for the local economy, with my friend Benson making a killing off all our investors who visited and needed taxi drivers for the weekend. At least Benson was now in profit thanks to our efforts.

Tsavo rhino chase

I joined two friends for a long weekend drive to Tsavo West National Park and then onwards to Malindi. My friend David worked at the international NGO called World Vision, which conducted a variety of projects all over Kenya from child education, to health services and even a significant amount of work in microfinance.

David had worked at Accenture but left to stay with World Vision, which was one of Accenture's ADP clients. We were joined by Melissa, my other friend, who was a little older than David and me. She also worked at Accenture in Nairobi.

We rented a Toyota Rav 4 and crammed into it with all our gear. I was finally going to see Tsavo where the man-eating lions killed all the railroad workers in the movie, *Ghost and the Darkness*. The drive down Mombasa road, which was mostly still under construction, was nothing short of terrifying. Sections of road went from tarmac to dirt without warning and there were no signs directing the lanes of traffic. The result was a dusty free-for-all of large trucks from the Mombasa port, buses, matatus, passenger cars and motorcycles. If you were in a larger vehicle, the smaller vehicles would give you right of way no matter what lane or side of the road you decided to use.

David took joy in driving as fast as humanly possible, while still keeping at least two wheels on the road. The police flagged us down at one stretch and informed David that he was going 130km in an 80km speed zone. The police had no way of proving this but wanted us to pay "something small" or a "chai kidogo" little tea, for them. None of us wanted to support the bribery culture of the police, but we probably were speeding. David pulled out a large handful of coins from his bag and walked over to the police officer. I was never sure why he had all of those coins but it seemed to work because David came running back. We drove past the police officer, who now had his hands full of coins. We made it to Tsavo National Park in time to catch our dinner at one of the older budget lodges in the park.

Early the next morning we set out in search of the Big Five, which is what the old colonial hunters called the five most difficult and dangerous animals to hunt. They include the lion, elephant, rhino, leopard and buffalo. I was never sure why the hippopotamus, crocodile, giraffe and cheetah had not made the list since they are also big and dangerous.

The landscape of Tsavo West reminded me of parts of Colorado, with rolling red hills scattered with scrub brush. Within ten minutes of driving, we came across a young leopard in the road that seemed to just be out for an early morning stroll. The soil in Tsavo is much redder than in other parts of the country and this turns most of the animals the same color. This leopard's blond patches were a little redder, which made the white spots stand out in the early morning light, the way neon light makes shirts and teeth glow. Leopards are the most elusive of the big cats in Africa so we were excited to see one up close.

David took us on a small side trail that clearly had not been used in a while. It was against the rules to drive off road in the national parks, but as long as there was a clear 4x4 trail most of the rangers did not seem to mind. We scratched the sides of the car with the sharp edges of the thorny bushes but David kept driving.

Eventually, we pulled into a clearing and stopped about thirty yards from a giant rhinoceros and its baby. All of us lowered our windows and started snapping pictures as if a Hollywood celebrity had just appeared. Rhinos have notoriously bad eyesight but this mother and her calf did not seem to mind us, so David crept the car closer. Then the mother lifted her massive head and gave us all a death stare that chilled my blood.

"OK, time to go David."

David put the Rav 4 in reverse and started to back away slowly. A loud beeping noise started with the reverse engaged. The mother rhino lowered her head at that and started towards us at a short gallop.

"Go, David, go!" shouted Melissa.

I was in the back seat and instinctively rolled up my window, although a small pane of glass would hardly stop the charge of a full-grown rhinoceros three times heavier than our car. David accelerated and the rhino was in full charge with its little baby running along next to its mother. David was not looking where he was going and we smashed into small bushes in reverse. The rhino, seemingly satisfied with our reaction, slowed and we continued to crunch past the underbrush.

No sooner did the rhino stop chasing us then we plowed into a tree and came to an abrupt halt. Fortunately, the spare tire was on the back of the car and it absorbed most of the impact, but the tree still left a large dent. Benson would not be happy, again.

"I think I need a beer after that," said David.

That evening we were the big celebrities among the safari guides because we had seen two rhinos and a leopard. Nobody else had spotted any significant game. We did not say anything about the scratches and rhino charge.

Rockefeller and the "Rockettes"

Around the same time as Acumen and Grameen's interest in Juhudi in 2009, one of America's largest private foundations was also interested. The Rockefeller Foundation is a $4.1 billion foundation that has been around since 1913. Normally the Rockefeller Foundation preferred to invest in impact funds (they provided funding to both Acumen and Grameen) but they had a relatively new Program Related Investment (PRI) initiative, which allowed them to make direct investments in select social businesses around the world. Rockefeller had a local office in Nairobi but it only focused on providing grants, while the New York office was the only entity providing the PRIs.

The PRI team was made up of two brilliant women, Barbra and Christina, who had considerable commercial banking and private equity experience. After Aleke and I had our initial phone call with them we were both excited, since Rockefeller was a big name globally and might give us some great recognition. Plus they could invest around $1-$3 million. Our business plan was really starting to look great and included a ton of information in the annex section, where I had outlined the investment returns on a specific cow, listed all of our competitors and their rural reach, as well as detailed financial model assumptions.

Once Rockefeller had reviewed our business plan, Cristina sent over her first battery of questions. There were over eighty questions. I had never seen an email with so many. Most of them had already been asked before and we had ready answers but others took a long time to research.

I was so excited to be having all of this interest from funders. I spent an entire weekend answering Cristina's questions, only surfacing to go and eat or buy groceries. Satisfied with my work, I sent a reply to Cristina on Sunday night so she could have it on Monday for follow up questions.

I did not hear anything for two weeks. Then Barbra wrote back asking for a date for their due diligence. I could not believe there were no follow up questions. My answers were surely not that complete to have fully satisfied them. Were they just asking these questions to sound smart? Was it simply a hoop to jump through to qualify for their funding?

Barbra and Cristina brought another woman from the Rockefeller team who focused on monitoring and evaluation for the foundation. Aleke called the trio the "Rockettes." Fortunately, their visit went smoothly and all three had a fantastic few days visiting our clients and meeting with our staff.

I think we were getting better at hosting investors.

Kilimanjaro – the roof of Africa

I had made plans to climb Mt. Kilimanjaro in Tanzania with two friends from business school in the summer of 2009. One had a job as an investment banker with Merrill Lynch and the other was a consultant with Deloitte. Both lost their jobs in the banking crisis and recession. Neither one of them felt comfortable spending money to travel to Africa now that they were without a job. But I still wanted to go, so I booked a trip. I would be placed with some other climbers for the trip.

With Mt. Kenya completed, I felt a little more confident about the success of my K-Rep stair-climbing training. Tanzania is said to be a lot like Kenya but much slower and larger. The nickname for the country is the 'sleeping giant' because of all the natural resources, arable land and population size. The Tanzanians knew right away, from my Kiswahili, that I was from Kenya. Apparently the dialect is different. Kenyans sound quite rude to Tanzanians, who speak the 'pure' and polite Kiswahili. To order a beer in Kenya I would say, "Ninataka Tusker" or "I will take a Tusker." But in Tanzania they expected me to say, "Tafadali bwana, naomba Tusker" or "Please sir, I beg of you for a Tusker."

At the climbing base I had dinner with nine beautiful American college students who were about to climb the mountain with their professor of biology. Unfortunately, I was not paired with this group but instead with a Canadian father, his wife, their 12-year-old-boy and the middle aged uncle, for the six-day journey. Our guide was a 30-year-old Tanzanian and Rastafarian with impressive dreadlocks. He said he had climbed Kilimanjaro over 500 times in the past twelve years working on the mountain and was quite knowledgeable. The two of us hit it off right away and he loved the fact that I knew some Kiswahili.

We passed a long line of Tanzanian men on the drive up to the main gate of the national park. They were all porters from the local villages looking for work on expeditions to the summit. I estimated the crowd of porters to be over 300 people that day. Kilimanjaro hosts something like 25,000 climbers per year and that does not include porters and guides. The summit success rate is around sixty to seventy-five percent and ten to twenty people die each year, so I figured my chances of at least surviving were not too bad. The mountain has become a significant source of income for many in the area. Not to mention the $100 per day park fees, which go straight to the Tanzanian government and probably disappear after that.

I had carried my own bag and gear up Mt. Kenya without much difficulty so I intended to do the same on Kilimanjaro. Our guide shrugged and said something in a local dialect I did not understand and then a group of porters started shouting and pointing at me. Apparently I had kept one of them out of a job that day, which did not make me feel very good. There is a fierce social structure for most mountain porters. If one of them steps out of line or upsets a more senior porter, the senior porter would throw the junior's bags down a ravine and make them retrieve it. I witnessed a few of these altercations during our climb.

The younger porters are made to carry more weight and the less comfortable bags than the more senior guides. We had a young porter in our group named Juma, who looked about fourteen, but was tough and had a good attitude. Our party of fifteen (five climbers, six porters, two guides and a cook) all set off on the Whiskey route up the mountain.

There was a constant line of people on the trail that, from above, must look like a long colony of ants carrying gear and supplies to the various camps on the mountain. The climb started in a lush rainforest and then broke through to the high-alpine tundra and cloud forest. We shared the first campsite with another eighty people on the climb and a massive group of forty from Qantas who were on a management-bonding trip for all of their top employees.

I realized then that I had certainly signed up for the budget version of the climb. The Qantas group had a massive dome tent that was 15ft high and easily fit all of them. They sat down to dinner at nice tables, metal chairs, white tablecloths and even little centerpieces with candles. Crates of wine and beer were opened after their meals and they had a grand party at 11,000 ft. My jaw dropped when I heard the rumble of a generator that powered a flat screen TV and DVD player. They all sat around the tent and watched movies before going to sleep. With labor so available and cheap it was seemingly easy to climb a mountain with all of the amenities of your living room. Like nearly all Australians, they were extremely friendly and invited me to share some beer with them. One woman in their group had a prosthetic leg and was the star of their video shoot. So we had a 12-year-old and a woman with one leg about to summit the mountain. As with Mt Kenya, I thought I had better be able to climb this thing.

The next morning we had fantastic weather and started a steep cliff scramble. The porters ambled up easily and one passed me with two spare prosthetic legs tied to his back. I imagined how great it would be if I could just swap out a leg when mine started hurting. Public toilets were limited mostly to pit latrines that were overflowing and surrounded with toilet paper. My favorite was an outhouse that was built on a cliff face. Everything that went down the toilet fell to 1,000 feet below. Of course the Australians had portable toilets with showers that were larger than my tent.

After a particularly grueling day, I noticed that the young porter Juma, with a massive load on top of his head, was starting to struggle up a slope. I was feeling great so I hiked down to him, picked up his bag and threw it on my head. I marched up the hill alongside Juma with his load and all my gear as the rest of the porters cheered. Juma thanked me profusely at the top.

Later that evening I looked down to where the porters were staying and saw a small skirmish break out. Juma pushed over another porter who then came at him with punches. I started to run down but the guide grabbed me. "No, let them go." I turned away, imagining the dialogue: "Hey Juma, you were too weak to carry your load so the mzungu client had to do it for you. You will never make it."

The next day Juma's face was a little bruised and bloodied. The whole incident made me realize the importance of first understanding the social and cultural context of the lives of the porters, before trying to help any of them. My good intentions ended up causing more damage than if I had done nothing.

At the last base camp before the summit was a place where all the trails come together. It was literally a tent city, with well over 200 tents in the shallow basin. The place was full of trash and there was toilet paper everywhere. I discovered that the ranger station sold cold beer at $4 each. I had one and quickly passed out into a deep sleep at 15,000 ft.

It was from here that the father and son started to struggle. Our guide, to my surprise, started cursing them both in Kiswahili to me. He said: "Those two should have never been allowed up here. It is dangerous. The boy is far too young and the man too overweight. The booking agents just get greedy and take everyone. Now I have to deal with them."

The final ascent was at night and we had a full moon to guide the way. The plan was to reach the summit by sunrise. About forty-five minutes from the summit, the father and boy needed to return and the mother joined them along with the head guide. The uncle and I continued on with the junior guide. Our pace quickened and we found an open section in the trail with no other climbers. The night became quiet and the brilliant sky, full of stars, seemed extra clear in the crisp air. I was closer to those stars than I had ever been before.

At the high altitude, I got a strange adrenaline rush and felt full of energy, which propelled me to the top. We crested the ridge of the summit just as the sun rose. Blinding rays of light lit up the ground below us and reflected off the massive bluish white glacier snow that sat on the peak. The snow had receded significantly in the past twenty years but the massive 30ft high block of ice looked like it belonged in Antarctica and not on the top of the volcano.

I looked down into the black crater below and did not see any snow. The junior guide said the ground was still warm from the lava. We were one of the first groups to reach the summit and we posed for a few pictures next to the famous sign that marks the summit. I tried to call my brother but did not get any service. A British couple followed after us and broke out some hot tea with cups, saucers, sugar and powdered milk. So classy. Still feeling great, I wanted to spend more time on the summit and take more pictures. I looked at our junior guide who was sitting with his head between his knees. The uncle looked at me and said: "We might need to help him down."

We each took an arm and slowly helped him down the mountain. He quickly improved before we made it back to the camp.

Just like on Mt. Kenya, altitude sickness can hit anyone and it usually is the more fit people who tend to climb too quickly. We all made it down that next day safely, having climbed the tallest mountain in Africa and the tallest freestanding mountain in the world.

The Rolex

I have always had friends who have joked about starting some various businesses after an idea comes up during dinner or at drinks. Usually the idea dies after the meal is finished or all the beer is empty.

Andreas, Jeremy and their roommate, Nick Sowden, had all recently been to Uganda and sampled a wonderful snack called the Rolex, which consists of wrapping a deep fried circular flatbread, called a chapati, around a filling of bananas and chocolate Nutella, similar to a crepe. One can also fill the chapati with eggs, bacon and cheese for a portable breakfast. There were many options for this delicious snack that resembled a burrito.

My three friends could not believe that the Rolex could not be found anywhere in neighboring Kenya. There is a good reason why the rest of the world is not scattered with Kenyan restaurants, like those of Ethiopian or even Ghanaian cuisines. For most foreigners the ethnic Kenyan food is bland and lacks imagination with only the staple, tasteless ugali alongside grilled goat meat, beef, chicken or fish. Sometimes a side of sukuma wiki or kachumbari, which includes diced tomatoes and onions, will round out the dish. Don't get me wrong; I came to love Kenyan food and still prefer a nicely grilled goat over lamb any day, but eating the same types of food everyday gets a little old.

It is against the law in Nairobi to sell street food (although not widely enforced), so it was nearly impossible to get a quick bite to eat without sitting down and ordering a lengthy lunch. Of course, one could always find fried chapati and snacks in the little shops on the street but they were hard to eat every day.

When Andreas, Jeremy and Nick began talking about starting a Rolex company, I agreed it was not a bad idea. What shocked me was that all three actually did it. They hired a guy to build a wooden, rollable food wagon/cart, and then hired a street vendor to make chapatis (after much sampling in the neighborhood). In a few days, the team had a logo, tagline, website, t-shirts, fans and a rich menu of delicious Rolex options, with fillings ranging from a pepperoni pizza to lemon zest and sugar. I quickly became one of their best customers and would regularly order about twenty Rolexes for my staff during lunch. I could easily have an egg and cheese Rolex for breakfast, a pizza Rolex for lunch and then the grilled hamburger and cheese (known as the Full Monty) for dinner – although eating more than two in a sitting was not advisable.

Somehow the guys managed to convince the owner of a popular nightclub in Westlands to lease them space each night near the entrance to the club so the late-night crowd could order a greasy Rolex on their way out. Sales were climbing and Jeremy built an SMS feature that tracked sales in real-time and reported the numbers on their website. The website picked up a lot of attention and even sparked a 'cease and desist' letter from some watch company with the same company name. All three of the young founders also had full-time day jobs and were struggling to stay on top of the increasing demands from the Rolex chapati business. So they hired a Kenyan manager to take over.

In the following weeks, sales started to dwindle on the website reports, even though lines were out the door each night at the club. The daytime lunch business never generated many more sales outside of my orders. Sadly, Rolex sold their food cart to the owner of another nightclub, where it now sits rusting in the back of his building. I hope someone will pick up the dream again in the future.

Rhino Charge

My embassy friend Doug had rolled his Defender earlier in the year, crumpling the frame but leaving the engine and just about everything else intact. His insurance paid for a new vehicle but he kept the old one, cut the top off of it and bought huge tires so he could drive it on some serious off-roading.

Doug entered into the Quattro Charge, which was a 4x4 competition outside of Nairobi. The competition had a series of stations about 100-200m long, with various obstacles like large rocks, rivers, hills, etc. that needed to be successfully navigated. You were scored on time and how many times you needed to stop on each course. All kinds of 4x4 enthusiasts were there with trucks of all shapes and sizes. Doug's Defender, now called Betsy, did great.

Doug then asked David, from World Vision, and me to be part of his team in the annual Rhino Charge. This was a major competition in Kenya that had been going on since 1989. Roughly thirty teams of six people per vehicle would raise a minimum of $5,000 for the Rhino Ark charity, which helped preserve the dwindling rhinoceros population in Kenya. The race takes place at a different location in rural Kenya each year. The location is not revealed until a few weeks before the competition to keep people from scouting the course. The course consists of about twenty checkpoints or GPS coordinates which need to be reached in any order. The drivers have twelve hours to reach each checkpoint and the vehicle that reaches the most checkpoints in the shortest distance wins. For example, if a mountain or ravine is in between the vehicle and the checkpoint it may be easier to go around the obstacle but it will cost the team more mileage than those who drive over or through the obstacles. There is a lot of strategy involved.

The driver and the team of scouts are responsible for helping navigate through the wild underbrush to find the best ways to the checkpoints. My job was to run in front of Doug and Betsy with a machete to scout paths. The race was in the hills near Lake Baringo, which was a dry and rough part of the country full of steep hills and unforgiving terrain, not to mention wild animals.

We woke up before sunrise to drive out to our designated checkpoint with a few other drivers. Most of the other vehicles were massive with tires that would reach my waist. We did not stand a chance. The race started, but unlike any other car race I have seen, nobody was in a particular hurry. The vehicles and teams ambled along and disappeared into the brush. We found a dry riverbed and decided to drive through that, since it was clearer than the brush. However, the river did not run in the direction we needed so I ran ahead to find a way out. I turned the corner and was alone in the riverbed when I spotted some movement ahead. It was a small black and white animal that looked like a big skunk. It was a honey badger. Normally they do not come out during the day but this one was in plain sight looking at me. I was terrified since YouTube had done such a great job outlining how vicious honey badgers can be. They eat snakes, chase lions and chew through everything. I could not make it back to Betsy without it running me down. So I held up my panga blade and tried to make myself look bigger. That was what I was told to do with the mountain lions or cougars, at least in Colorado. It seemed to work because the honey badger scampered off down the river.

We managed to find a small boy from one of the nearby villages, who directed us to the first checkpoint. The checkpoint was full of spectators and volunteers with water, cold wet towels and meat pies. This was easy. We set our GPS coordinates and headed off towards the next destination. We climbed up a steep hill and when we could go no farther, Doug hitched up a winch with a rope and tied the other end to a tree on the top of the hill. Then we pulled Betsy up the steep hill with the winch. On the way back down the hill we put the winch on the back of the truck to lower it down. It worked incredibly well.

The landscape seemed to attack anyone or anything that tried to get through it. The two-inch spines from the acacia trees were everywhere, but my worst enemy that day was another thorny tree that had spines in the shape of hooks or barbs. As soon as it brushed your shirt or skin it would grab hold and dig the spikes into you. Getting extricated took great care.

Doug decided to drive through another deep ravine and this time we were not so lucky. The thick foliage kept us from driving very fast and we had to use the winch over and over again. It took us three hours to go a few hundred feet. We still had a lot of checkpoints to hit and were burning daylight. Exhausted, dehydrated and lacerated, I was wondering why on earth I signed up for this thing.

We finally emerged from the brush and crashed onto a service road near our third checkpoint. Another competitor flew by on the road and covered us in dust. Apparently the winning strategy that year was to find the dirt service roads and use them to get close to the checkpoints and not drive through ravines. We only made it to three checkpoints that day but it was actually better than some teams, who had to stay an extra night to have their turned over vehicles towed out by a local tractor.

At least I showed that honey badger who was boss.

Maralal Camel Derby

Maralal is a sleepy frontier town in Northern Kenya, close to the border with Sudan and Ethiopia. Once a year the town is filled with foreigners racing in the Maralal Camel Derby. I had heard about this race from some friends and even had a number for one of the best camel wranglers in town. I emailed a few of my friends to see if we could get a group of five people to make the eleven-hour drive for a long weekend.

Two weeks later I had a list of forty people who wanted to go and even a waitlist. Fortunately Benson's taxi business was now booming and he'd recently purchased a tour bus that could seat forty people. So we all loaded up for the journey and Benson himself came along with the driver.

We left early in the morning because we knew parts of the road were bad. I had no idea how disastrous it would be. After close to ten hours of driving we found ourselves on a very dusty road with no sight of civilization for miles. The bushes seemed to close in around us and even scratched the sides of the bus. We had no mobile phone service and no map to guide us. Then the bus came across a river. It looked too deep to drive over.

One of my friends had the suggestion that we should get out of the bus just in case it does not make it across or tips over. It sounded reasonable, so we all got out of the bus and the driver rammed through the water at full speed. He made it to the other side and we all picked our way across rocks to join the bus. This river crossing happened once again a few miles later. It was getting dark and we had been driving for over thirteen hours with no sign of Maralal or civilization.

Northern Kenya is not the best place to be for security reasons since the area is famous for hosting bandits known as Shifta or terrorist groups from Somalia. It was especially not advisable to take a busload of Americans at night to this area. If anything happened it would be my fault, since I did the organizing.

Finally, we hit a paved tarmac road and picked up mobile service again. Benson called a few people and a security escort came out to ride with us for the next hour to Maralal. The security escort consisted of three police officers crammed into a small Subaru but one of them had a rifle. We made it to Maralal just as our hotel started giving away our rooms to other guests. I received a fair share of complaints that night about the trip but everyone was happy to be alive and, finally, to be in Maralal.

The next morning was total chaos.

The entire town showed up for the event and my busload of expats was something new to them. It also meant there was a shortage of camels. I learned that camels come in very different varieties and speeds. My camel wrangler gave me one of the lighter-colored speed camels, while a majority of our bus received the darker slow camels. The 'saddles' consisted of two sticks tied together over the camel's back forming an X to hold and then a blanket folded over a few times to sit on. Rudimentary stirrups were then tied to the sticks. Each camel came with a young boy who directed, pulled and hit the camel with the stick when needed to get it moving. The rider just held on for dear life and tried not to get in the way.

The race started with a bang and we were off and running. My camel, named Sudan, sprinted to the front of the pack, and at one point left the boy driver behind us. Sudan veered toward a large tower of spikey cactus, which the camels like to scrape against to rub their skin. The boy caught the reins just as I was about to be skewered. The race circled the town to make a 10k loop.

Camels are probably one of the most uncontrollable animals to ride. Unlike a horse that has more of a front to back rocking motion, the camel is straight up and down which makes for a really sore backside after only a few minutes. I decided to stand in the stirrups for the last 5k with the rough canvas cutting lines in my legs. For some unknown reason I'd brought a vuvuzela, commonly used in sporting events around the world to make an obnoxious trumpeting sound, and strapped that across my back. I felt like an Arabian night riding into battle on a galloping camel with my sword across my back.

Sudan closed in on the lead camel that was also of the racing breed. I could see the finish line; we were definitely running faster than the leader. My poor young guide boy was on the verge of collapse and barely keeping up.

The crowds were lining the streets at the finish and I thought this would be a good time to blast my vuvuzela to give Sudan a final battle call.

I blew the vuvuzela and Sudan swiveled its head back at me with a foaming mouth and tried to snap at my leg! I jumped back, almost falling out of the saddle. Sudan had had enough. Nearly 300 feet from the finish line he sat down.

Just sat down.

The young boy was pulling at it and yelling at the camel, but no luck. Two camels passed me and then another. Finally, Sudan decided to get it over with and stood up to cross the finish line for 5th place. So disappointing. Most of my friends with the 'slow' camels did not finish because their camels sat down or their saddles broke. Amon decided simply to run 7k alongside his camel and finished in the top ten. Other events of the day included a tri-camelthlon which incorporated a bike and run into the camel race. My backside took a few weeks to recover but it was well worth all the turmoil.

I may have completed twenty-two due diligence reports in twelve months, but my social escapades were singularly lacking in such precautions. Still, it made for an adventurous life.

Chapter 10 | International Rockstar

T hings started to look up in the weeks after the camel race. Acumen, Grameen and Rockefeller all concluded their initial due diligence with very positive results, and Kiva graduated us out of the probationary period to become a full partner. This move increased our monthly limit to $20,000. Another review was scheduled for late June potentially to increase the limit again. We now needed $4,973,000, but had some new lenders, and even some donors, interested in providing some small grants to help. Based on the good news, I told my parents that I would stick around Kenya another three months to see what happened with Acumen, Grameen and Rockefeller.

Acumen's microfinance experts dug deep into my financial model and did not find anything wrong with our projections. That was a relief. The only critical feedback we received from any of the investors was that we should hire another credit compliance officer and think about setting up an internal audit function. These were quite easy to do and would not take more than a month.

Fortunately, a few of the small grants came through which helped us get to June with a surplus of cash that would last a few more months. Kiva reviewed our limit again based on our stellar performance in the first six months. Our normal monthly limit was removed and we had a new overall cap of $500,000 we could raise with Kiva during the year. Our field team worked hard in July of that year to raise nearly $60,000 through Kiva. I ran the numbers and berthed a tentative sigh of relief when I saw that we might even survive to the end of the year if we kept on with our Kiva fundraising.

It was now late August and Amon said they would present to their investment committee in September. "You'll be able to get the funds in the next few months," he predicted. It was perfect timing to keep us from worrying about our next financial doomsday. With all the heavy lifting done for the fundraising, I decided it was probably time to start looking for new offices.

We were now ten people in the main office and eleven when Rachel was around, so things started to get a little tight at K-Rep. Also, since we were doing a little better (financially anyway) than some of the other pilot programs, we were constantly being asked to share resources with them.

I loved the Kilimani area and, with Acumen and K-Rep so close to each other, I thought it would be best to remain in the same neighborhood. Rachel and a few of our staff found a beautiful 3,000 square foot house nearby with a massive garden. The owners had converted an old colonial home near the Kenyatta Market area (walking distance to my favorite Nyama Choma place). All of the bedrooms had been wired for phones/internet and the garage was sealed off and converted into a boardroom. The space was actually too large for us but just felt perfect so we took it and then looked into subletting space to a few other organizations.

We called the house Juhudi Gardens, for the grassy two-acre backyard full of guava and avocado trees. I was allocated the master bedroom, complete with closet space and a shower. Kiva also moved in and we subleased the rest of the space to a technology startup called Kopo Kopo. Soon, we discovered the power supply was continually dropping, the internet connection was terrible and the roof leaked. The first week we were there, Isika and the security guard were robbed, kidnapped and driven all over Nairobi in our company vehicle.

The muggers asked Isika: "What ATM card do you have?" so they could go to a specific bank and take out all of his money.

"K-Rep Bank," stammered Isika.

"That bank does not have any money. We will let you go now."

Some of that was true as K-Rep was one of the few banks in Kenya not to turn a profit in 2008 and it was still struggling in 2009.

Kopo Kopo was frightened by the security issues and fed up with our connection problems so they moved out. A non-profit organization – Jacaranda Health which sets up maternal health clinics in Nairobi – moved in shortly after.

The field operations were also continuing to perform. We kept adding $20,000 to our loan portfolio with the clients, and repayment rates continued to register at about ninety-five percent.

It was early September of 2010 and I was invited to speak at an event sponsored by GBF in Washington DC. I had not made many trips home in the past twelve months and the US had started to feel a little more foreign to me. The big cars, loud people and thousands of options in the grocery stores struck me as odd. Flying through the glitzy, space-age city of Dubai between the US and Kenya felt like I was time traveling to different worlds or realities. The jetlag and general disorientation added to the effect. Harold was starting to raise money for a new fund, since he had almost finished spending and investing his first round of money. GBF wanted to showcase some of their successful investments and, apparently, we were one of them. I was asked to give our investment pitch to the participants in the GBF conference even though we were already well on our way to closing our investment if Acumen, Grameen and Rockefeller all came through.

It seemed like Acumen and Grameen would provide the $2 million in equity and Rockefeller would contribute the $3 million in debt. A nice, round $5 million to meet our goal.

My presentation had come a long way since the beginning. I now had lots of clear historical numbers and client case studies supporting both our financial projections and our social impact story of how a cow generates wealth over time for the farmers.

Grameen was at the conference, so I was confident about giving my presentation. At the end of the pitch someone from USAID stood up and asked in a gruff voice: "So what is the point? What's in it for me?"

A little confused and insulted I said: "I just presented the point. You can get whatever you want from financing Juhudi. If you are a donor you can improve the lives of 100,000 rural Kenyan farmers who do not have access to finance and if you are an investor you can get our twenty percent for equity and ten percent for debt."

Juhudi was not a 'project' but in fact a business that also had a very positive social effect on the lives of rural smallholder farmers. The social business concept seemed to be a little new for some of the donors in the room and I was not so sure they bought into it.

Steve and I met afterwards. He told me that Juhudi had been approved for an investment by Grameen Foundation, alongside Acumen. Acumen would provide $1.2 million and Grameen $550,000 in convertible debt that was structured very much like equity. That is, it could be used for anything to help the business, subordinated to senior debt (the senior lenders would get their money first if Juhudi went bankrupt) and had a long-term repayment of five years. This was all the news I needed to hear to get my mind off the rather unpleasant person from USAID.

I made plans to fly back through New York, so I could meet with Acumen and Rockefeller. My meeting with Acumen was a lot of fun. Everyone in their fancy Chelsea office seemed to know who I was and that Juhudi had just been approved by their Investment Committee for an investment. Even the well-known Jacqueline Novogratz came out to say hello and shake my hand.

Dressed in my best Kenyan suit, I took a fifteen-minute taxi ride from Acumen to Rockefeller at One Rockefeller Plaza. The office was stunning, with great views of Manhattan and a massive bronze waterfall statue at the entrance. I sat down with the Rock-ets to tell them about both Acumen and Grameen. They both looked at each other and said" "Well, we also have some good news for you. Rockefeller has approved Juhudi for a seven year loan of $750,000 with an interest rate of eleven percent."

I paused because I was expecting to hear more than three times that amount from them and the interest rate seemed really high. I had worked so hard during their due diligence and they knew how much money we needed. How can a $4 billion dollar foundation that gives out around $200 million each year decide to skimp us on $2 million? That was pocket change to them. We were not asking for charity either but paying them for a loan. Rockefeller was over a hundred times larger than Acumen but was providing us with substantially less than Acumen.

"What is wrong?" they asked.

"Nothing. I was just hoping it would be more. Is there any way to go up to $1 million at least?"

I regretted saying it as soon as it left my mouth because we really did not have any other option for lenders other than Rockefeller, and their loan would likely bring in more investors in the future. The $750,000 was better than nothing.

"Why don't you start with the smaller loan and we can always consider a new loan after a year of two depending on how the business is running?" Barbra offered. While the Rockefeller due diligence was a brutal process, Barbara and the rest of her team were quite pleasant in person. They all seemed to genuinely want to help Juhudi.

"That sounds great," I replied as we all stood to leave.

We shook hands.

Well that was a great trip, I thought to myself as I rode in the taxicab through downtown Manhattan. I had just raised almost $3 million for Juhudi.

I sat back and looked out the back window at the setting sun over the city skyline. I thought of all my friends in that city who had lost their jobs in the financial crisis and here I was raising millions for a company in Africa. We were still almost $2 million short of our goal but at least the new money would allow me to stay in Kenya for another eight to twelve months and raise the remaining funds. I eagerly anticipated my long trip through space back "home" to beautiful Kenya where I knew one of Benson's drivers would be waiting to meet me at the Nairobi airport with a smile.

Meru NP

The K-Rep Group rewarded my latest successful fundraising trip with a promotion from CFO to CEO of Juhudi Kilimo. I think it was more that Aleke was tired traveling back and forth between our new Juhudi office and KDA. The previous six months of fundraising for survival had kept me from sleeping much, or doing anything enjoyable over the weekends. Now with a little breathing room after the US trip, I badly needed some fun in my life. I started to go out again and meet the new crowd of young expats who had recently arrived in Kenya that summer. Now a seasoned veteran of life in Nairobi, I was a wealth of knowledge for the hopeful young professionals looking to make a difference in Africa or seeking adventure, away from the boring jobs in the US. My favorite new friends in Nairobi, Elizabeth and Sebastian Gregarek, invited me, and my new girlfriend, Charlene, on a camping trip to Meru National Park (it turned out that my previous girlfriend had been taking extended layovers in London on her way from the US to meet up with an ex-boyfriend, while dating me, so that was the end of it for me).

Charlene, a MBA Haas Berkeley grad, was working for a non-profit organization called KickStart, which produces low-cost treadle pumps for rural farmers to irrigate their crops. The organization operated all over Africa and had won multiple awards. Not many of the Juhudi farmers were interested in the $88 pump because for $140 they could buy a petrol pump and use their time more efficiently than manually pumping water. The difference between the two pumps based on a monthly payment for a loan was about $4, which did not hinder the farmers' monthly cash flows.

Charlene and I had met at a conference and hit it off, since we had the rural agriculture thing in common. Charlene went on to be the social mayor of the Nairobi expat community. I think she knew just about every American expat in the city by the time she left four years later. We had also adopted a baby elephant together, named Kainuk, from the David Sheldrick Elephant Orphanage. This meant we paid $50 to get monthly updates about Kainuk and have extra visiting hours with the elephant in the evening, after the rest of the tourists had left. We could also visit the restricted region of Tsavo East National Park, where the full-grown elephants were released into the wild.

My friend Elizabeth was a fiery redhead banker from New York. She had turned to a life of microfinance in Kenya by working for one of the rating agencies. She spoke fluent German and French and met her husband, Sebastian (who is French), in Switzerland. The combination of all the European experiences meant that the two were fantastic cooks and very interesting to talk to.

I was very much looking forward to this trip to one of the more remote parks.

The main campsite in Meru National Park was probably the best campsite I have ever been to in Kenya. They had an outside pool, open-air kitchens with running water, and a little ranger station with solar power to charge phones. After we had set up camp and eaten an amazing meal that included a French flourless chocolate cake, we settled down under a clear night sky full of stars. Then baboons splashed loudly in the pool.

The guards had disappeared into the safety of their cabin for the evening. This camp did not have any electric fence and I was not so sure the guards would come to our rescue if anything attacked us. I drank a lot of water (and French wine) during the evening, so around 2am I woke up, needing to go to the bathroom. I started to switch on my headlamp but then froze. From what sounded like right behind my tent, I heard the unmistakable roar of a male lion, which literally shook my bones. A lion's roar is an unmistakable sound in the wild. Deep and guttural, it strikes terror in the hearts of any hearing it up close.

On a previous safari, with Greg in Samburu, we had been robbed by a baboon who had jumped into the back of the car while my back was turned and stolen a bag of marshmallows and cheese nibs. I felt so defenseless at that moment that, when we were back in Nairobi, I purchased a Maasai club, called a rungu, to fend off any future baboons. Now in the tent, I reached for my trusty Maasai rungu, which I slept next to every night. It was practically useless against a lion, but if attacked, at least I would go down fighting. I thought about how thin the lining of the tent was. It reminded me of a plastic bag with a sandwich inside. For the lion, I was that sandwich.

I stayed awake not moving until about 5am, when the sun started to come up. I heard some footsteps and rustling around the tent and expected it to be the guards coming to my rescue. I unzipped my tent and stood up to thank them. However, instead of the guards I was surrounded by a massive herd of fifty impala and a few larger water buck. They all lazily looked at me as if expecting me to say something. Then they went back to their grazing and rolled through our campsite. It turns out that everyone else had a wonderful night of sleep and did not hear a thing.

Sebastian and I thought it would be fun to drive to the far south of the camp and exit out of a separate gate on our way back to Nairobi. We asked the camp rangers and they drew up a rudimentary map for us. Then we took off through the park.

We drove for a solid three hours, not seeing many animals but enjoying the views. The road started to become more overgrown on the sides. Clearly, very few vehicles had gone this way. The road dropped down a very steep ravine and entered a dry riverbed before it seemed to disappear. We could not see where it crossed or where it came out on the other side. The hill back up was far too steep to drive back so we were stuck in this riverbed with no phone service and nearly out of water.

Elizabeth was five months pregnant at the time, so things were getting a little serious. Sebastian and I found a trail that went up the opposite bank but it seemed more like a trail an elephant would make with one track than a road with two tracks. It was just wide enough for Sebastian to push our small white Pajero 4x4 through. The car filled with the dangerous tsetse flies and we were all bitten a few times. I was not sure how long the deadly sleeping sickness would take to kick in but I hoped we could be nearer civilization when it did.

After a few more hours of bushwhacking we finally crashed onto a road. We found a sign pointing to the southern gate. Exhausted and relieved we all greeted the rangers at the gate. It was close to 3pm and if we pushed we could make it back to Nairobi before it got dark. The rangers clearly had not seen many people at their gate and were asking us where we were going.

"Through the gate and back to Nairobi," I told them.

"No," one responded. I thought maybe there was a problem leaving from a separate gate but it turned out that one of the main bridges had washed out a few weeks ago and the road back to the main highway was impassable. We needed to go back to the northern gate and exit that way.

We were crushed.

The rangers gave us some water and pointed us in a better direction than the way we had come. It was too late to get back to Nairobi that night so we stayed at a hotel in Embu, which is a few hours between Meru and Nairobi. The car ride home was very quiet.

Savannah Sands

The new office was a twenty-minute walk from my apartment and the wild dogs of Ring Road. I found another fantastic place just five minutes from the Juhudi Gardens, called Savannah Sands. Since one- and two-bedroom apartments are hard to come by, and are usually more expensive than three- and four-bedroom places, I had to settle for a three-bedroom on the top floor. To this day it was one of my favorite places to live. Charlene and I had ended things and I got to know five American girls who lived in my apartment complex and were all involved in public health.

My neighbors at Savannah Sands were a fun group of people to spend time with and learn about the research work they were doing with the Center for Disease Control or evaluating the public health facilities in Nairobi. The six of us rented a van and spent a day visiting the famous family-owned Brown's cheese farm, which is one of the leading brands of high-end cheese in Kenya (and East Africa).

The farm consists of a few small houses that have been converted into a cheese processing plant. We toured the facilities and watched them make over a dozen types of award-winning cheeses. The lunch consisted of food freshly picked from the family's garden. That evening, I took my five women to a party along with another girl I had met earlier, who was also in public health, named Neeta Bhandari. She was Indian by descent, was born in Tanzania and spent most of her life in Northern Virginia and New

York. Neeta was smart, accomplished and astonishingly beautiful. She had a way of attracting the attention of an entire room when she was talking. I am sure it was not easy growing up as an ethnic Indian from Africa and speaking with a thick American accent. It made it difficult to answer the where-are-you-from? question. Yet this background also allowed her to connect warmly with every type of person in Kenya. Everyone loved her – the Maasai security guards, the elite Indian business community and the expatriate diplomats at the US Embassy parties. In her first three months in Nairobi, she had also managed to become friends with Charlene, however, so she was a little off limits to me.

I took all the girls out dancing later to a few clubs in Westlands. In parts of Kenya, polygamy is still practiced and socially accepted but after that weekend I am not sure it would ever be a great idea. At the bars I was constantly being asked to tell unwanted suitors to leave my girls alone. One of the girls tried to tell an overly aggressive Kenyan man that she was married and he replied "don't worry, so am I," then showed her his ring. Infidelity is also socially accepted in Kenya and happens everywhere. I am not sure it is any different than other countries, but the Kenyans are a little more open about it.

The next day we visited Ngong Racecourse, which offered fun Sunday afternoons of racing. My friends and I enjoyed betting and watching the racehorses make their way around the functional, though slightly run-down track. I never won any money but had fun picking the best- named horse in each race. There also happened to be a nine-hole golf course inside the track and hitting the horses with an errant shot was not outside the realm of possibilities. I played the course a few times with a friend, Brian Dempsey, who worked at a rival microfinance company and Jesse Moore, who ran a solar lighting startup company called M-Kopa, which allowed its customers to pay-as-you go and pay down the light over time. If a customer missed a payment then the light would be remotely shut off or repossessed. Needless to say, this was an effective strategy.

That same week AMSCO invited me to travel to Helsinki for their annual board meeting with representatives from the IFC, UNDP and African Development Bank.

The AMSCO program was under review and they needed one of their sponsored managers to come and give a few presentations about how the program was helping to develop Africa. They loved the Juhudi story, but I think they also needed someone who could travel to Finland on short notice without needing a visa. I thought it would be a nice opportunity to showcase Juhudi to these international big shots.

In proper UN fashion, I was booked at the most expensive hotel in Helsinki and given a $250 per day cash allowance. Helsinki is a beautiful city, especially in the summer when the sun does not start to set until well past 11pm. Then it rises again at 3am. I gave my two presentations, showcasing Juhudi's performance and how much money we were able to raise over the last year. I also talked about how we had used the capacity building grants to improve the performance of our staff and how that moved our client repayment from eighty-eight percent to ninety-six percent. The donors loved it.

Each evening I was taken to lavish dinners with ambassadors and senior level Finnish government representatives for international affairs. I ate reindeer and some spectacular smoked salmon. Life with one of these big international donors was grand if this is what they did every week. Unfortunately, I was not able to generate any new leads from investors on the trip. I still had in the back of my mind that even if everything worked out with Acumen, Grameen and Rockefeller, Juhudi still needed another $2 million in debt. Hopefully the presentation put our name out in the European investment community. At least AMSCO seemed happy with my visit.

Mobius

As Juhudi attracted more interest from investors, I somehow became the guy for young entrepreneurs to talk to about starting a company in Kenya. A 24-year-old guy from the UK, working on the Kenyan coast in Kilifi, named Joel Jackson somehow got my email and phone number. Joel was working for a fantastic organization called Komaza, which works with farmers on barren sandy lands around Kilifi and helps them plant trees along with teaching them about agro-forestry. Joel, a political science and computer science major, was sick and tired of the appalling infrastructure and limited transportation options in rural Kenya. The rough roads wreaked havoc on the public transport vehicles making for uncomfortable rides. In fact, some roads were simply impassable during certain parts of the rainy season.

Joel decided that he wanted to design a low-cost Kenyan-built vehicle that could better deal with the harsh environments of the public roads in Kenya. Once again I found myself thinking this guy was crazy, much like Andreas, to think he could start a car company in Kenya. The automotive industry spends billions each year on developing new vehicles and has perfected large-scale manufacturing to absurd levels of detail. How could someone possibly compete with the likes of Toyota, Isuzu or Mitsubishi, which make up close to seventy percent of the vehicle sales in Kenya?[iv]

I met with Joel anyway. He turned out to be a charismatic smooth talker with a sophisticated British accent. Joel had done his homework about building cars and could spin a compelling story for his idea. I loved

---

[iv]   Matt Gasnier, "Kenya 1st Half 2015: Toyota Hilux teases Land Cruiser 70 for #1," Best Selling Cars Blog, July 25 2015.

the concept of having a low-cost and reliable vehicle for rural transport in Kenya. It would make the lives of my loan officers much easier and could even be financed to our smallholder farmer clients to help them deliver milk or bring supplies back to their farms.

Later that year Joel officially founded Mobius, which was coined after the Mobius Strip, by Joel's advisor Andrew Youn, for the three dimensional strip's properties that provide an infinite number of surfaces it could travel. When Joel came by our office later that year offering pre-sales of his new car, I was the second person in line (after Andrew) to pay my deposit of $500 and sign up for an order to be delivered sometime in the future.

Our Juhudi client with a cow financed by a Kiva loan

Juhudi farmers in their tea fields in Kericho

Group of Juhudi farmers in Murang'a

*Me (left) with Mike Jelinski (middle) and Andreas Zeller
(right) on top of the Mobius*

Doug and his modified Land Rover at the Rhino Charge

House in the tree

With the Nairobi friends at the Lamu castle

On the top of Mt. Kilimanjaro

With Stephen on the hike to Mt. Kenya

The Maralal Camel Derby

Following a loan officer from KDA through the streets of Kibera

Roadside mechanic with Neeta near Maasai Mara

Milk delivery truck near Meru

Camping near the Mt. Suswa Conservatory

With Neeta on the Kenyan coast

*The Juhudi Executive Team. From left to right: Nat
Robinson, Gilbert Ambani, Shadrack Mutunga, Nancy
Butama, Benjamin Kimosop*

Throwing a frisbee on the shores of Lake Jipe by Tsavo West National Park

Having a meal of nyama choma with Benson from La Playa Tours

A Juhudi loan offier using a tablet in the field at a client's home

My mom stuck in the mud after torrential rains in Laikipia

Juhudi clients

A Juhudi farmer carrying tea leaves to sell

Steve Wardle (middle) and Brian Dempsey (right) working with our pilot Joel (left) on our plane in the barren lands of Turkana

With Andreas (left) and Brian (right) after a GP Karting race

The Juhudi field team after being made Pokot elders near Lelan

A celibration dance after opening an FSA in Mabera

*Aleke Dondo and the Mabera District Officer after an FSA
launch*

*Aleke (center) after Juhudi Kilimo won the the Social
Entrepreneurship Award*

*Standing at the site of the Lelan cooling plant with the
Lelan Highlands Dairy Cooperative Director*

Chapter 11 | Patient Capital

The Juhudi field staff ratcheted up their performance with the flowing Kiva funds. Our client repayment rates were as high as they ever had been in the past, at ninety-six percent. Our monthly income had improved and now we were losing less money each month. I asked Aleke if K-Rep would be interested in giving me some shares in the new company, now that I was CEO. He said that he too wanted shares. In many public and private companies, shares are provided to the senior management over time to build a long-term incentive for the management and closely align the directives of the business to the rewards of the management. I was not entirely sure how well this would work in a social business, since our primary goal was to help farmers. If, for whatever reason, Juhudi became wildly profitable, it would probably mean we were charging too much interest to our clients or being too harsh on our collection practices. I did not want to be part of the company if that were the case. Nevertheless, the K-Rep Group was supportive of the equity idea but suggested we conclude things with the new investors first in case they had any misgivings.

My role as CEO was not all that different than CFO and General Manager, only now I did not have Aleke to help me make as many decisions. I usually felt lost and alone with most of my regular management decisions. But I did my best to learn quickly from mistakes and move on. The local business association, AMFI, was looking for fresh leadership so they elected me to their board and appointed me as their treasurer. This brought me into closer contact with the other CEOs of financial institutions from around the country who happily acted as my mentors and supporters. I focused my attention at Juhudi on building my individual rapport with each manager and employee through regular one-on-one meetings or casual walks in the garden. This was something I think I learned how to do well in college as a fraternity president who was responsible for almost forty drunk college kids. My "management style" often ended up with me spending long hours in the dean of students' office trying to explain my way out of the previous night's utter destruction of the fine arts theater from a party that got a little out of control. Dean Edmonds was a big man and devout Southern Baptist African American from Tennessee, with a Lifetime Achievement Award and a world-class debater. Edmonds was one of those people you did not try to argue with as a student. But he had a big heart and much like Aleke, took an interest in helping me make my way through life.

Cash was still a problem at Juhudi. I had to caution our management to keep growth slow since the only money we had was from Kiva. While Acumen, Grameen and Rockefeller had all received official approval to invest, we still needed to draft agreements and agree on the rest of the terms of the investment. The investment teams at Acumen and Grameen estimated that we could have the money in our bank account before Christmas, if everything went well. Three more months of austerity measures were bearable if I could give hope to my staff that the money was on its way.

It turned out that the AMSCO visit to Finland helped us with our funding shortfall. While Acumen, Grameen and Rockefeller were still working to get their investment documents drafted, Oikocredit, from the Netherlands, had recently sent us a twenty-page loan agreement. They were offering a two-year loan for $350,000 at 14.66% floating rate which was pegged to the Kenyan Treasury bill. So if interest rates charged by the Kenyan government went up the interest went up. If they went down the interest rate did not drop below fourteen percent. Even though the loan was for two years, the first payment was due after three months and interest due after the first month. There were also a lot of new legal clauses such as personal guarantees, a lien on all assets, etc.

Aleke and I were desperate for cash, so this seemed like a good deal. Agora finished their due diligence and asked if we had any other lenders who were about to provide us with any loans, so we shared the Oiko loan agreement with them. Agora was shocked at the structure of the loan and felt the terms were almost predatory. We were literally about to sign the agreement with Oiko that day.

That same afternoon Agora sent over a legal agreement for a loan of similar size but for thirteen percent interest and over five years. We could not absorb both loans into the business at the same time, so the Juhudi board opted to take the Agora loan first. This crushed Oiko, who had spent several months and invested significantly into the due diligence process. Our investment officer said that we "had just left her standing at the altar." I felt horrible about it but it would have been irresponsible to the business to take the higher interest and shorter-term loan when we had a much cheaper option on the table. More importantly, Agora was interested in making an equity investment in the future, whereas Oiko did not have an equity fund for Kenya at that time. I really liked the team from Agora too. One of their investment officers was a former CEO of a major microfinance institution in Cambodia and the other was a banker from the UK who had gone to my high school in Colorado for a few years before moving to London. The Oiko team was also amicable but I was not able to connect at the same level as I did with the Agora team. The personal relationships seemed to become an important factor in selecting Agora in addition to the more favorable terms in the loan agreement.

I should have known that things never go smoothly for very long when running a business.

The legal agreements from Acumen/Grameen included a 122-page loan agreement and a forty-three-page shareholders' agreement, since they were investing in convertible debt. Rockefeller only had a sixty-two page agreement, but they insisted on putting in place an onerous thirty-page inter-creditor agreement. This agreement required Rockefeller to approve any loan in the future to Juhudi and for the new lenders all to agree and sign the same inter-creditor agreement. The theory was to protect Juhudi and the lenders but in practice, for such a small company, it was quite inconvenient.

I was also not quite sure why these agreements were much longer than Agora's (UK) and Oikocredit's (Netherlands), which were both under ten pages. Perhaps it was the need for the US to keep so many lawyers employed? We did our best to go through the lengthy agreements with K-Rep in detail but it took forever to review them. I also thought it would make things easier if Acumen and Grameen came in together on the same terms so we could save time.

I was wrong. If we proposed a change, Acumen would need to review it with its lawyers and then Grameen would need to review it with their lawyers. Then Grameen's lawyers would need to agree with Acumen's lawyers on any proposed changes. I felt like I should get credit towards a law degree after spending so much time with each investor's legal team on the transaction.

Acumen and Grameen are nonprofits so to cut costs they both used outside pro-bono legal services. This meant that they received free lawyer time from some of the top law firms in Washington DC and New York. These firms handle investment deals of hundreds of millions of dollars so they pumped our investment documentation with the same language and sophisticated structure of an investment many times the size of small investment deal of $1.75 million.

The lawyers were essentially donating their time to Acumen and Grameen, which meant they would review the agreements when their paid jobs were not demanding their time. The result? It took us over six months just to get the agreements aligned. Once we finalized the agreements and structure with Acumen and Grameen I sent the documents over to Rockefeller, so they could see we had some convertible debt. This would make the Rockefeller loan more secure since the loan was senior and paid out first in a bankruptcy.

Barbra was not happy. She told me that, "Rockefeller was very uncomfortable with the structuring of the subordinated debt." Barbra would use that word, 'uncomfortable', with nearly everything that happened to Juhudi from that point forward. In the five years Rockefeller was a lender I do not think they were ever comfortable. However, she did have a valid point on the structuring because Rockefeller was providing a seven-year senior loan and Acumen/Grameen were providing a five-year subordinated loan. A situation could occur where Acumen and Grameen are paid out before Rockefeller, which was not right.

I expected Acumen and Grameen to talk to Rockefeller and we could work out the differences. Acumen and Rockefeller were only fifteen minutes away from each other in New York. I was wrong again.

The situation deteriorated quickly and both parties took defensive sides with egos at stake. Acumen and Grameen thinking that their investment was structured correctly and Rockefeller was wrong, while Rockefeller believed their investment was structured correctly and Acumen/Grameen should change. Since there were no communication lines at all between the investors in the US I found myself scheduling conference calls from Nairobi to try and work out the issues.

Agora's $250,000 loan gave the company a good boost but it essentially just cleared part of the backlog of farmers waiting to take loans. The money went out the door much faster than I had anticipated. That meant back on the monthly life support cash of Kiva. I had no idea how much longer the Acumen/Grameen/Rockefeller drama would last and if we did not get another boost of cash by December, we were once again looking at our death spiral of doom. In mid-October I made the tough decision to slow our growth again to a trickle. We were only issuing a few new loans to farmers each week in order to conserve our cash. This move also hurt our financial sustainability, which had been the highest ever during the previous three months. Not that it made a major difference, but I also froze my salary to help the monthly burden on cash. For the negotiations, I did not care one bit about the five- or seven-year structuring. I just wanted the money so we could survive this year. Finally, Acumen and Grameen broke the deadlock with Rockefeller and agreed to increase their term to six years and then Rockefeller would make their first loan repayments in year five.

Back to the lawyers again. We had lost another three months of valuable time.

Just as we resolved the Rockefeller structuring issue we had some more drama. I found out later that the way the debt converted to equity was not very common. The K-Rep Group directors were not happy. The convertible debt had an interest rate of thirteen percent and carried with it the option for Acumen and Grameen to convert to equity at a pre-negotiated price with K-Rep of 1.6 times the book value of equity for the 2009 audited accounts. What this means is that if things went well and Juhudi became profitable, Acumen and Grameen could decide to be the majority owners of the business with around ninety to ninety-five percent of the ownership. However, if things did not go well and Juhudi did not reach profitability, Acumen and Grameen could keep their money structured as a loan and be repaid after six years. K-Rep had guaranteed the loan, so K-Rep would be paying back Acumen and Grameen if things really went off the rails. It was kind of like betting on cards at a

Black Jack table. If the dealer dealt you a winning hand of twenty-one, then you would receive ninety to ninety-five percent of all the winnings and give the rest to the player sitting next to you. But if you lost the hand to the dealer, then the player sitting next to you would pay all your losses for you. Acumen and Grameen could not lose in this scenario.

Agora thought that this kind of pricing and structure was predatory and taking advantage of Juhudi and K-Rep's weak cash position. Once converted to equity at a future date, Acumen and Grameen could own anything between sixty and ninety-five percent of the company, depending on when we broke even and converted, unless K-Rep put in more money. Our other lender and interested equity investor, Agora, was also not happy with how Acumen and Grameen had structured their investment. Nobody seemed to have a right answer for the correct structuring of these investments, so it was one fund's word against another. I was pulling my hair out, since all of this felt like kids calling each other names on the playground. Hopefully, not all entrepreneurs have to go through this and it is just unique to the nascent industry of social enterprise and impact investing.

Agora gave us a counter offer to K-Rep that they would invest straight equity of around $2 million and only take fifty-five percent ownership of Juhudi. The K-Rep Group (who owned one hundred percent at the time) did not want to give up their control of Juhudi. Since we had about six months of money left we did not have much time to find another investor for a better deal. I personally thought that either option would be fine, especially for an early stage business like Juhudi.

The K-Rep Group wanted to try and keep a majority ownership for a few more years and hoped they could invest later to avoid being diluted by Acumen and Grameen. Most of K-Rep's income came in the form of dividends from their partial ownership of K-Rep Bank (which was still losing money) and from a few rental properties it owned around Nairobi that did not produce much.

There was also a major perceived benefit in taking investors like Acumen and Grameen. They had higher profiles and large professional networks, which could help Juhudi. After a number of deliberations, K-Rep decided to go with Acumen and Grameen over Agora, who were shocked and disappointed that K-Rep would select a more expensive investment over what they had provided. I had invested a lot of time in the Agora relationship and really liked the partners running the fund. Agora still had their $250,000 loan with Juhudi, which they graciously said we could keep on our books until the money from Acumen and Grameen hit our accounts. Then they wanted the money back.

Everyone was happy by the end of November and we had all agreed on the documentation. I wanted to have some cash in the bank by December because our farmers seasonally demonstrate a much higher demand for loans that month. There seems to be more cash in the Kenyan economy around that time, which means clients are also more willing to pay their loans. This extra holiday cash could be attributed to the annual tea bonuses that came in November. It paid many of the tea farmers in the country for their harvests earlier in the year, which were dependent on global tea prices. Many of our farmers were in the tea areas of Kericho and Litein, so they were affected. The rest of the cash could be from increased remittances abroad or from family in Nairobi during the holidays as Christmas gifts.

I told my staff to be ready for a large influx of cash from Acumen and Grameen so we could meet the demand for our clients. After I told them, I suddenly had the sinking feeling that perhaps Acumen and Grameen might not be able to get everything done over the holidays. So I went back to my list of interested investors and reached out to a contact I had recently made at the major investment bank, Deutsche Bank. Deutsche Bank had a small social investment arm capable of quickly providing small loans of $100,000. The investment officer was a terrific guy named Ben, who said if we worked extremely fast, he could get the approval to us before the close of the year. I quickly sent over the droves of files I had prepared for all the previous investors. Then held my breath. We pulled off a Christmas miracle and received approval from Deutsche Bank before their board left for the holidays. I took a vacation trip to see my family in Colorado and was on the phone with Ben on the ski lift when he told me the news. Now we could provide some of our eager farmers with cows for the holidays. However the $100,000 would only tide us over until the end of January. We needed Acumen and Grameen's big investments.

Nothing came in January.

I was crestfallen. We had received the investment committee approvals in September and finalized all the documentation. What was happening?

My staff lost confidence in me and we went back to restricting loans to our exasperated clients again in early February. Our Operations Manager, who had become a good friend of mine, had started in the business as a loan officer and then worked his way up to work in the Head Office, suddenly resigned. He left a letter on my desk one Friday saying that he was giving his notice. This hurt because he was smart, hardworking and quite passionate about the business. However, he had a young family at home and after seeing what was happening with the business he could tell we were in trouble. His father-in-law had helped him get a job at the Central Bank that paid better and probably would not run out of money. So I took on the Operations Manager role in addition to the CFO and CEO role. It was exhausting.

We did not get the money until April 2011.

December through March we lost probably around $500,000 in potential business due to the delays in funding disbursements. It took the Acumen Fund twenty-two months from our first serious meeting with Amon in June of 2009 to their disbursement in April of 2011. I would certainly understand if Acumen had concerns with our business or wanted to wait and see how our numbers turned out before investing, but that was never the case. Acumen's motto is 'patient capital' because they are willing to invest over the long term and let businesses mature. I think the patient capital motto refers to how long it takes to receive the funds.

To Acumen's credit they have dramatically improved the amount of time it takes to disburse an investment and have hired more in-house legal counsel, which helps speed up their process.

Amon called to say they could finally wire the funds. I told him to "press the button" and send them over. We held a small party in the Juhudi Gardens to celebrate.

Ford Foundation

The Ford Foundation is one of the largest foundations in the world, with assets of $12.2 billion, second only to the Bill and Melinda Gates Foundation with $41 billion. The Ford Foundation funds a variety of civil society organizations globally. It has done a lot to fund social microfinance institutions including Juhudi's largest competitor, Kenya Women Finance Trust (KWFT). The Ford Foundation had also funded KDA at one point and still had a relationship with Aleke.

Similar to the Rockefeller Foundation, Ford had a local Kenyan office which only managed the grant making aspects of the foundation and the PRI lending team was in New York. Ford had a fast yet sophisticated due diligence process overseen by the Director of the Financial Assets Unit, Frank DeGiovanni, who had decades of microfinance experience, and Christine Looney, who was also an expert in the field. Ford was very interested in the social impact story of Juhudi and helping us better measure the non-financial benefits of the Juhudi loans. We had full approval from Ford in seven months after the first serious meeting and funding after a total of fifteen months. This seemed extremely quick to us when compared to the other impact investors.

Ford was interested in a major loan of $2 million, which was all we needed to close our fundraising goal of $5 million. Ford was offering a ten-year loan with an eight-year grace period on the principal payments. It would have an interest rate of one percent. Ford was also not at all concerned about the subordinated debt maturing before its loan. It was a spectacular deal and game changer for Juhudi.

I was curious why Ford and Rockefeller had such different concerns and structured their investments so differently, when both had identical legal structures and similar missions. I was especially curious why Rockefeller would charge us eleven percent on a loan and Ford would charge one percent on a much longer and larger loan when they were investing in the same company. Barbra stammered out an answer that the interest, "needed to pay for the investment staff and support services". I think it gives more evidence that none of the impact investors knew how to structure their investments and price risk accurately with Juhudi.

Once we closed on the Ford investment I went out with Amon to Brew Bistro and ordered a twenty-dollar hamburger made with truffle oil. It was fantastic.

Social Performance

Surprisingly, none of our initial impact investors asked me for any tangible impact studies or data on how the Juhudi loans improve the lives of farmers. For many, it was implied that access to finance had been proven around the world to benefit low-income communities.

Rural smallholder farmers in Kenya were among the poorest and most economically exploited groups in the country. So by providing loans for assets that increase incomes and build wealth, Juhudi had to be helping. We also had lots of great case studies about farmers who started out with very little farm income and could not send their kids to school. Then after three or four loans the farmers had increased their income by four to five times and were sending their children to school and investing in their homes.

I was interested personally in going a little further to show how Juhudi was different to every other microfinance institution in Kenya. Most Kenyan microfinance institutions were similar to those such as SKS in India and Compartamos in Mexico, which provided loans to low income communities but did not necessarily help all of their clients to have a better life. The loans certainly insulated the clients from economic shocks but most of the high-interest loans went to finance personal consumption (dowry payments, health care costs, school fees, rent, etc.) While the personal consumption activities are certainly important expenses to a low-income family, they normally do not help the family to generate more money to pay the interest and fees on the loan. This situation forces the family to borrow a new loan from another institution to pay off the first institution. The end result is a low-income client who is mired in a cycle of debt.

Microfinance had been criticized extensively for burdening the poor with debt and the *New York Times* featured an article on the topic and targeted Kiva for one of its partners in Nigeria with high interest rates. Unfortunately, trying to get a strong academic study on social impact is terribly expensive. A study conducted by a reputable research firm could cost anywhere between $50,000 and $300,000, depending on what is being evaluated.

Aleke and K-Rep stopped evaluating their own programs altogether, because any self-evaluations are always open to interpretation and criticism of the evaluation methodologies. It seemed that every impact fund or social research firm had started to develop its own model and methodology for evaluating impact. So I looked for low-cost options that were accepted around the world and found two that I liked.

One was specific to microfinance, called CERISE. It was a self-administered evaluation that told how well a microfinance institution was carrying out its social mission as an institution. CERISE was developed in France and was being pushed by Kiva on its partners to help them achieve their social mission. The second was the Progress out of Poverty tool or PPI (I am not sure how they came up with that acronym), which was being pioneered by the Grameen Foundation. This tool was a set of ten questions that could be asked to a microfinance borrower about their household items and the response would tell how likely the borrower was above or below the poverty line. The ten questions were developed after a major analysis was done on income levels and household item correlation in each country. For example, if someone had iron sheeting on their roof and owned a TV they had a much higher likelihood of being above the poverty line than a household that did not have these items.

We were the first institution to translate the Kenyan survey into Kiswahili and started trying it out on our clients. Initially it was a little harder to explain to clients why we were asking for random household items like frying pans and towels but apparently those items had a high statistical correlation to poverty levels.

PPI and CERISE are just two components of hundreds of different tools, assessments and methodologies for measuring impact. Rachel Brooks took a liking to social performance and did wonders for Juhudi by keeping our data organized and updating the assessments. The impact investing community was also working hard to standardize everything and find a way to compare social impact across investment companies and portfolios.

We were asked by Acumen and GBF to be a beta test company for a new Global Impact Investing Rating Standard (GIIRS), which was working with a new movement in the US called the B-Corporation, run by the nonprofit B-Lab. A B-Corporation was a way to certify, license or legally structure a company that is demonstrating some significant social benefits from the work being done. This could be through carbon-emission-reducing solar companies or fair trade coffee companies looking to return more money back to the rural low-income farmers.

I really liked the concept and volunteered Juhudi to participate. We had a 300-question assessment plus several rounds of in-person interviews by the GIIRS team. Luckily, we had Rachel, who was still volunteering after her Kiva Fellowship, to help drive the process. Rachel helped the GIIRS team to develop their microfinance addendum of their assessment based on the CERISE evaluation. We finally became GIIRS certified, with a rating number that investors could use to compare us with other rated companies. This also qualified us to become a certified B-Corporation – the first in Africa.

This actually did not mean anything in Kenya, but it qualified Juhudi to receive some software license discounts with a few US firms and some other perks. However the real reason we went through the GIIRS process and B-Corporation certification was to show the world that we were a different kind of company than all the bank and microfinance institutions, who just provide savings and loans. We wanted to send out the message that we had a strong social mission and were dramatically affecting the lives of rural Kenyans. Hopefully, some day, groups like GIIRS and B-Lab will be able to drive more investment capital to social businesses or perhaps help a Certified B-Corporation access governmental tax advantages around the world for the social benefit to society.

One of the greatest social performance tools I found for microfinance was through an initiative called MF Transparency, which gathered and published the true interest rates and fees charged by banks and microfinance institutions all over the world. Microfinance is notorious for hiding fees and complicating interest charges for the low-income borrowers. Juhudi was one of the first institutions to submit data to MF Transparency's review of Kenya. I was worried that if no other institution submitted data or if they falsified data then we would look like the most expensive lender in the market. I knew our interest rates were no higher than the market microfinance rates and even lower that most of our competitors. To my surprise, the initiative was able to capture the pricing data from a vast majority of the major institutions in Kenya. Juhudi scored the highest transparency score for the entire country. However being the most transparent in a country that regularly ranks in the bottom quarter of Transparency International's annual rankings probably did not help us very much. Still, it was a start.

SEDF

Stephanie Koczela (the Kiva boss who made me cry) put me in touch with a new person who had just moved to Nairobi from Liberia and was working for the Soros Economic Development Fund (SEDF). This fund was associated with the billionaire and mega investor, George Soros, but run by one of his sons. The purpose of the fund was to support the economic development of developing countries around the world. They had focused most of their investments around Eastern Europe but now were making a big push for investments in Africa.

The fund already had a major office in Johannesburg, South Africa, and had now started operations in Nairobi. SEDF was also getting much more interested in social businesses but their minimum $2 million equity investment size was preventing many early stage businesses from accessing their funds.

The young SEDF portfolio associate in Nairobi was named Brandon Matthews. He was from California but had spent most of his life working in New York and investing in microfinance in South America. Like all of the portfolio staff of the impact funds we had worked with, Brandon was incredibly smart and quite diligent, but also young, in his late twenties. Brandon certainly knew a lot about microfinance at a strategic level from his experience in South America. Brandon and I met at a bar and hit it off right away. At that time Juhudi was not really needing another equity investor, but I was drooling over SEDF's massive $700 million fund and capacity to provide follow-on investments of $5 or $10 million in the future. This was something that Grameen and Acumen could not provide.

Brandon and I spent a long weekend rafting the White Nile in Uganda where we both bungee jumped into the river from over 100ft. During that trip Brandon said that while Juhudi was probably a smaller deal for them, he was going to present it to their investment committee anyway.

We were approved and I set out to try and justify why we needed another $2 million in equity from Soros along with Acumen and Grameen. Both Acumen and Grameen were excited and eager to tap into Soros' deep pockets so we went ahead with the due diligence.

It was a little awkward having Brandon change from being a friend to a hardnosed investor asking questions about Juhudi and my job. Brandon was only a few years younger than I was, but he really took advantage of the fact that he had all the money and we needed it. Brandon was not one to be politically correct or diplomatic with any of his criticism or questioning. He went through my business plan and told me that "it reads more like a grant proposal than a business plan", even though this business plan had already raised close to $5 million. I had to smile and nod.

Brandon was also critical of our management, saying that we were 'unproven' and while our Chief Accountant and Operations Manager were fine we "needed five more just like them" and the rest of the team was weak. To my surprise, Brandon was actually the only investor directly to question my own credibility, since I did not have any experience before Juhudi in microfinance, agriculture or in running a business.

It was all very valid criticism but the way it was delivered bothered me. I thought his tone came off as extremely arrogant and condescending. But having spent enough time in corporate America and business school, I could manage the blunt and direct approach of his due diligence. However, my Kenyan staff, Aleke and the board of all-Kenyan senior statesmen did not appreciate this approach whatsoever. Still greedy for the money I brushed this all aside and assumed that if SEDF did invest they would not put a 27-year-old like Brandon on our board. After the due diligence had finished in October of 2011, they went strangely silent. I did not see Brandon or get an email for almost two months. We assumed that SEDF was not interested any longer.

One of the other investors from the speed dating event, Alterfin, had finally set up their equity fund called FEFISOL and were interested in Juhudi. So we went through our 22nd due diligence of that year with Alterfin.

It turned out that Alterfin was not comfortable investing while Kenya was going through a referendum to put in place a badly needed new constitution. Alterfin even curtailed their current loan, forcing us to pre-pay before the referendum. They were the only lender who was concerned and it probably stemmed from the fact that Alterfin did not have any staff in East Africa, so the idea of a Kenyan vote terrified them. I personally attended the referendum ceremony, which went without a hitch (other than a tank catching fire in the parade). But Alterfin suddenly went silent and would not provide us with a timeline on their investment.

In February, Brandon finally broke his silence and made contact. They had decided they wanted to co-invest, with the same terms as Acumen and Grameen, both of whom had closed almost a year earlier. But they requested to change some of the legal documentation to be more consistent with their previous investments. I thought there would be no way this could happen but lots of money brings influence and both Acumen and Grameen agreed to have SEDF join their investment terms.

So we embarked on another round of edits and negotiations but now with three legal teams. SEDF had its own in-house lawyers who were quite experienced with the general deal documentation. We still had not heard anything from Alterfin, so we went ahead with SEDF. It turned out that Alterfin was still working to close their fund and had to put the investment decision on hold. Of course, one week after we had agreed to take on SEDF we did hear back from Alterfin that they had approved their equity investment. I even tried to convince Acumen and Grameen to take on Alterfin too, as another shareholder, since it would help us with the Central Bank requirements which favored numerous shareholders.

The Belgian head of Alterfin gave me a hard time for seemingly not being transparent with our equity raise process and limiting the investors to a small group of Americans. While it may have looked like that on the outside, the reality was that we had no idea what we were doing, had no process, and were just responding to investors on a first-come-first-served basis.

These were all good lessons I would use for our next rounds.

We finally had all the money we needed and a strong group of equity investors who shared in the social mission of the business along with K-Rep. I thought this would be a good time to ask the board again for some shares of the company for Aleke and myself. The new investors suggested that we wait until the conversion happened, then we could talk about incorporating an employee share ownership plan. We had a lot to prove and did not even know if the company would make it. The way the convertible debt was structured with Acumen, Grameen and Soros was that the debt could be converted when the company hit profitability, which was loosely defined as revenues exceeding expenses for at least three consecutive months.

I was worried that my financial projections were wrong and we would need much more than $5 million to reach profitability, so the investors put in another clause that allowed them to convert their debt to equity if the company needed to raise more debt to reach profitability. My theory on the business was to raise the $5 million, scale the number of loans to clients without adding any more offices and focus on improving staff efficiency through training and improving our systems. The other was simply to increase our interest rates charged to our clients, which would allow us to reach profitability sooner with less money. I saw this as a last desperate option and selfishly wanted to prove to everyone that we could offer loans at market interest rates to rural farmers and still make a profit, something the banks and microfinance institutions in Kenya have never been able to do. The last six months of performance at Juhudi was starting to prove my theory. We had substantially grown the loan portfolio to our clients in 2011 with Acumen, Grameen and Rockefeller's money so that our financials were really starting to improve. Our monthly cash-burn (the amount of money we were losing each month) was down to a few thousand dollars compared to an average of over $30,000 a month the year before. We had increased the client base from 1,000 clients to 7,000 clients without increasing our staff size, which also helped the profitability numbers. Additionally, the loan portfolio reports were very positive and client repayment rates had stayed above ninety-four percent for the past eleven months. Now with the new funds from Ford and then Soros we increased growth even more.

By February 2012 the company reached its first ever monthly profit, or at least the break-even. It was a huge milestone and I thought all of our lenders and investors would be ecstatic. Unfortunately, nobody seemed to care much.

I think everyone was exhausted from the months of negotiations and contract structuring. Our portfolio size was $4.5 million, which was just under my projected size needed to get to profitability.

March and April rolled by with even higher profits and in May we made $18,000 in a month.

The first thing I did with the increased funds was to hire a management team. We had been getting by with some very talented and hardworking but quite junior staff in IT, finance, and HR. Rachel was running all of our social performance work and doing most of the company marketing without any formal training in the field. She was doing a great job but was still a volunteer and only part-time, since she had a family with young kids to take care of at home.

We had a very difficult time hiring any Kenyan managers because most of them were much more expensive than our junior Kenyan staff. As soon as any professional had achieved any technical or managerial experience in Kenya, they would either leave the country to work in the US or Europe or get hired away by an international NGO working in Kenya and paying exorbitant Western salaries, which our business model could not support. The solution was to rely on the heavy flow of foreign volunteers who were eager to work in Kenya for the experience and then use junior Kenyan staff who could be trained into technical managers.

The process worked quite well while we were growing slowly, because it took time for the junior staff to mature and develop the skills needed for the company. Now that we were growing faster we needed more experienced talent. We still did not have an Operations Manager and to add pressure to our management team, our Chief Accountant had just resigned.

The Chief Accountant was a young and ambitious Kenyan that I had encouraged to apply to be an Acumen East Africa Fellow. This was a wonderful leadership development program, sponsored by the Acumen Fund along with several other corporate donors, to help build leaders in social enterprises across East Africa. For nine months, each week the participants in the program would spend time listening to motivational speakers such as Jacqueline Novogratz and work on their own personal leadership styles. It was a very competitive program and, like most of Acumen's work, received a significant amount of PR.

The local newspaper had featured the names and profiles of all the Kenyan participants, which elevated them to celebrity status overnight. Several months into the program our Chief Accountant started getting calls from headhunters working for large multinational companies and NGOs. Unilever, which is a donor to Acumen, poached our Chief Accountant and offered him more than double the salary we were paying him. We could not even provide a counter offer without upsetting our entire salary structure.

Shortly after our Chief Accountant left, Njambi, our HR Manager, decided that she did not want to do HR as a profession any longer and returned to office administration. This was certainly fine, but we had just hired someone else to run the office administrative work and front desk operations. Njambi ended up finding a job with the Grameen Foundation, which was now opening up a full office. While it was hard to be losing another friend and strong employee to one of our investors, I supported the move since Njambi wanted to follow a career in office administration. I was now left needing to hire a Finance Manager, HR Manager, Operations Manager and probably an IT Manager. My sleep and social life were sacrificed once again.

Celebrities and new visitors

Acumen had a wide and powerful professional network, which unfortunately did not help Juhudi as much as I had hoped. However, a random connection did send a very unique and brilliant volunteer to work with us from the top global strategy consultancy, McKinsey and Company.

One of Acumen's fundraising staff worked out of a McKinsey office in Dubai and came across one of the junior consultants from Pakistan, who wanted to work in Kenya before going to business school. His name was Ghalib Hafiz and he had very strong recommendations from various managers in McKinsey. We took him in for a few months to see how he would do in Kenya.

Ghalib showed up on his first day wearing a dark suit and not saying much to anyone other than politely answering questions when asked. My team tried to inquire about his experience and interests by asking what types of businesses he worked with but his response was always, "I worked in every sector and did everything." I was not so sure how long this guy would last at Juhudi and in Kenya.

Rachel and I took Ghalib for drinks after work one day and he finally loosened up. Ghalib was one of those people who think on an entirely different level. I put his brilliance to work in developing our strategic plan for 2013, reworking our financial model and identifying some key operational areas for the company to improve certain elements, such as how client repayments are posted into the IT system. He quickly became loved by our Kenyan staff and assimilated to become part of the family.

Though Ghalib helped plug some of our management team weaknesses, I was still concerned that there were gaps in knowledge that would hinder our long-term growth. One additional problem was that since Juhudi was a service business, it depended heavily on high quality staff to interact with our clients. It was not easy to find this caliber of staff in Kenya.

I thought it would make sense to start with an HR professional who could then help us hire a Finance Manager and IT Manager. We used a website called Brighter Monday, along with circulating the job description of an HR Manager to our local networks. I was looking for a more strategic-thinking HR professional, who could make human capital management a core strategic function of the business.

After a few disappointing rounds of interviews, a motherly figure who was working at a major health insurance company in the HR department sat down for the interview. Her name was Nancy Butama and she had a very strong physical presence about her. She proceeded perfectly to demonstrate her deep understanding of how managing human capital can drive every aspect of a business. When finished, Ghalib, Rachel and I all looked at each other, amazed. We knew we had our person. However, there was a problem. Nancy was coming from a large corporation and her salary expectations were beyond what we had budgeted. Nancy loved the social mission of Juhudi but was not willing to compromise much on the salary since she was paying for her two children's school fees by herself. After the interview I met with Aleke thinking that maybe Aleke could convince her to take more of a pay cut. His response was: "Give her the salary she wants. We need to have her. She will be well worth the investment." Nancy Butama joined us as our HR Manager a few weeks later.

Like most African countries, Kenya lags behind the rest of the world in terms of gender equity. I quickly realized that a majority of our high-performing employees in the branch offices were women, yet very few of our managers were women. When Juhudi was still part of KDA, nearly sixty percent of the employees were men and less than ten percent of the managers were women. Two years after Juhudi spun off from KDA, we had increased the total number of women employees to over sixty percent. With Nancy now as a new executive, forty percent of our management were now women. My next challenge was to get our all-male board to be a little more diversified.

Around that same time, we were fortunate to have a few international celebrities join the team. Matt Flannery, who was running Kiva.org, sent me a contact through one of his friends in San Francisco. This guy was a brilliant Stanford graduate working as a software developer at Google who wanted to come to Kenya for a sabbatical. What made it even better was that he was prepared to volunteer. This meant that not only would he solve some of our management issues, but it wouldn't cost us any of our stretched budget. His name was Kevin Gibbs and he had created amazing things for the world, like Google Suggest which helps complete the sentence you are typing into a Google Search, as well as the Google App Engine, which we were using at the time for our Juhudi website and some of our web-based tools, such as Echo Mobile.

Kevin was coming out with his wife Page, who was interested in working for a healthcare related organization. I set her up with Jacaranda Health, which was in our building. Once Kevin had settled into life in Kenya, he set about building a mobile-based app that ran on the Android operating system, which helped our field staff connect directly to the head office accounting system on their mobile phones. It was some beautiful software, which he called Simple MFI.

Kevin worked closely with Ghalib, and between them they developed a new way to think about the role mobiles could play in the business. Ghalib helped develop the strategy to roll out the new system to our offices and it paved the way for Juhudi better to utilize the quickly expanding mobile infrastructure in the country. When I first arrived in Kenya it was difficult to send a large attachment to GBF or have a cheap phone call with my parents without a three- to five-second delay. Since Kenya had received fiber optic cable from Dubai, the internet and mobile phone services and coverage had improved dramatically. I could call my parents in the US with perfect clarity from my Kenyan mobile phone and the call would not cost much more than a local call in Kenya. In fact, the mobile phone reception is significantly better in Kenya than my home state of Colorado, where large sections of land have no access at all.

Like many developing countries, Kenya's mobile telephone infrastructure was much more developed than its landlines. The country found it easier and cheaper to build a few towers than to string wires across the country. Nearly eighty percent of the population have a mobile phone, and I would argue that ninety-eight percent have access to one through a neighbor or family member.[v] A vast majority of the population pre-pays for their airtime with small scratch cards versus the traditional post-paid system of the US. The small airtime kiosks were so ubiquitous it would be hard to throw a rock and not hit an agent. Even in the small rural towns it was quite easy to purchase scratch cards.

I also arrived in Kenya just as M-Pesa was taking hold of the country. This revolutionary way of sending money to someone via a mobile phone became a runaway success in Kenya and has yet to be replicated in many other countries in Africa or the world. Academics have published literally hundreds of research papers evaluating the M-Pesa phenomenon. So many moving parts need to be right for something like M-Pesa to flourish; the quality of the service carriers, the regulatory environment, the saturation of mobile phones in the population and the lack of other payment platforms, like credit card services. What I certainly feel is overlooked in the research about M-Pesa is the role that Safaricom played in the phenomenal success, not some high-tech secret. The main value is the 85,000 agents around the

---

[v]   Communications Authority of Kenya, "Quarterly Sector Statistics Report First Quarter of the Financial Year 2014/2015," January 2015: 6.

country who serve the 19 million registered users.[vi] Like little bank branches all over the country, these agents accept cash and transfer the cash into digital cash on your phone to be sent to anyone else with an M-Pesa account.

If someone wants to convert the digital cash into real cash they just visit an agent. In addition to the agents, Safaricom invested heavily in raising awareness of the service and training millions of users through marketing. The company drove semi-trucks throughout the country registering people and teaching them how to use the service. The original plan for M-Pesa at Safaricom was not to make money but to get more people to join their mobile network. Now M-Pesa generates around $250 million in profits each year for Safaricom.[vii] It worked out well for Safaricom and for Kenya.

****

Our next big visitor to Juhudi was also connected to us through Kiva. Kiva had attracted a world-renowned author, travel writer and Jeopardy star named Bob Harris. He was writing a book about Kiva's experience of lending money to people all over the world. Bob spent a year visiting hundreds of Kiva borrowers in multiple countries and writing about their lives and how Kiva's money had made a difference.

Bob turned up at our office dressed in full khaki safari gear with pockets filled with cameras, maps and other necessities for the wild. He looked ready to take on the Serengeti or travel through the Sahara for a few weeks. I spent a few hours talking to Bob, who turned out to be one of the nicest and most supportive people ever to visit Juhudi. I was fascinated by his life and latest job as a hotel reviewer for *Fortune* magazine. He was being paid

---

[vi] Claudia McKay and Rafe Mazer, "10 Myths About M-PESA: 2014 Update," CGAP, October 1, 2014.

[vii] Lesley Stahl, "The Future of Money," 60 Minutes, November 22, 2015.

to travel around the world, to stay at the most expensive hotels and write reviews about them for *Fortune's* readers, aspiring to be rich and famous. I found myself also interested in some of his stories about a few of the other microfinance organizations he had visited.

The Kiva loans were overwhelmingly positive and helpful to some disenfranchised entrepreneurs but he also came across, with other institutions, a few cases of fraud or where the loans were not used as they were intended. Fortunately, Bob's visit to our clients in rural Kenya was an enjoyable experience for him and for all our staff, and he outlines his adventure in the tea country of Kenya with Juhudi in his bestselling book, *The International Bank of Bob*.

Barclays

Between Acumen's PR, Bob's book and a few awards, Juhudi had received some attention from other organizations and some multinational companies. A fantastic group called Leaders' Quest, which works with global executives of massive multinational companies and tries to provide international leadership experiences or quests to developing countries, contacted us about hosting a group of executives from Barclays, the global bank. I was thrilled. Who knew what great kind of partnership could come from this? Maybe Barclays would want to deliver the Juhudi loans through its bank branches or perhaps give us a low-interest loan. I worked hard with the Leaders' Quest team to develop the two-day itinerary, which included a visit to one of our nearby offices and client groups in Murang'a. A group of security specialists even came to do a walk-through and evaluate any potential risks.

Barclays has had an interesting history in Kenya and Africa. The bank was ever present in most of the former British colonies and provided fantastic banking services to high net worth individuals and larger corporations operating in Kenya. About ten years earlier, Barclays had made a big push to expand its branch networks in Africa to help reach the millions who were 'unbanked'. Barclays reached a point where they were opening a new Kenyan branch almost daily and had built a significant network in less than a year. Then a number of things happened, including some tough economic times, and Barclays ended up closing nearly all of its branches in Kenya. This was right around the time that Equity Bank was making its début. It swooped in and picked up all the branch locations and banking staff that had been let go by Barclays. A few years later Equity became the fastest growing and most successful bank in Africa.

I was able to meet the Barclays executive for Africa who managed this exit from Kenya. I spent all day with the Barclays team answering questions and telling them about the Juhudi business model, which they loved. I received some interesting questions about Kenya such as, "Why would a poor rural farmer want to use a mobile phone?"

We did our best to answer that by talking about the business needs of a farmer to check market prices or coordinate a milk delivery with a buyer. But we also informed the group that the rural poor of Kenya still had the same need as a rich banker in the UK, to stay in touch with family and friends on a mobile phone. In fact, this need is so important that some households will forego a meal in order to purchase more airtime on their mobile phones or pay for mobile phone charging if they do not have electricity.

We made plans to follow up on more partnership ideas and, potentially, some funding options. I emailed a few thank you letters but never heard back from any of them. I was frustrated once more at having wasted management time over the visit. We have had the same problem with every large corporation we have tried to work with. They would demand that we spend time explaining our business and hosting their visits, but when it came to finding a way for us to work in tandem there was no reciprocation.

They knew that many entrepreneurs saw the large companies as sources of markets or funding, which only made the executives cringe at the idea of allocating some of their budget to a start-up.

Acumen also tried to get us to work with General Electric, Unilever and SAP but each time we would spend a lot of time brainstorming ways to work together and each time I would never hear back from the executives. The larger companies viewed the social enterprises as a way of improving their PR, which turned off the entrepreneurs who needed strategic partners and not charity.

While at Accenture, I had learned how larger multinationals operate, so I was aware of the politics and bureaucracy that must be managed for external partnerships to succeed. It was therefore not that much of a surprise when each of these potential partnerships failed. No doubt other social enterprises had more luck (like M-Kopa and Safaricom) in this area of corporate partnerships, but I could never get them to work. They certainly seemed like game changers; someone who could leverage a distribution network like that of Unilever's or tap into the technical prowess of SAP to help with a social business. Perhaps our failure to engage with the large multinational corporate partners was due to my own aversion to the corporations, brought on by my dismal experience with Accenture. However I felt we did give Barclays, General Electric and SAP a substantial try.

Both the large company and the small social enterprise need to be able to see the direct benefit of a partnership that can be easily communicated to all levels of the organizations. It takes a lot of time and energy on behalf of the companies and entrepreneurs to make the partnerships work and keep them going. I later attempted to answer this dilemma of partnership engagement through the creation of an interim solution, with Juhudi Labs, which will be discussed in later chapters.

One of Acumen's newest investment companies was involved in urban sanitation, and it was making waves in the corporate sector. They were doing a much better job than we were of mopping up all the high-profile partnerships and PR opportunities.

Three MIT MBA students had come to Kenya several summers earlier to work on a new business idea that had won them recognition in a business plan competition. The business proposed to collect human excrement from the slums in Nairobi and turn the waste into energy through a biodigester. This way the company could provide a solution to the sanitation problem in the slums with nice public toilets and at the same time sell renewable energy to the grid in the city.

It was a difficult and complex business model to execute but the founders were exceptionally competent. David Auerbach, Ani Vallabhaneni and Lindsay Stradley, all had excellent credentials: degrees from Princeton and work experience with some of the top investors in the US. For them, anything was possible. The company was named Sanergy, combining the words Sanitation and Energy. The trio of founders quickly became a great addition to the growing Nairobi social enterprise community, all centered in my neighborhood of Kilimani, where a few other expats also lived.

Chapter 12 | Awards

Juhudi continued to hit its growth and repayment rate targets each month. Word was out in the social enterprise community that Juhudi had broken the profit barrier and was making the final transition from a non-profit to a for-profit social enterprise. Apparently this does not happen very often. More funders continued to call and email but by this time we were flush with cash and did not need them anymore. It was a very nice position to be in after the previous two years of panhandling. I estimated that we had all our funding lined up for the next two to three years of growth, with the undisbursed funds from Acumen, Grameen, Soros, Ford and Rockefeller. Now that we were profitable, all we needed to do was convert the convertible debt from Acumen, Grameen and Soros to equity by September, which would release another $2 million from Ford and Rockefeller. Seemed easy enough.

But of course not. I started thinking of what could go wrong and how quickly we could end up in another economic death spiral if that conversion delayed. To be safe, I started replying to the new potential investors and keeping the relationships warm.

One of the groups who approached us was the Charles Schwab Foundation, who encouraged us to apply for their annual award recognizing successful social enterprises. I thought it might be a little premature to start celebrating but it was worth a shot. The Foundation award was to be judged on a number of criteria, outlined in their lengthy application process. The award did not provide any money to Juhudi but it was a good way of helping our reputation. The World Economic Forum hosted the winners each year, which might even grab the attention of new investors. With all the money we were raising and the unique business model of financing productive assets for rural Kenya, maybe we had a shot. Additionally, we had Rachel Brooks who was a talented writer and already knew Juhudi well.

When we were completing the application we struggled to outline the actual entrepreneur behind Juhudi. The company was started by an institution (K-Rep) and the incubator (KDA) was managed by Aleke Dondo. Although Aleke was spending less than ten percent of his time on Juhudi, he had certainly contributed the lion's share to its initial development. So Rachel and I wrote about Aleke and all he had done to start Juhudi. We highlighted the role he has played in Kenya in terms of supporting the microfinance industry in general and promoting innovation in the financial services sector to help the poor. It seemed to work because we made it to the second round, which required more documents but also an interview with Aleke. Luckily, Aleke was more than willing to get involved and he won the hearts of the selection committee.

In March of 2011, he was awarded the Schwab Social Entrepreneur of the year Award, which was presented at the World Economic Forum in Cape Town. We could not believe it. Juhudi was such a small company but our numbers did look great and we were receiving so much traction in the impact investor space. Aleke attended the awards ceremony and was granted much-needed recognition for Juhudi and his work at KDA over the years.

While the endorsement was nice, I was also expecting this award to bring in some new partners or some funding. No such luck.

Mulago

The founder of One Acre Fund, Andrew Youn, was connected through a mutual friend, since both of our organizations focus on helping rural smallholder farmers.

One Acre Fund had received millions from the Gates Foundation, MasterCard Foundation and USAID, as well as being named one of the Top Ten Most Innovative Companies in Africa by *Fast Company*. Andrew Youn was a few years older than me, and would go on that year to be named on *Forbes Magazine's* Impact 30 list, which recognizes leaders for their social impact on society.

Andrew is from the Midwest of the US and he fully embodies its kind, considerate and laid- back reputation. When we first met for lunch, Andrew was wearing Teva sandals with socks, trademark apparel for him. Andrew and I hit it off and shared a few ideas together. He was interested in how Juhudi organized its loan groups and I provided him with the sample group constitution, that we had borrowed from K-Rep. I believe One Acre Fund is still using this document today. Although Andrew was an extremely busy person, with over 50,000 clients and 400 employees to manage, he went out of his way to introduce me to investors and donors interested in supporting rural smallholder agriculture. His generosity was something I deeply admired and, to pay it forward, I have since then always offered to help other social entrepreneurs by linking them to investors or helping them work out a problem we may have solved in the past with Juhudi.

One evening, Andrew told me that I needed to meet a person named Kevin Starr, from the Mulago Foundation. I was happy to be flexible, as Kevin was on a very tight schedule and the meeting needed to be the next day. It happened to be a Saturday. The only time that we could meet was on the taxi ride to the airport. The plan was that I would ride along in the taxi from downtown Nairobi to the airport and would have twenty minutes to pitch Juhudi. This was going to be awkward. Fortunately, Kevin's breakfast meeting was canceled and he had an opening.

Kevin was a tall, middle-aged, blond American with a Californian accent. I may have confused him for a surfing bum who had spent the last thirty years on the beach. Kevin was a medical doctor who 'accidentally' got into the world of philanthropy and impact investing through a climbing friend of his who tragically died on a hiking trip, leaving Kevin in charge of his family's endowment, now called the Mulago Foundation.

Our breakfast was fun. We spent most of the time talking about Colorado and life in Kenya. He was already familiar with the Juhudi business model and really only wanted to get to know me better. Kevin told me about their Fellows program, which brought social entrepreneurs and nonprofit founders together for a week in California to hear from business leaders and work on common issues as a group. Mulago could then provide small to medium-sized grants to help the participants build their organizations or try out some of the ideas they had together.

Three months later I received an email from Kevin's administrative assistants asking me why I'd not yet booked my flight to San Francisco. She explained that the program was starting the following month. There'd been no application or follow up call, yet I was accepted into this elite group of fellows. I realized later that this is how Mulago works. They rely on their professional networks and previous fellows to recommend their new fellows. Andrew Youn was a past fellow and had apparently spoken highly of me and of my work.

The Mulago Foundation and my two annual trips to a wonderful place called Bolinas, California, was a highlight of my time at Juhudi. Kevin Starr and his deputy, Laura Hattendorf, both had tremendous experience and insight into what types of models work well and the kinds of support that are needed at each stage of development. It was also very nice to spend a week without email and think about larger strategic issues with the business, instead of focusing on the minutiae of daily crisis.

I would highly recommend that any social entrepreneur make sure to plan some of this time away, once in a while. There was another benefit to being surrounded by other like-minded entrepreneurs, and that was to share ideas and commiserate together. I cherished the network I was able to build through Mulago with people like Andrew Youn and David Auerbach, the co-founder of the urban sanitation company I discussed earlier.

Mulago also supported Juhudi with several small but transformative grants, which helped us build our capacity and experiment with a new type of approach to innovation and product design. Mulago is one of the few great donors in the world that does not require a lot of burdensome reporting or highly structured proposals and budgets. They invest their grants more like an equity investor simply by asking the entrepreneur to focus on growing their business and hitting their milestones with their grants. It is unfortunate that more donors do not offer flexibility like this for early-stage businesses.

The Parents Finally Visit

After more than three years, I finally convinced my patient and supportive parents to visit me. They had grown up in New Jersey, were high-school sweethearts and together moved out to Colorado in their twenties for the adventure of the mountains. My dad served in the National Guard before practicing law with a small practice in my hometown of Evergreen. My mom was a primary school teacher in Denver. Both were great athletes and fantastically supportive of my twin brother and me. My parents had traveled to Europe a few times before, but like a majority of American families they did not spend much of their lives traveling outside the US. My twin brother traveled even less and I was not sure if he even had a valid passport.

According to some studies, roughly ninety-eight percent of the news about Africa that is shown in the US is negative or about poverty.[viii] So

---

[viii]   Karen Rothmyer, "Hiding the Real Africa: Why NGOs prefer bad news," Columbia Journalism Review, March/April 2011.

my family had spent their whole lives hearing about child soldiers, pirates, Al-Shabaab, Boko Haram, Ebola and people living in tents or mud huts and being eaten by lions.

My family and friends back home were regularly impressed with my pictures of tall office buildings in downtown Nairobi and stories of using my mobile phone to send money. Having visited nearly all of Kenya's national parks, I felt I had a good understanding of where to go and what to do with visitors from abroad.

My parents used their airline miles to book the thirty-hour journey with multiple stopovers. I had become friends with the family who owned the Tribe Hotel and Village Market, who were kind enough to offer a great 'family and friends' discount. So my parents spent their first night in a five-star hotel situated inside one of the most western malls in Kenya. I hoped this would limit their culture shock. Several months earlier, my brother's fiancé, Ginny, and her girlfriend came to visit me but could not find Benson's driver in the middle of the night at the Nairobi airport. Benson's driver had somehow translated 'Ginny Domm' and her friend 'Toni' on his signboard to 'Jimmy Bomb and Tiny Tony.' When Ginny and Toni arrived they saw the sign but assumed the driver belonged to another passenger in a red jump-suit and his shorter side-kick who was loaded down with gold necklaces. To make things worse, I also had a typo in my phone number in my last email so Ginny could not reach me. Fortunately, before they jumped in a car with some random man trying to take them to a hotel in a rough neighborhood, Ginny was able to find an internet café and see an email from me with the description of Benson's driver. My brother would have never forgiven me if I had caused his future wife to be kidnapped or worse.

I introduced my parents to all of my friends and some coworkers at a wine and cheese event at one of the upscale Nairobi restaurants in the Junction Mall. Their opinion of the country changed dramatically. Instead of taking them to the ever-popular Maasai Mara or Tsavo national parks I opted to take them out to one of the smaller reserves in the Laikipia area. Little did I know the area would receive the most rain it had seen in over fifty years. It rained every day. Bridges were washed out, lodges flooded and all the animals sought shelter in the deeper brush, making the game drives more difficult. My parents were good sports and bundled up in rain jackets and blankets for the safari rides and enjoyed the landscape, regardless.

The first evening, we were visited by a young leopard that was climbing on a large boulder outside the lodge. Then a rare striped hyena jumped up on the same rock to challenge the leopard. Both animals stood roaring at each other on the top of the rock, outlined against the silvery setting sun. It looked like something right out of *National Geographic*. I must have shouted something in my excitement because both animals suddenly looked at me and then ran off in separate directions. My parents and the other guests all shook their heads at me in disappointment.

The next morning we had a beautiful day for a game drive and we set out in search of some lions. Our driver deftly maneuvered the old Land Rover, avoiding mud and sinkholes. We drove down by the river that had overflowed its banks and was still carrying large trees along its roaring currents. Just as the guide was explaining that this area was where they had spotted lions earlier, the vehicle lurched forward and sank deeply into sandy mud. We all were thrown in the direction of the rushing river and had to lean toward the bank to keep from toppling in. So there I was again, stuck in the mud in lion territory, this time with my 65-year-old parents. We had no mobile phone reception and were outside any signal for radio contact with lodges in the area.

I took out my rungu and grabbed a curved panga from the back seat to stand watch for animals while the driver tried to get us free. He spun the wheels in the mud but only drove the vehicle deeper, up past the axles.

We sat there on the riverbank for a few hours and I began thinking that we would be spending the night in that place. We could defend one side from the lions or anything else that came out of the dense brush, but what would happen if a hungry crocodile or territorial hippopotamus approached from the river? To make things worse, it started to rain again.

By random luck, a truck full of rangers spotted us and came to investigate. After trying unsuccessfully to free us – and almost getting their own truck stuck in the process – the rangers offered us a ride back to our lodge so we could get dry and call for more help. We all made it back to Nairobi safely.

After that stressful safari, I thought my parents might like a few days on the Kenya coast before their long trip back to Colorado. My dad was an avid golfer and I found a fantastic course on the coast near the town of Vipingo. We stayed at a house on the beach, which was a short drive to the golf course. I had no idea how rural and devoid of taxis the town of Vipingo was. Even Benson did not know anyone in Vipingo. We would need to call a taxi from Kilifi or Mtwapa, which were both about thirty minutes away and would cost close to $30 for a fifteen-minute drive. Finally, I connected with a driver who said he could drive us to Vipingo in the morning for $10, which seemed to be our best option. The three of us waited on the road and heard a large vehicle rumbling down the road. A twenty-five passenger purple bus full of artwork and a slogan that read "haraka haraka haina baraka", which is "hurry, hurry no blessing" or the equivalent of haste makes waste. The driver and his assistant opened the door and asked, "Robinson?"

"Hi" I replied, and we piled into the bus.

The Vipingo Ridge is an exclusive golf course with a few security checkpoints along the way. It took a lot of convincing in my best Kiswahili to get our giant purple bus inside the gates. We pulled up to the clubhouse, got out and strolled inside with all the golfers and guests staring incredulously at our transport.

We had a wonderful day playing golf but on the 12th hole one of our local caddies suddenly shouted at my mom: "Down mama, down!"

I looked all around wildly expecting to see some pirates or Al-Shabaab with guns pointed at us. My parents and the caddie were all face down on the ground with their hands over their heads.

"Bees," my dad shouted, and I dropped down just as a massive swarm of African killer bees swarmed over our heads. I looked over at a lake nearby and wondered if the bees started attacking if I could jump into the water. There were probably crocodiles or poisonous snakes in there. My dad was allergic to bees and a sting could be deadly. How were we able to still find so much danger on the coast at a golf resort?

But the danger passed and we ended up having a great day and our purple bus was there to drive us back to our house. The owner of the beach house eventually let us borrow her 1987 white Mercedes, along with its expired insurance sticker, which raised our adrenalin when we drove slowly through any police checkpoints. At least we did not turn as many heads the next day at the golf course.

The adventure and drama with my parents' visit continued up until the last day. It turned out that when booking our flight back to Nairobi to connect with my parents' international flight I had confused the time of 05:30 hours with 5:30pm. When I realized my mistake on the morning of our flight it was too late to book a later flight that day. We still had most of the day so I called Benson to see if he could help find someone to drive us the seven hours back to Nairobi before the flight. Normally, the Mombasa taxi drivers would take advantage of a situation like this and charge triple the price. Benson managed to find someone on short notice to drive us all the way to Nairobi. Mombasa Road was still under construction in places and we had long stretches of rough dirt that were packed with massive semi-trucks flying around us in all different directions. My parents were good sports and called everything an adventure, but I suspect they were quite ready to be done with the adventures and get back home.

Echo Mobile

Rachel had finished her three-month tour of duty at Kiva and decided to stay on with Juhudi as a volunteer. We had well over 2,000 active Kiva loans and the mandatory journaling for Kiva was a difficult process, because it meant our field staff would need to travel out to each client's farm and ask a series of questions for Kiva. Their answers then had to be transcribed, simply to be posted on the Kiva site at the head office. So it was not exactly a top priority. To encourage us to prioritize it, Kiva decided to send us another Kiva Fellow for three months to help us capture more 'journals' from our clients about how they had spent the Kiva loan. The new Kiva Fellow was named Jeremy Gordon and he was an engineer from Stanford. Given how great Rachel was, I remained a little skeptical that Jeremy would fit in as well and be as effective. Jeremy turned out to be a brilliant software developer and went on to be one of my close friends.

Jeremy quickly realized that the paper-based journaling system was not efficient for Juhudi since our rural client bases were too difficult to survey regularly in person. However, building on the development of our mobile research, we knew that about ninety percent of all our clients had mobile phones. Jeremy started to look around for software that would allow us to send an automated survey by text message from a computer in the head office. Frustrated by what was available on the market, Jeremy decided to build his own mobile survey software.

The software would send out a text message in Kiswahili saying: "Hello Juhudi Kilimo client. Would you like to take a survey for Kiva on your phone? Please reply Yes or No to this message." If someone responded yes, the software would send the first question asking about how they used their loan. The responses that came back would be catalogued and easy to copy and paste into the web form for the Kiva profiles. It worked very well, most of the time. The one problem was that we had to run the system through a mobile phone that was connected to a laptop. This meant that when the power went down, which it did often, the whole thing stopped working. Over time, we learned a lot about how to design the surveys to improve the response rate (usually around thirty to forty percent) and found a way to reverse the SMS tariffs so that Juhudi paid for all of the messages. The survey tool was a low-cost and effective way to capture direct client data from a rural population.

Rachel started to get interested in the survey tool, seeing a need for the service with a number of organizations in Nairobi. The only challenge was that the mobile phone/laptop infrastructure allowed for a maximum of five surveys to be sent out at once before the modem became too backlogged. We needed to invest in a short code and SMS gateway, this was a service provided by the mobile networks that would allow us to have a much higher volume of text messages. It also looked more professional to get a message from an official short code that was labeled 'Juhudi Kilimo' than some random mobile phone number.

Rachel, Jeremy and I applied for a challenge fund grant from our old friends at GBF and were awarded enough money to invest in the new technology and infrastructure to scale up the operations. Jeremy and Rachel then went around Nairobi selling the text message survey service to social enterprises, businesses and international NGOs. It was very popular. The natural next step was for Rachel and Jeremy officially to launch a new company, called Echo Mobile. The company serves fifty clients from eight different countries providing them text message survey services as well as analytics, voice recognition surveys, push marketing and a variety of other great options for learning more about consumers.

In his free time, Jeremy built our first website, designed our first logo and enhanced a number of our IT capabilities. Jeremy came to Kenya for a three-month Kiva fellowship and ended up staying for the next four years, a common expat story in Nairobi's social enterprise community.

New Guys and Fraud

With our Head of Finance department gone from the Acumen Fellowship program, we were scrambling to find a new replacement. The board helped to hire the finance manager of a local investment fund, who seemed to have a great deal of experience. The interview panel was not quite sure about his cultural fit, especially as he had never worked in microfinance or a socially oriented organization. However, we were pressed to hire someone quickly and went ahead anyway. This turned out to be one of the many mistakes I made in hiring our executive team.

The candidate turned out to be quite competent and in the first week he overhauled the finance department and changed everyone's job, to help boost productivity. But this created anxiety among the finance team. The changes were actually good and in line with international best practices, but the difficulties arose more from the way the new manager addressed the change process. The staff were threatening to quit, checks and payments were not being processed and even the new manager was getting frustrated.

I explained to him that he should first get to know the staff and learn how microfinance was a little different than mainstream financial services, before making more dramatic changes. During this time, I started to get a clearer picture of the problem. I felt that the new manager looked down upon our finance staff. He'd come from a more structured environment and he felt that we had weaker processes and people. Some of that was certainly true, but to treat the junior staff with such arrogance prevented anyone from trusting or respecting the new manager.

Less than two months in, we started to look for a new person. Fortunately, the Grameen Foundation helped out and sent me a résumé for a Kenyan who had interviewed for a position with Grameen but did not fit their criteria. His résumé and background seemed ideal for Juhudi. He had over eighteen years of microfinance experience. He'd worked with big institutions such as KWFT and was currently the acting CEO at a medium-sized institution in Burundi. His name was Shadrack and, as soon as I spoke to him, I knew he was a perfect fit for Juhudi. I set up an interview with Nancy and one of our board members and they both agreed. We let go of the current finance manager (who quickly landed another job) and two months later we had Shadrack as our new finance manager at Juhudi.

Fraud in Kenya is estimated to affect fifty-two percent of the 124 chief executive officers from large companies surveyed in 2014 by PricewaterhouseCoopers. [ix] From my experience on the business association board of AMFI and at Juhudi, I estimate that gross fraud affects ten percent of any workforce in Kenya. Even these numbers are likely too low since a majority of fraud goes undetected or unreported. Sadly, it is a reality of doing business in Kenya. My management team and I prided ourselves on complete transparency when dealing with investors and partners. During the due diligence visits, we shared everything that was asked for, both good and bad. If something bad happened, such as an employee stealing money, I

[ix] Humphrey Liloba, "Survey shows Kenya lax on fraud," East African Business Week, March 3, 2014.

would report this right away to our board and investors. Getting all of our dirty laundry out in the open also helped us to improve as a company. None of the fraud cases were particularly large and usually involved a loan officer collecting cash from the clients (which was forbidden) and not reporting the repayments. We had never lost more than a few thousand dollars in any case and the loan officers were always terminated on the spot.

Shortly after Shadrack joined we were hit with the largest fraud case the company had experienced.

We had a loan officer that had started with the company as an administrative assistant. Her name was Christine Bosibori but everyone called her 'Pinky', because she loved the color pink and everything from her phone to her shoes were pink. Christine's manager had recently been fired for a fraud case, which had been picked up by our new internal audit department. The sacking had thrown the department into chaos but Christine had showed great leadership and led the office through the transition. As a result, she was quickly promoted to a branch manager and sent to start our new office in Kilgoris in the Transmara area of Kenya, which is home to many of the country's Maasai tribe.

Juhudi had created some great new groups in the area and we were excited to expand into this new territory. Shortly after we transferred Christine to Kilgoris, our junior loan officers started reporting some problems with her old groups. The books had a high number of discrepancies and some of the groups appeared not to even exist. Our internal audit reviewed the office and discovered an elaborate scam involving Christine, several group officials and a local Savings and Credit Co-operative, known as a SACCO.

The group officials were colluding with Christine to collect all the correct documentation required for loans from unsuspecting farmers in the area. Christine would complete the loan applications and, as soon as a check was issued to a client, the group chairman would cash the checks on behalf of the clients. This of course is illegal in Kenya but the chairman had a relationship with the directors of a local SACCO, who would illegally cash the checks for a fee/bribe. Christine and the chairman would then take the money and slowly pay small amounts of the loans each month, so they would not show up as delinquent in the Juhudi accounting system. It worked like a Ponsi scheme. As long as the two could keep processing loans they could keep taking money. The total amount taken from this scandal was originally estimated at $200,000.

It was heartbreaking to see a young 25-year-old like Christine with so much leadership potential engaging in such unethical behavior. Shadrack found a solution to the SACCO loophole. It included stamping our checks as 'Non Negotiable', which meant our clients needed to cash them or deposit them with regulated banks. This cut down significantly on the poorly regulated SACCOs, but we still had the occasional teller fraud with the main banks.

In the wake of the fraud we were able to collect a significant amount of money from the chairman, but Christine fled the country. It is extremely difficult to prosecute someone in Kenya for fraud. The costs involved with hiring lawyers and the risks of working with the local law enforcement, who will likely also steal money from the employee or clients, were too much for us to justify. The only option we had was to put a picture of Christine in the local newspapers saying that she was no longer an employee of Juhudi Kilimo and not authorized to transact any business on behalf of Juhudi.

I later discovered that Christine had eventually returned to Kenya and found a job with another microfinance organization in Mombasa. I suspected that they did not bother with background or reference checks. Our company was still forced to write off over $100,000 as a loss and our reputation in the region suffered.

Fraud was a huge problem for us and, over the years, I guess that we had to terminate the contracts of about ten percent of the workforce due to losses. This was actually better than some institutions in Kenya. I was once told that Equity Bank fires about one teller a day, due to fraud.

I always felt that the best protection against fraud is good systems with checks and balances along with a strong anti-fraud company culture. This is easier said than done in a country that has enormous social pressure to provide economic support even to distant relatives. When our staff is faced with providing health care payments for a dying uncle or school fees for young children who lost a father to HIV, it is tempting to steal money from a rich company. Aleke once told me that about ten percent of people will steal from you no matter what and another ten percent will never steal from you. The remaining eighty percent will only steal if there is a low likelihood of being caught. Our goal was to remove as much of the temptation as possible and try our best to screen out the bad ten percent of characters before hiring them. In the years to come I would continue to be shocked by the people I had hired, trained, trusted and become friends with, who would later defraud the company.

Chapter 13 | A Conversion to Disaster

By June 2012 the company had made a steady stream of monthly profits and it was finally time to convert the debt from Acumen, Grameen and Soros to equity. I certainly felt like an exhausted marathoner who just turned the corner to see the finish line. We had accomplished what all of those investors said we could not. I had raised enough money. Our staff had translated that money into cows and farm equipment for our farmers. The farmers had repaid their loans at remarkable repayment rates. The new wealth generated by the farmers allowed us to pay our staff, operations, taxes and our lenders. After all that, we still had some money left over as a small profit each month for the equity investors. The miracle of the business system worked. Each entity involved benefitted in some way. We were also paying thirteen percent on the convertible debt, so it was in the company's interest to convert that to equity and then draw down on the next rounds of debt from Ford and Rockefeller, which was cheaper. Everyone was excited.

We had taken a long-shot company idea and turned it into a profitable business. I was regularly being asked to speak at conferences with the World Bank, top business schools and several local conferences sponsored by investors. Juhudi was attracting a lot of attention and even more interest from future funders. The operations were running smoothly and had experienced some of our fastest growth in the company's history.

This success did bring its own problems. If we kept growing at the same rate, we would need another $1 million or so by September. This did not bother me since the Ford Foundation had had another $1,250,000 waiting to send to us as soon as the conversion was completed. Also, Rockefeller had another $350,000 remaining to be disbursed under their agreement if we needed it. Acumen, Grameen and Soros had another $500,000 waiting too if Ford and Rockefeller delayed anything. All this money was just waiting to be sent to us as soon as the equity conversion was finalized. We had hit all our required targets and all Acumen, Grameen and Soros needed to do was sign the paperwork to convert their debt to equity. The heavy lifting on our part was all done and now it was up to the investors to carry out the rest of their investments agreed in the contracts. Nothing could stop us now.

It was at this time that events out of my control started to have an impact on the business. Amon, one of my closet allies in the business, told me that he was leaving the Acumen Fund in Nairobi. I would miss working with Amon, whom everyone called my 'wife' since we spent so much time together at work and socially. Shortly after Amon's departure Biju, who was a very strong diplomat on our board with a high degree of understanding of Juhudi, also left Acumen and as a consequence resigned from our board to seek other opportunities.

I had no idea how much of a blow this would be for Juhudi.

There were also some new changes at K-Rep. The company had recently transitioned its Chairman of the Board from Bethuel Kiplagat to Kabiru Kinyanjui (both of whom were also on the Juhudi board) and with it came some changes to the KDA strategy. K-Rep suddenly decided that they wanted to retain a majority ownership in all of the KDA spin-off companies. They felt they were losing control and losing money when they sold their interests in the spin-off companies to foreign investors. At the time, this new strategy did not worry me since K-Rep had already signed the reams of legal documents agreeing to the investment terms of Acumen, Grameen and Soros. However, unless K-Rep invested more in Juhudi they would be heavily diluted as a shareholder after the planned conversion, moving from owning one hundred percent of the company to just five percent.

Another change that seemed to be of limited concern at the time was in regard to Kimanthi Mutua, who was a K-Rep Group director and Juhudi director. Considered in Kenya as one of the founding fathers of microfinance, he had recently resigned as the CEO of the K-Rep Bank. He had done tremendous work for the sector in Kenya by spearheading the 2007 Microfinance Act, which allowed microfinance institutions to be regulated to take deposits (like a bank). He was a brilliant banker and provided Juhudi with a lot of good advice in its early days. Like most of the K-Rep directors, however, he was extremely busy and rarely came to board meetings, unlike Aleke who attended nearly every one.

One of the occasions he attended was when Juhudi was being recognized for its innovative work in agriculture financing. After seeing how many mainstream investors were now interested in Juhudi, Mutua suddenly realized that they were sitting on a potentially valuable company. It was now in K-Rep's interest to try and fight for more ownership. I thought the convertible debt agreements with Juhudi were a little predatory and in retrospect the US investors had seriously taken advantage of the Kenyan founders by fixing the share price really low in advance of the conversion. It looked more like a takeover than an investment.

Most of the convertible debt investments I witnessed in the social enterprise sector set their conversions to a future valuation method, or triggered on a multiple of the next round of investment. However, it can be argued that our US investors did take a risk up front by investing so much in an early stage company that was losing money, even if their loans were one hundred percent guaranteed by the K-Rep Group in case of default. K-Rep did understand all of this and agreed to the terms of the investment. They had another option at the time for equity from Agora that they could have accepted instead. It seemed to be a little greedy of K-Rep to now decide that they were interested in maintaining more ownership over Juhudi.

We had a cordial board meeting and decided that we could still work everything out to keep K-Rep happy under the current agreements. After the board meeting Steve from Grameen, Brandon Matthews, Aleke and I were sitting around the table talking when Brandon sat back and in his classic arrogant tone told us: "You know that there is no way Soros will convert with Bethuel Kiplagat on the board. He needs to go."

"What?" shouted a shocked Aleke.

"He is too much of a political risk for us."

"Don't you think it would have been a good idea to share this before we were about to convert or before we even added you as an investor?" I asked.

If we had known that this would be a precondition to the Soros conversion I do not think we would have signed with Soros. Soros mentioned that they were a little concerned with Kiplagat before their investment but never said anything about him being a barrier to investing or converting. Perhaps Soros thought K-Rep would transition off the board of Juhudi, since K-Rep was intending to only be an interim board until new investors joined the company. Brandon crossed his arms and said: "Look, I don't really care. This is coming from my higher ups and there is nothing I can do. Get him off the board."

At age 76, Kiplagat was a senior Kenyan figurehead who was a former ambassador and extremely well connected politically. It would be considered profoundly disrespectful to order him to leave. In our board meetings, Kiplagat was usually our chairman and a very good one. He always provided constructive insights about how to expand to new areas and explore new partnerships with various food processors to help our clients.

Kiplagat was also a former Permanent Secretary in the Ministry of Foreign Affairs who had been implicated in a savage military massacre by the Kenyan military in Somalia in 1984 called the Wagalla Massacre.[x] However, Kiplagat had been cleared by any wrongdoing by the high courts and it seemed only Kiplagat's political opponents raised it now to tarnish his reputation. For whatever reason, the Soros Open Society Foundation (which has tremendous influence over the investment arm of SEDF) decided they did not like Kiplagat. Aleke thought it might be a tribal or political ploy by the Kenyan staff of the Open Society Foundation. Whatever the rationale, I did not particularly care for the politics, it put Juhudi in a terrible position since this issue would probably delay the conversion. We were planning on needing the new money from Ford and Rockefeller in September and probably could survive until October but any delays after that would mean another halt to our lending to our farmers. How could this happen to us again? The financial death spiral was once again looming. The thought of telling my field staff and clients we could no longer give out loans again crushed me. I was not sure I would even be able to explain the delay this time. We had lots of money under contract, the new investors had agreed to convert their debt to equity but because of some board politics we could not execute anything and had to wait. I felt as if a meteorite had fallen out of the sky and struck me as I was reaching for the finish line in the marathon.

Aleke and I were left with no option but to face the task of asking Kiplagat to leave. Aleke did his best but Kiplagat was an elder and twenty years his senior. It was culturally unacceptable for Aleke even to approach Kiplagat. Somehow the news found its way to Kiplagat and the K-Rep Group anyway. They were furious. I was dragged into a heated meeting with all the directors of the K-Rep Group and targeted. "You Americans with all your money, just think you can come here to Kenya and push us out like this.

[x]   John Oywa, "Secrets of the 1984 Wagalla massacre emerge," *The Standard*, June 11, 2011.

You and your investors have no respect for what we have built and the effort that was put into KDA and Juhudi." I did my best to explain that these were social investors and they wanted to improve the lives of rural farmers. I had thought that this ideal was aligned to the mission of KDA and the K-Rep Group. It fell on deaf ears. Egos had already been bruised.

All sides of the conflict turned to their lawyers and began to examine the legal contracts. We held another heated meeting where a senior official from Soros, named Cedric de Beer, flew in from South Africa to help with the negotiations. Acumen had still not appointed a new board member, so it was Steve, Cedric, Aleke, Kimanthi and Kabiru (Kiplagat refused to meet with Soros, given their demands that he resign). We reviewed the documents, which clearly stated the new investors could convert at will after the company started to make profits. Cedric was a very seasoned finance professional with nearly fifteen years of experience running a housing finance company in Johannesburg. However, he carried the same blunt approach to diplomacy which Brandon had demonstrated earlier and that put the K-Rep Group members on edge.

It was difficult for me to pick a side. I felt badly for K-Rep, getting a bad deal and being pushed around but I also felt obligated to Acumen, Grameen and Soros, since I had brought them into the company in the first place. I also felt that the agreements had been signed by all parties and in good faith. Cedric emphasized this point at the meeting. Kimanthi Mutua's reply was something I will never forget...

"This is Kenya. Contracts can be broken."

"I can't believe you just said that," Cedric responded.

In truth, Kimanthi was right. If K-Rep wanted to tear up the contract they could. Kimanthi and Kiplagat had enough political influence that the lawyers and courts would no doubt defend their position over the American investors. Acumen, Grameen and Soros could spend a lot of time and money in legal fees fighting this in court and they may not win the case in the end. It is my view that it is this level of dirty politics and corruption that has kept Kenya from becoming a great country. It is almost expected that as soon as you have a position of power, that you abuse it. The general public is so used to seeing corruption cases in the newspapers that they have become indifferent and quickly forget about incidents in the past.

I had now lost all respect for Kimanthi and the K-Rep Group. I wanted nothing to do with them ever again. I still find it ironic that Kimanthi sat on the board of the African Microfinance Transparency initiative.

For the next three months we held more tense meetings where the K-Rep Group would identify details in the contract, such as how the date of the contract was three days before the last signature on the page. This was not a material problem and did not invalidate the contract and was more about the fact that all but one signatory signed the contract on a Friday and the last signed on a Monday. The reason for the difference was Kenya laws are a little archaic in that the ink signature is the only valid signature. This makes getting physical signatures from New York, Washington DC and Johannesburg quite difficult.

September came and went with no resolution and we were quickly running out of money. Our lenders were furious because these delays put their money at risk. I could not share much of these confidential board discussions with my staff so they did not know what was going on. I ran the numbers and realized that we could slow the loan disbursements to our clients and stretch our cash another three months, until perhaps late January of 2013. If we did not resolve our issues after that, we would have to stop lending altogether and completely run out of money by April or May. A slow and painful death loomed after such a wonderful year of achievement.

By early October 2012, I made the decision once again to slow lending to our clients and to freeze my salary again to conserve cash. This utterly demoralized our field staff, who had been busy taking in new clients and approving their loans. My staff kept wondering if we needed more investors to provide more money. We had $2 million waiting to be sent to us after the conversion. Several new lenders and investors literally started begging to provide us with money to keep our operations running at full speed. I had to politely refuse since I knew that no new funding could be passed through our board until they resolved the current K-Rep and impact investor stand-off. We just had to wait. .

The sad thing was that the K-Rep Group was so stuck in their position that they were willing to let Juhudi completely collapse over the shareholding issues. This seemed incredibly self-centered, considering the thousands of rural smallholder farmers who were benefitting from our services. Unfortunately the farmers were the last people considered in our board debates. I even contemplated mobilizing our farmers and staff to stage a protest outside of the K-Rep office to try and push things along. Fortunately, we still had an open dialogue with K-Rep (through their lawyer, as they would not speak to Acumen, Grameen or Soros directly).

K-Rep cannot be blamed for the entire conflict, since it was Soros' hostile demands that Kiplagat leave the board that had sparked the fight. Acumen had not officially replaced Biju or Amon so they were unable to play a role in the negotiations, and with Cedric in South Africa (Brandon relocated to New York), the investors relied heavily on Steve from Grameen. At 34, Steve had lived in Kenya for less than a year and was known for his hard-nosed negotiating tactics (something I had faced earlier when negotiating for the Grameen investment). The combination of being tough, young and American did not sit well with the K-Rep directors who were all respected elders in society. I found myself mediating across the cultures and age gaps but at one point, one of the K-Rep directors who had not participated in the earlier meetings confused me for one of the white American investors. He proceeded to berate me for not-respecting K-Rep's history and trying to steal the company away from them. K-Rep was still the majority shareholder and as CEO, I was a K-Rep employee and had been loyal to K-Rep for the past three years. I had spent a lot of time working with Aleke and Kiplagat to try and understand the position and politics of the K-Rep Group. Aleke was losing influence with K-Rep because of his closeness with me and the US investors.

We still had three months of cash and Juhudi's future was not looking good. If we could not resolve the shareholding issue there would be no reason to try and stretch our survival to March or April of next year. We would be done.

I convinced the board and lenders to allow us to consider a round of bridge financing to give us more time for the negotiations. Once again my friend, Ben at Deutsche Bank's development finance division, miraculously got approval for a $350,000 loan to tide the company over for a few months. It turned out to be enough to get us to January or February but not much after that. Loans to our farmers would stop.

I was not sleeping or eating much with the stress. We had nearly sixty employees with families depending on them for income. Not to mention the thousands of farmers we had convinced to work with us. I started talking to my parents again about coming home, since it seemed like my time in Kenya was over. I hated this idea. I had put so much of my life into this company, which could so easily have a bright future helping hundreds of thousands of farmers. We had proved that the model worked. Then to have this selfish ego-battle at the board level destroy all the good work of my staff and clients over the years was sad. I could understand going home if I had failed to raise the money for the company or the business model had not worked. Even something as unfortunate as a military coup or outbreak of Ebola in Kenya would be a better reason for me to return home to the US. But not for this. It was like flying a mission all the way to the moon and putting down the landing gear only to be told to abort because NASA was in a fight about their budget between the president and congress. I wanted to go home after either personally failing at the business or reaching a point where I could leave Juhudi in good hands to continue and thrive without me.

Then I got a call from Aleke who said to call Kiplagat.

Kiplagat seemed to be getting over the Soros demands and was more interested in ensuring that Juhudi survived than in protecting his and K-Rep Group's ego. He had an idea he was going to run by the K-Rep Group: to sell all their shares in Juhudi for a premium. This way, K-Rep could save face and the new investors could convert their equity and own one hundred percent. It was the only solution we had, so I called up each of our investors to get their take on the proposal. Fortunately, all of them liked the idea.

By late October, everyone had agreed in principle for K-Rep to exit Juhudi. But we were far from done. We still needed to get formal investment committee approvals from the US investors, to negotiate a sell price, draft the documentation and go through Acumen, Grameen and Soros's painfully slow lawyers to get all the documents finalized.

The K-Rep exit was some good news I could now share with Ford, Rockefeller, Kiva and Alterfin. I was also hoping to beg them to disburse some of their loans early to help with our cash situation. Rockefeller, of course, was still uncomfortable but Ford seemed to be open to the idea. They wanted some official documents or notices talking about the exit and the new investor's commitment to convert, which was easy enough to get.

Acumen and Grameen both received their investment committee approvals in early November to go forward with the K-Rep buy-out and conversion. For some reason, Soros was dragging their feet on the approvals. It was not because Soros had any concerns about the proposal.

In fact, Brandon had done a nice job in seeking acceptance from each individual committee member. It was due to the fact that the committee members could not find a day to meet before early November.

Juhudi was losing money every day while we waited for this decision to be made, but Soros could not seem to schedule a conference call to make the decision. For whatever reason they insisted on meeting in person. It ended up taking Soros a full three months to finally meet in January of 2013 and approve their side of the transaction. I sent all the documents to Ford and they generously squeaked out $500,000 to help us stay afloat.

Juhudi ended up paying the thirteen percent in extra interest on the Acumen, Grameen and Soros loan from the month of June through December of 2012 and this restricted growth from September to December. These actions forced the company to start taking losses in November and December, which meant the company made an overall after-tax loss of $15,800. Although this figure was a big improvement on the loss of nearly $200,000 the year before, it was still heartbreaking after all our hard work in getting to a profitability that was now being eroded by the shareholder drama.

Lamu Castle

In October of 2011 a French tourist was kidnapped by Somali pirates, probably linked to Al-Shabaab, from a resort island off the coast of Lamu on the Northern coast of Kenya. This sparked the Kenyan military response and invasion of southern Somalia, targeting Al-Shabaab militants. Looking at the long-drawn-out wars in Iraq and Afghanistan I was not sure at the time if this was such a good idea for Kenya. Especially given how difficult it is to defeat militant groups without any connection to country or government.

Kenya also had some very porous borders. Essentially anyone who paid an immigration official $50 could get into the country. Of course, the international media was all over the Lamu kidnapping and my parents seemed to know more about what was happening than I did, living in Kenya.

Tourism in Kenya took a plunge and especially the island of Lamu, which had an economy heavily dependent on foreign tourists. The US Embassy staff and the employees of many international organizations were forbidden from visiting Lamu and the coast. This meant many of the hotels were offering huge discounts on their rates just to stay alive.

I had been to the beautiful beaches of Lamu a few years earlier and loved the quaint downtown Stonetown and quiet Shela areas. There was a massive replica Swahili castle built right on a large beach on the northeast part of the island. There were no other buildings for nearly half a mile, which made the castle seem more like a beach defense fortress looking towards the Indian Ocean and surrounded by sand dunes. Imposing fifty-foot walls surrounded the building with a massive twelve-foot front door, tipped on the outside with large metal spikes. When I was there last, I worked up the courage to walk over and ask a massive security guard what the castle was used for and he told me it was a private residence. If I was interested in renting the castle I could contact the owner directly.

Now that the prices were lower I decided it was time to take a break and make a beach trip to get away from everything. I called up the castle and spoke with a very nice German woman. I negotiated to rent the whole place (which slept up to eighteen people) for a weekend at a discount of more than seventy percent of the original price. This was apparently just enough to pay for the staff for the weekend and still make a little cash. Neeta (whom I had finally convinced by that time to be my girlfriend) and I rounded up fourteen of my friends and we all headed for the castle. Mac Perish joined us. He was a tall blond guy from California who had graduated from Stanford and was now working for Kiva in Kenya, managing many of its partners including Juhudi Kilimo. I could never seem to get away from any work-related relationships on social trips in Kenya.

Inside the massive iron doors was a beautiful open-air courtyard garden that ran the length of the castle. A glimmering pool stretched out inside the garden and all the rooms looked down to the pool from the second floor of the courtyard. The decoration was a mix of Swahili/Arabic design with hints of North African influence from the large rugs and glassware decorating the hallways. The upper floors had wide windows that looked out into the rolling dunes or off into the distance of the Indian Ocean. The rooftop parapet, my favorite, ran the perimeter of the castle, with guard towers at each corner. The towers, which offered spectacular views over the ocean, were where all of us gathered to have sundowner cocktails as we watched the sun disappear over the desert hills.

As the organizer of the trip, I was granted the master bedroom, which sat at the end of the long corridors overlooking the pools. I had a grand balcony where I could stand and shout orders to all the rest of our guests. The best part of the balcony was that it was just high enough for me to make the 15ft jump into the pool. The pool was deep enough so I didn't worry about hitting the bottom. I proceeded to wake everyone up each morning with a cannon ball splash.

One evening we persuaded one of our friends to bring out her guitar as we sat in the 'round table' room: a perfectly cylindrical brick room at the base of one of the towers. The large round table and great wooden chairs made us all feel like knights.

If any of the pirates came to kidnap us, at least we were in a well-fortified castle on the beach. Fortunately nobody bothered us.

Back in the game

Now that Ford had sent their money and all the investors and shareholders had reached a resolution, I felt better about where things were going. We still had tremendous demand for loans from our clients but were being cautious about managing our cash. K-Rep and the investors were still negotiating the sale price that was to be included in a large document, called the Share Purchases Agreement. Once the agreement was finalized and signed (more lawyers) we would then need to go to the Government of Kenya to seek approval from the Competition Authority. This agency would make sure that any change in majority ownership of a company did not undermine the competitiveness of a sector by creating a monopoly.

We did not think this would be an issue because we were not creating any kind of monopoly. Still, I dreaded a potential eight-month process of bureaucracy and corruption that would prevent the deal from closing. The Ford Foundation money would run out in another four months and if there were more delays in the conversion, we would be in trouble with cash again. With all our shareholder drama going on, I thought I would try to line up our next round of funding for later in the year.

Our growth numbers had started to improve and profitability was slowly returning on a monthly basis. In addition, some of the positive PR had reached investors. I emailed and called all those investors who had told me to talk to them when we were profitable: Oiko Credit, ResponsAbility, Triple Jump and Triodos. In a matter of two weeks, I suddenly had six term sheets for loans that ranged between $500,000 and $1 million each. Apparently word was out that we were looking for money and there were now lots of investors willing to play. This was quite a different story from the first round of financing.

We had hit the magic three-year milestone, secured our first round of equity financing and broke even. It was fun finally to be able to pick and choose our investors, based on their loan terms and what other experience or grants they brought to Juhudi. The current round of investors was much more 'commercial' than our initial one and this showed in the terms and speed at which their transactions were completed. We did not have much of a range in interest rates, which were all two-to-three-year loans with similar covenants, within one percent of seventeen percent denominated in Kenyan Shillings (commercial banks were lending at eighteen percent so this was a competitive rate). Many of the 'social investors' had difficulty investing more than $1 million and I wanted new investors who had deeper pockets and could provide follow-on financing if we needed it in the future.

We concluded all of the due diligence, not without hiccups. I thought it might be a good idea to invite two lenders to meet with our management team on the same day to save time. It turned out to be a bad idea. Both lenders insisted that they get individual time with each manager without the other lender in the room. So the plan backfired and ended up consuming twice the amount of management time for the meetings that day. Fortunately, we passed the due diligences and all received investment committee approvals.

We still had not finalized the share purchase with K-Rep (but were getting close) and I had no idea how long the Competition Authority would take. Seeing this dilemma, ResponsAbility, arguably the most commercial of the lenders, with one of the highest interest rates, offered to disburse their loan after the share purchase agreement had been signed, but before the Competition Authority. This pushed them to the front line of lenders. The $600,000 from ResponsAbility was timely and kept us going as we finalized the documentation. The Competition Authority then surprised everyone. It took the government agency one week to process our application and they were very professional about the whole experience.

Chapter 14 | Survival

With the equity conversion and K-Rep exit on its way, I figured it was time to spend a little money where we needed it badly. Our two-year lease at Juhudi Gardens was coming to an end and the landlord was asking to more than double our rent to KShs 360,000 ($4,200). She told us that this is what the market was paying and for us to either sign a new lease or get out in three months.

At the time, Nairobi was experiencing a boom in commercial real estate development especially in the Ngong Road and Kilimani areas. One of the first buildings I looked at was a beautiful brand new curved building called the Priory on the main Argwings - Kodhek road near the Yaya Centre. The offices had large open spaces with lots of light. The landlord had told us that the space was going for 120 Kenyan Shillings per square foot or KShs 500,000 for the space, which was out of our price range. I remember thinking how amazing it would be to have a company that could afford nice office space like this and I could move into one of the many apartment buildings within walking distance.

We looked at a few more houses and office buildings but all of them were either completely run down or far too expensive for our budget. With a month left on our lease I noticed that the Priory building still did not have many tenants. The landlord said they had lowered the price to KShs 110 per square foot. I negotiated them down to 100 or KShs 400,000 for the 4,000 square foot space. This was not much more than we would be paying for the Juhudi Gardens and the Priory had more space, better security, a backup generator, faster internet and we could sign a seven-year lease. The board agreed and we started plans to partition our new place.

Life in the Cloud

In my time at Accenture I had participated in a few IT system integrations for large corporations. This was a painful change process where Accenture would help the company install a new IT system, which meant training all the employees how to use the new system and get them to give up the old system. This process creates a lot of anxiety for the staff, which then builds up resistance to the new system and can be devastating for management. I really wanted to avoid changing systems at all costs to try and spare everyone at Juhudi this headache.

We had hired a reputable IT consulting group in Nairobi to evaluate our systems and IT department as part of one of the multiple due diligence requests. The report came out clean saying that our Microsoft-based system was providing all of the required functions but we should think of hiring more staff for the IT department.

Both Kevin Gibbs, from Google, and Ghalib, from McKinsey, struggled tremendously to implement new initiatives with the system. We were having some serious challenges with our IT system. Since our IT system was licensed under Microsoft, if we wanted to make any changes we needed to hire a local IT consultant to make these alterations. The local groups we worked with were slow, did not attempt to understand our business and were extremely expensive. We were locked in an abusive relationship with these consultants who charged us every time we sneezed. Most critically, the Microsoft system did not integrate very well into other external systems.

Kevin's Simple MFI was working very well but was not optimized for the current IT system. Ghalib was in the process of improving our mobile money integration with M-Pesa but was having a very difficult time with the local Microsoft IT consultants who seemed to break more things with the system each time they were called in to fix something new. To complicate things, our leaky server room and frequent neighborhood power cuts meant our internet and systems were down several times a week, or sometimes for an entire weekend. Our clients were repaying loans nearly 24 hours a day with M-Pesa and we needed a system to keep up with the demand. The new office would help with the power and internet, but our IT system came under review by the management. Ghalib and I had been in talks with Salesforce and Sanergy about installing a cloud-based leads management system to help our staff track and manage new clients. None of this was very easy to do with our current system and I was beginning to see the need to explore other systems as we continued to grow.

We hired some new IT consultants to help us with selecting a new system (something I would highly recommend). At the same time we started to recruit for a Chief Information Officer, who could participate in the selection and installment of the new system. Once Kevin Gibbs had left, nobody at Juhudi had any deep technical knowledge of IT to help with the interviews so we used the head partner of our consulting company to sit in the interviews and ask the hard questions.

Ghalib, Rachel, Aleke, the consultant and I, then held a series of interviews and were shocked at the salary expectations some of the candidates were anticipating. I could not justify hiring someone with only five years of general IT work experience at a salary level nearly twice that of our regional managers who had well over ten years of work experience. We settled on a candidate who worked at a bank but was a specialist in IT security. I thought he had answered all of our questions well but the consultant did not think we should hire him. I loved the energy and extroversion the candidate had (rare for an IT expert) and we ended up hiring him anyway.

The new system selection process did not leave us with many great options that fitted all of our needs. It came down to two strategic decisions. We could either spend $500,000 to $700,000 on a robust banking system that would continue to support us if we ever decided to transform into a bank or deposit-taking microfinance institution. The banking systems also required significant investments in hardware like servers and more IT staff. Or, we could go with a lower cost ($200,000 to $400,000) system that was more flexible but probably would not pass the requirements for the Central Bank if we decided to become a bank in the future. This would mean we would need to change systems again. The more flexible system also seemed to integrate a little more easily into third parties, which we liked.

Our board made the decision that Juhudi would not become a bank in the next three to five years, so we should look at the lower cost systems. Of those systems, one stuck out for everyone. It was a web-based system called MFI Flex, which operated on the Salesforce.com platform. We had just started testing the use of Samsung tablets with our field staff on some of the leads management program and Simple MFI. The initial results with the tablets were encouraging. I thought our staff would lose them, drop them or they would get stolen, but none of that happened in the first six months. I liked MFI Flex because it could be run on the tablets and would allow our field staff and management to access the system anytime and anywhere. The mobile networks in Kenya were found in all of our remote areas of operation and data bundles were cheap. However, MFI Flex was run by a very new company and that posed some risks. But I was comforted that the system was built by a large software company like Salesforce.com so if for whatever reason MFI Flex went under as a company, we might still be able to salvage everything with Salesforce.

Our board liked the proposal and we selected MFI Flex to put together our new IT system. This new system would allow the company to better track the loans to clients and see reports in real-time on tablets or laptops. The current system required a loan officer to send an email to the head office staff to pull a report and email back to them, a terribly slow process.

We had a conference call with our new CIO and MFI Flex teams from India and San Francisco in January of 2013. We were told that the system would be up and running in three months. I believed them. By July of that year it was clear something was not working, since we were still going back and forth between MFI Flex, our local IT consulting company and our IT staff. After a number of frustrating phone calls, the truth of the matter came to light. It turned out that MFI Flex had not actually built their system yet and were designing on the fly. Since the delays were with the software company we were not charged anything but the project was still far behind schedule. Suddenly the head project manager at MFI Flex was fired and one of the founders and brilliant software engineers took over the installation. It was as if all the lights had been switched on. Things started working and we were on track for a 'go live' in October. I was amazed at the difference a new manager can bring to a seemingly dying project.

Our CIO had applied through CIO Magazine for the CIO 100 Awards, which recognize companies from all over the world who are using technology in an innovative way to generate business value. Our CIO thought our recently deployed Salesforce leads management system and the tablets in rural Kenya would make a good application. He was right. We became a finalist and were then selected in August 2013 to come to Colorado Springs to the five-star Broadmoor hotel to receive our award at their annual conference.

The ceremony would be held in the building next to the Colorado foundation at which I had worked for nearly ten years earlier. It was an extravagant event with companies like IBM, Boeing, AT&T and Accenture all receiving awards. My parents came to watch the ceremony. I was by far one of the youngest people and I am sure everyone at the conference was wondering what I was doing there.

The fanfare continued when I got back to Nairobi. We had just hired a new marketing officer, who had worked as the brand manager at Coke and was well connected with the media houses. I was on national television and in all the local newspapers for the award. We were the only African company that year to be recognized.

Juhudi was now being talked about everywhere. Neeta was living with her parents and grandmother in Nairobi. Her parents had grown up in Dar es Salaam and later moved to Kenya. Neeta's grandmother made a point of clipping out articles about me to share them with the rest of her family. I loved going over to the Bhandari home for dinners where aunts, uncles and cousins would all come together and sing and dance until late in the evening. Neeta's father, Anil, came from a large family of nine brothers and three sisters who all lived together in the same small home. Anil went to the US to get a Master's degree in civil engineering from MIT and a PhD in transportation engineering from Perdue. He taught for a time at the University of Dar es Salaam before returning to the US for a job at the World Bank developing roads and infrastructure. Anil was still a consultant for the World Bank and would tell us stories about his recent journeys to Afghanistan to advise the Afghan government about its road infrastructure.

Acumen sent us an experienced technology volunteer under their Global Fellows program who had previously worked at Accenture. Her name was Nicole Iden and she quickly gathered up the loose ends of our new system implementation project and got everyone in line, including our CIO. After Nicole's program had ended, I hired another smart Kiva Fellow as a consultant to help us with a credit scoring model. It turned out that this fellow also had a significant level of IT experience after working for a major bank in the US. I have had the privilege of managing a number of different people from all over the world, but nobody as unique as Varick Schwartz. In typical American fashion, he gave his opinion bluntly. I found this refreshing, although his style offended many of the senior staff. It was difficult to argue with anything that Varick said due to his sheer brainpower and the fact that he was right about almost everything.

We ended up postponing the October go-live until November. We were having some serious problems with the internet connectivity at the head office. For a web-based system to work it needs to have a very fast and reliable internet connection. It was a mystery, because the tenants in the same building were not having any issues and they were all using the same service providers.

One morning Varick took me aside. Clearly he was upset about something. "Your CIO has to go," he said "He is incompetent, he is abusive to his junior staff and this entire system implementation is at risk because of him. Just ask any of the other IT partners. They all know it but feel awkward saying anything to you about it. I don't. The internet connection is just one example of something he should be able to solve but can't."

This was a shock to me as I had become friends with the new CIO who had assumed the role of the office MC and energizer. I took Varick's advice to heart and casually talked with the junior IT staff over some beers after work to get a sense for how they were being treated. Sure enough, the vendors all complained that they were not being treated professionally, and it was affecting their work. The most jolting news was that they were so demoralized they were begging their friends at other companies to hire them away from their misery. Apparently the CIO would tell them how little they knew about IT and, whenever one of the junior staff came up with a good idea or solution, the CIO would take it as his own to make him look better to the board and me. The CIO was a fantastic talker but had held seven jobs in the last ten years, which should have clued us into his job performance. I talked to the CIO to encourage him to step back from the new system implementation and the internet problems and let Varick try to manage it all. Within two weeks we were back on track for the go live and had had our first week of uninterrupted internet connectivity.

The junior staff loved working with Varick, who was taking time to coach them and encourage them in their day-to-day activities. This put me in a tough position because now I was puzzled as to what the CIO had been doing for the past nine months at the company. It turned out that the Acumen Fellow had been covering for his work for the year and she was too nice to tell me. I informed the board of what was happening and they were supportive about letting the new CIO go. So on Christmas Eve I sat down with the CIO to give him the news. I thought that by telling him before the holidays I would give him time to start thinking about his next move while surrounded by friends and family.

I made the mistake of being too diplomatic and not very direct about what was happening to him. I talked about changing strategy and reorganizing the department. This only confused him and I had to have a more firm conversation with him later, outlining his poor performance as the reason for dismissal. Treating the junior staff so horribly really angered me. And I felt guilty too. The blame for hiring someone who is a bad fit and then allowing them to stay with the company for nine months fell squarely on my shoulders. I had told myself after our CFO mistake months before, that I would never make an impulsive hiring decision again. But I had let my response to his personality get in the way, in spite of the major faults our IT consultant had identified after the interview. At least the situation had been resolved now.

By default, Varick would assume the CIO role for the next six months until the new system stabilized and we could find a more permanent CIO.

The system went live in late January without any major problems.

Varick and the IT team worked tirelessly to get it up and running. We were fortunate to have someone like Varick who could jump in and motivate the IT team to make such a dramatic organizational change.

MFI Flex was a beautiful system. I had real-time portfolio reports on demand from my laptop or even my phone anywhere I had an internet connection. The reports were easy to build and understand, which allowed our management team to start making more informed decisions. If I were to start with Juhudi again I would start with a robust system and then build the people and processes around it. Some may say cash is king in an early-stage business, but in rural microfinance, system is king.

Maasai Mara

It was August, around the time that the wildebeest make their famous annual migration from the Serengeti in Tanzania up to the Maasai Mara in Kenya. Over one million animals make the spectacular journey and feed predators along the way, who gorge themselves on wildebeest for several weeks. *National Geographic* has made this natural phenomenon famous by televising the dramatic river crossings where wildebeest are devoured by crocodiles as they try to escape the waters and scramble up the banks to the other side.

Neeta and I had visited Maasai Mara independently several times before, but neither of us had ever witnessed an actual crossing. With all my game tracking experience from the other parks, I thought it would be fun for the two of us to take my Honda CRV out for a long weekend to see the migration.

We drove out to the northwestern part of the park where we would stay for two days and then drive back to Nairobi through the southeastern gate. As anyone will tell you who has driven to Maasai Mara recently, the last 100km of road to the reserve is deplorable. It has, of course, something to do with corruption and disputed rights/ownership of the road between the Maasai and some local politicians. I had just put new shock absorbers in and the mechanic said they were guaranteed for life. He even gave me a plastic card (all in German), authorizing my guarantee. I feared for the shocks after the brutal five-hour drive. We made it to the lodge just in time to watch the sunset from a hill over the wide expanse of the Maasai Mara savannah.

Most commercial game drives begin at 6am, to have the best chance of viewing game, especially big cats, before the day becomes too hot for the animals and they escape to dense bush for shade. Then, the tourists return to the lodges for breakfast around 8 or 9am. Neeta and I were tired from the drive so we slept late, had a leisurely breakfast and left for our game drive at about 9am. We passed all the tourists on their way back as the sun was now starting to bake the lower grasslands.

Within a few minutes of driving we stumbled upon a great herd of elephants and cape buffalo making their way along the road just a few meters from our car. On the opposite side of the road stood an opposing rhino staring threateningly at the elephants and buffalo.

"So there are three of the Big Five," I told Neeta. "But they usually do not like each other like this."

I remembered my last encounter in a car with a rhino and decided to keep driving. Neeta was now navigating with crystal clarity from Google Maps and receiving full 3G service produced by a mobile network tower out in the savannah disguised as a large palm tree. I had not seen any other palm trees growing in the grasslands but I guessed most tourists did not even realize it was a fake. We turned the corner and Neeta spotted a hunting party of lionesses, reclining in the shade under an acacia tree with a freshly killed wildebeest at their feet. We took a few pictures and I wondered if our tourist friends had seen them on their drive. I glanced over and noticed a strange cloud of dust coming from the opposite side of a thick grove of trees.

A white safari van with a few tourists pulled up behind us and I pointed to the lions. They slowed to take a few pictures and then sped off towards the trees. I was wondering what could be more exciting than seeing lions under an Acacia tree in the Maasai Mara. Then I remembered why we were in the Mara that time of year.

I drove down the road towards the dust and trees until the road stopped on a high bluff overlooking the bank of the great Mara River. The other safari van had stopped along the bank too and they were all looking across the opposite bank.

"Maybe this is where the crossing is," Neeta commented.

Sure enough a huge heard of wildebeest and zebra crested a small hill on the other side and came running down the bank towards the river. Several zebra were in the lead but stopped short of the riverbank and parted to the side to let the wildebeest charge into the water. I was not sure if this was intentional or if the zebras were just a little smarter than the wildebeest.

Dozens of wildebeest jumped in and started swimming against the current to make it to the other side. A few minutes later the first of the swimmers made it to the opposite bank and started up the steep rocky bank not far from our car. Like a stream of ants or lemmings the wildebeest followed each other into the water and up the bank making their bugle calls, which sounded like a cross between a sheep 'mew' and cow 'moo'. The animals looked exhausted after crossing and I thought about how well the lions we saw earlier were positioned down the road. Neeta and I took pictures, videos and felt like we were in the front row of a *National Geographic* video. We could not have picked a better location to watch one of the Seven Natural Wonders of the World roll out at our feet.[xi]

[xi]   Serengeti Migration, Seven Natural Wonders, 2014.

Just as Neeta was saying "they picked a good spot to cross, because I don't see any crocodiles", a massive crocodile slowly swam downstream towards the crossing wildebeest. I expected it to jump right in and pick one off but it swam under the crossing animals and circled around downriver of the crossing. A few minutes later I understood why.

One of the younger wildebeest could not make it up the steep bank and, left without many other options, decided to swim back across to the original bank. It was clearly tired and the current swept the animal downriver as it struggled to swim. The crocodile struck and the wildebeest struggled to keep its head above water before being pulled under. Two other crocodiles joined in the watery buffet along with dozens of large vultures waiting for something to be killed.

The sheer volume of animals crossing was astounding. We must have watched several thousand cross the river and still there were thousands more waiting to cross on the other side. Upstream I saw a dark shape moving underwater and realized it was a massive twelve-foot-long crocodile with a full-grown wildebeest sideways in its mouth. Somehow the powerful beast was swimming quite gracefully against the current with the wildebeest dragging.

By 10.30 we had seen four of the Big Five and had a front row seat for the wildebeest crossing. I broke out the gin and tonic and we toasted our luck.

My CRV was an old car and made plenty of noise. This made sneaking up on animals quite difficult. The road from the southeast gate in Maasai Mara to Nairobi was all washboard and in terrible condition. We passed a few mud huts and wooden sheds just outside the gate with various little shops. I chuckled at one that read 'mechanic', which consisted of a man and a toolbox sitting outside the mud hut.

We drove on for about thirty minutes on the terrible road and my car kept making more noise. Suddenly there was a loud pop in the back of the car followed by a louder rattling noise. Neeta and I looked at each other in dismay as I stopped the car. I peered around back and noticed right away that one of my new yellow German shocks was sticking through the coil spring with one side resting on the outside body of my car and rubbing on the inside of the wheel. It looked terrible. We were probably two hours from the nearest town and I was not sure if the shock or wheel would hold. Then I thought of the mud hut mechanic back at the Maasai Mara gate. If he could not fix it, maybe we could catch a ride back with one of the tour vans to Nairobi.

The mechanic was thrilled to see me and started jacking up the back of my car right away. In a few minutes, he had taken the wheel, shock absorber, spring and a few other pieces of my car apart. Neeta put up with it all very well and was practicing her Kiswahili with the mechanic's wife.

As the sun began to dip on the horizon, I became concerned that we would be making the four-hour trip home in the dark. It is generally not the safest plan to be driving at night in Kenya especially along roads that do not get a lot of traffic.

The mechanic had identified a metal washer on the shock absorber that had snapped in half as the problem. He brought out a box of old nuts and bolts and dug through for a washer. He found one of perfect size and a little sturdier. I was intrigued to see how this guy would compress the large coil spring that went around the shock and put it all back in my car. The mechanic took a long piece of old rope and wrapped it several times around each coil. The spring slowly compressed a little with each wrap. When it was down far enough he slid the shock absorber inside and bolted everything together. He then cut the pieces of rope to let the coil flex to its full length again. By 5pm we set off again, after paying the man his asking price for the service of $10 plus a $2 tip for working so quickly.

We drove along the terribly bumpy road, and at times veered into the jungle to avoid a particularly bad section. I have terrible night vision and felt apprehensive. We would be an easy target for bandits or thieves on the road.

"Should we pull over and spend the night in the forest until morning?" I asked.

"No, let's go on," Neeta replied.

The car continued to make more noise and I started to question my recent $12 investment. Neeta's parents would not be happy with me for getting her killed this way when I knew better than to drive at night.

"This isn't good," I said, as the car juddered over corrugations.

"Look," Neeta pointed. A paved road was coming into view. "That must mean we're near a town."

Sure enough, this signaled the end of the terrible road and about thirty minutes later, we reached Narok.

The next morning we arrived in Nairobi and I took the car in for service. It turned out that we had blown two of the shocks and done some damage to the steering mechanism. The German company did honor their guarantee by sending four new shocks for free but said these new shocks were no longer guaranteed.

Chapter 15   Back in the Game

In October of 2013, the board and K-Rep finally concluded their buy-out. K-Rep had negotiated to sell its majority stake in the company for around 2.6 times the book value of the equity of the company. This means that it would get paid out in cash almost three times what the company was worth at the time, which equated to about $425,000.

I was happy to have it all done but at the same time a little frustrated. Over the last several years, if you looked at how much of its own money K-Rep had put in to Juhudi it was only about $114,000. The rest of the money had come from international donors who apparently did not mind that their grants were included in the valuation, in effect they were now a cash gift to the K-Rep Group. I decided it might be a good time to approach the board again for management shares. This time I asked for shares for Aleke, me and the Juhudi Executive Team (now called JET). Acumen, Grameen and Soros grumbled and thought it could be a board agenda item for 2014. It was odd having to push these investors so hard for a few shares of the company for the management so that we all could feel like small owners of the early stage company we were running. Perhaps noticing my displeasure, the board then offered to give me a small performance bonus for helping them through a nearly disastrous year. With our cash still tight, I thought this was a terrible idea. Instead, I asked if they would put it towards some shares in the company when the employee share ownership was developed. They agreed.

2014 was looking to be a great year. We had concluded the shareholder drama, we had a fancy new IT system in place and all the money we needed to grow as much as we wanted. My management team and I scheduled a company-wide retreat to get everyone motivated for the year. We closed 2013 with 14,000 clients and the board approved our plan to reach 50,000 clients by the end of 2015. The target was ludicrous but still held the glimmer of possibility, especially as Juhudi never once had an opportunity open up its potential without being constrained by cash, systems or board drama. I ran the numbers and the monthly targets seemed feasible to our field teams. I would still be happy even if we only reached 30,000 clients but there were millions of farmers to reach in Kenya who badly needed loans to purchase productive assets.

Our optimism took a hit just a few weeks into the new year. Since the company had continued to take losses for most of 2013, due to the equity conversion delay and slowed growth, a key ratio was now below acceptable levels. This was the solvency ratio that measures a company's equity base against its total assets. This is similar to a debt to equity ratio and essentially tells if a company can meet its debt obligations. I knew we would need new equity later in 2014 but it was a little hard to talk to our shareholders about bringing in new investors before they had concluded the purchase with K-Rep. With our debt-to-equity ratio below a safe level it meant I would need to find a new equity investment of at least $2 million before June. I had thought our fundraising needs were at an end. All I wanted was a few quiet months in 2014 to focus on growing the business and not spend so much time fundraising. Not a chance.

I&P

I put out word that Juhudi was now looking for equity among my big list of equity investors. Out of the blue, I received an email from the French investment fund I&P, who four years earlier had devastated me at their meeting at the Serena Hotel. The investment officer dug up my last email to him and replied saying: "I hear that Juhudi has accomplished great things and you are now looking for more equity? I will be in Nairobi in three weeks and would love to meet." My initial reaction was to ignore the email or write something back saying "you had your chance four years ago, sorry!" but I remembered Aleke's advice so I let go of any personal grudges and agreed to meet with I&P.

The tough investment officer was just the same but this time the meeting went more smoothly. I was able to answer many of his questions with ease since we now had so much operational experience. I&P scheduled their formal due diligence on their next trip to Kenya two months later. Things were looking good. It was hard to believe that this investor, who had been on the bottom of my list, was now one of the likely candidates for our next round of equity financing.

Nairobi also had a new fund called Progression East Africa, which was set up to invest large amounts of money in early-stage microfinance institutions. It was comprised of partners who were former microfinance CEOs and had deep operational experience running institutions. They checked all the boxes for me.

Progression was even based in Nairobi. The company's focus was microfinance and the staff (potential future board members) could support management with their backgrounds in the industry. Progression was also a social investor with a much more commercial leaning. They were looking for a specific financial return. Progression had clear return expectations that they wanted to hit for each investment and a five-year time frame to make it happen. This clear focus was quite different from Acumen, Grameen and Soros, who were investing grant money without expectations of a return or a planned duration of investment. In fact, to my knowledge, none of these investors had ever exited an investment profitably.

Victoria Falls

That Easter I took advantage of Mulago's travel support for its fellows and went to Zambia to visit one of my classmates who ran a fantastic organization called Rent-to-Own Zambia. This company was quite similar to Juhudi Kilimo in that it provided financing for equipment to rural Zambians but it also supported all the equipment distribution and sales.

For example, we were dependent on working with cow breeders and equipment manufacturers to get assets to our farmers. Rent-to-Own provided everything their clients needed regarding the equipment or assets that were being financed. Rent-to-Own could make money on the equipment sales and on the interest from the financing, which was nice. However this business model also was a little harder to operate because their staff needed to be able to sell the assets to the client while also evaluating them for credit risk. These are two different skill sets that sometimes give conflicting messages to the clients, especially if the client stops paying. This is why many car dealerships will offer financing for a car but you will need to work with a separate business entity for the financing.

I spent several days with the Rent-to-Own team, sharing our experiences of fundraising and learning more about how they were using mobile technology in the field with their staff. They had found a great way to scan and store loan agreements, payment receipts and other documents all on a mobile phone. It was also quite interesting to see how limited the banking and microfinance sector was in Zambia, compared to Kenya.

I took advantage of the long Easter weekend and Neeta came down with me to see Victoria Falls in Livingstone, on the Zambian side. We rented microlights and flew over the falls, which threw mist nearly fifty feet into the air with the thunderous power of the falling water. The indigenous name for the falls is 'Mosi-oa-Tunya' – the Smoke that Thunders – and it's very apt. It's a very impressive sight. It was the rainy season and the Zambezi was overflowing its banks, making the falls even more spectacular. Trails and walkways allow tourists to walk below the falls and get drenched in their spray.

We rented kayaks and floated down the river with a tour group above the falls. I could not believe how silent the falls were just a few hundred meters up river. If I were exploring the river for the first time I certainly would not have noticed the 360-foot drop until it was too late.

Several days earlier two young male hippos had been fighting up river and accidentally slipped over the edge to plunge to their deaths. Crocodiles now lined the banks in the slow pools, making the river even more dangerous. As an experienced white water guide from Colorado, I felt comfortable in the inflatable kayak but the water flow was easily twenty times that of the Colorado River. Towards the end of the tour, our guide pulled away to cross to the bank. "Careful of the waves!" he shouted to us. "Paddle to the bank."

Neeta and I tried to paddle after him, but we were slammed by a massive standing wave in the middle of the river, which knocked us both to the floor of the kayak.

"Bloody hell! You OK Neeta?" She was drenched, but nodded, her hair slapped across her cheek. We had to prevent the kayak from turning sideways and capsizing with the next wave. "I'll try and square up into the waves – you keep paddling, hard!" I shouted above the roar of the water. I thought of the hippos and crocodiles waiting for us on the bank and the devastating falls down river. Not the safest place to flip over in a kayak.

I struggled to my knees and heaved my paddle. We had to keep our momentum but the bow of the boat lifted so high out of the water that Neeta and I were barely able to make a solid paddle stroke. I cursed the guide under my breath for putting us in this position. Fortunately the waves subsided and we were able to push for the far bank. We were exhausted but safe.

Zambia borders Botswana, which is home to both the Kalahari Desert and the Okavango Delta, both famous for their wildlife. We had found a package deal for a flight and two nights at a remote lodge in the delta, which could only be reached by plane or boat.

The delta looks like a vast spider web of rivers and water channels that sprawl out for hundreds of miles in every direction. It is home to enormous populations of waterfowl, hippos and elephants. The lodge where we were staying was managed by a young ex-soldier from the UK. Small boats and canoes from the lodge would take guests to various islands or to view the hippos from the waterline. The wetlands teemed with activity and there were no other man-made settlements in any direction for hundreds of miles.

I was hoping to try my hand at fishing for the African tiger fish. The manager was also an avid fisherman and I convinced him to take Neeta and me out for an evening of fly fishing as the sun set on the delta. We took the boat up river for several miles and then cut the engine. The meandering bank was covered with high pillows of grass and there were no large rocks in the water. This allowed us to float down the river in silence, bouncing off of the soft grassy banks as we made our way back to the lodge. The setting sun bathed the water in a soft orange hue. Elephants silently moved along the banks as we passed. The manager strung up a few spin-casting rods and opened a beer for himself.

I cast my lure towards the deep undercut bank where, in the Colorado River, I would expect to find the big fish. A huge green head snapped at my lure just seconds after it hit the water. I pulled back and then fought to bring the fish to the boat. It was a long thick African Pike, which looked more like a crocodile without any feet and rows of razor sharp teeth. The guide smiled at me. Two minutes later I had hooked another fish, this one much larger, close to five pounds, which received a nod of respect from the manager. The fish would strike aggressively a few times at the lures in the water so once a fish was interested, it was difficult to miss it. We continued floating through the tranquil valley, catching more of the aggressive pike and each time we prepared to cast, I had to take care to remember that I was in Africa as we passed some elephants with their trunks in the water. I would not want to have one of those on the end of the line.

Neeta gave a frustrated cry as she managed to send one of the barbed treble hooks through the skin in her knuckle. Both the manager and I grimaced when we saw how deep the barb had gone. It would not come out easily and certainly not without a lot of pain. I remembered thinking that we were a plane ride away from any medical facility and hopefully she could survive until then. Neeta did not seem to be bothered. "Just pull it out," she said. I looked at the manager and he just shrugged. I held Neeta's hand and the manager yanked until there was a pop and the hook came free. The manager and I squealed like little girls. He got down on his hands and knees like he was going to empty his stomach over the side of the boat. "Oh come on guys it was not that bad," said Neeta. The manager and I both took long sips of whiskey but Neeta was already back to casting again.

I managed to land fourteen pike that evening and the guide asked if I wanted to be his partner next month at an annual fishing tournament with some of the other lodges. The trip made me want to plan another tiger-fishing visit with my twin brother. Too bad my brother hates to travel.

Westgate

On September 21st, 2013, Neeta and I were talking about our friend CJ, another American living in Kenya who was about to launch a Subway Sandwich franchise in Nairobi. It was fantastic news since it would be the closest thing I would have to a quick lunch since the Rolex disaster. I then got a text from Benson saying to stay away from the Westgate mall because there was a guy with a gun robbing the major grocery store, Nakumatt.

One of the many benefits to being a partial founder of La Playa, along with Benson, is that I had access to the network of drivers dispersed throughout Nairobi at any given day. So when the students of Nairobi were protesting and throwing rocks at cars, I would hear about it before anyone else through Benson's drivers. I was able to inform all my friends to avoid certain areas. I also discovered that I could find out which of my friends had gone to which bars the night before, if I wanted.

I told Benson to keep me posted and forwarded the message to all of my friends.

Neeta and I had had brunch at Westgate the Sunday before and I remembered commenting to her how dangerous it seemed to have a major road passing right by all the outdoor restaurants at the mall. Someone could easily drive by and lob a grenade into the mall. The Al-Shabaab attacks had escalated since the Kenya military invasion in Somalia and several public places had been attacked with grenades.

As the Sunday morning rolled on I started to receive more texts from friends saying that the Westgate mall incident was much worse than just a robbery. It was thought that terrorists were involved in a hostage situation and were blowing up parts of the mall. I spoke with Benson about the situation and he told me that two of my friends had gone to the mall in the morning but their taxi drivers were still waiting for them to come out. One was Jen Cantwell, who was the East Africa Managing Director for a technology social business called Samasource and the other was a great guy named Ravindra Ramrattan or 'Ravi' who worked at the UK based research group called FSD. I had been out with Ravi two weeks earlier at a party and he was one of those amazing people who always had a smile on his face and was usually laughing about something.

By the afternoon, the international media had picked up the story and my parents awoke in the US to see live coverage of the Westgate mall terrorist attack. I was in regular contact with Benson, who had informed me in the evening that Jen had made it out but he was still not able to track down Ravi. Two other groups of my friends were in the mall that morning but all made it out safely.

The siege went into the evening and all kinds of conflicting stories were circulating. I first heard that the Kenyan military had moved in and had killed everyone. Then I heard that there were still hostages being held in one of the stores. Benson had visited every hospital in Nairobi looking for Ravi. He had found his name on a list of patients admitted to the Aga Khan Hospital that had been treated for gunshot wounds. However, Ravi was not at the hospital and clearly had been moved somewhere else.

At 2am on Monday morning, a very somber Benson informed me that had finally found Ravi listed in the Nairobi morgue. He had been shot in the mall and transferred to the Aga Khan hospital, where he passed away. I had lost a few close friends to tragic accidents but nothing ever like this. I could not sleep the rest of the night and kept thinking about how I had just recently spoken with Ravi. That could have easily been me and Neeta at that mall.

The next afternoon I was having a conference call with Sapna from Acumen, who lived across the street from Westgate. We had to pause the call several times because the gunshots and explosions in the background were drowning out what Sapna was saying. Thick black smoke could be seen rising above the mall nearly three days later. Yet still nobody actually knew what was happening and if the terrorists were still engaging with the police or military and if there were any hostages left.

After the fourth day everything seemed to be over. The death toll stood at sixty-seven, thought to be caused by four terrorists linked to the

Al-Shabaab group from Somalia. The event shocked the Nairobi expat community. Additional security could be found everywhere and nobody wanted to visit any of the malls. Several of the expat volunteers working for the various social enterprises decided to leave the country and a group of consultants from New York postponed their trip. My own cousin and his wife were in the middle of planning their honeymoon to visit me and take a safari in Kenya but decided to cancel.

I could not blame any of them. The security situation in Kenya was horrible and who knew if something like the Westgate attacks would happen again. It was difficult to stop a group like Al-Shabaab, who were ever-present in Kenya with its porous borders and weak police force.

Bolinas

The Mulago Foundation partnership and Rainer Arnhold Fellows Program was one of the more helpful and personally enjoyable experiences I had with an external partner at Juhudi.

I had just completed my second and final trip to Bolinas, California to meet with another group of outstanding entrepreneurs and founders of high-impact organizations from all over the world. This time, in addition to celebrities Andrew Youn and David Auerbach, we were joined by a fellow Coloradoan named Madison Ayer. Madison was somehow managing to be the CEO of two fantastic social enterprises in Kenya.

One was called Honey Care Kenya, which financed farmers and trained them on how to raise beehives. Then the company would buy the honey and sell it on the open markets. The other company was Farm Shop, which was setting up retail and distribution centers around Kenya for small-scale farmers to buy high-quality farm equipment and inputs like seeds and fertilizers. Finding good quality seeds, fertilizers and equipment is a major problem for the rural small-scale farmer who easily becomes victim to numerous scams and counterfeit supplies.

At the end of the Mulago retreat, Kevin Starr gave a speech in which he talked about how early organizations tend to spend more of their time on testing, developing and innovating with their products and lab services. Then, as they discover what works, the organization starts to streamline processes to achieve more scale, like that of a factory. As the company grows it becomes important for the organization to continue innovating to keep up with the demands of the clients or beneficiaries, so they develop more labs. This resonated with me since Juhudi had a successful loan product of financing assets for rural smallholder farmers, which we were now scaling up. Very quickly we would need to diversify with other loan products to meet our clients' needs.

Product design (or any kind of designing) was not my specialty, but I met a husband and wife team at the Mulago retreat who were running a fabulous organization in Burma, called Proximity Designs. The organization had been developing water pumps and other equipment specifically developed to meet the unique needs of the Burmese rice farmers. So I used another one of Mulago's fabulous travel grants and went to Burma to learn more about their design thinking and process. It was fascinating.

The country had been closed off from the rest of the world for years under military rule. It generated some tough farmers who had been forced to survive without infrastructure or any kind of government or international aid agency handouts. There were no banks or ATMs and a sim card cost $1,500, where in Kenya you could pay $1.20 for one. Despite the surface differences, the Burmese had many of the same challenges as the Kenyan farmers with regard to access to credit, access to market and the need to upgrade their rudimentary farming techniques to increase productivity. Proximity was just starting to launch a new arm called Proximity Finance that would finance the farmers to purchase seeds or equipment from Proximity Designs. I told them everything I knew about Juhudi. I certainly left with a wealth of knowledge and ideas to bring back to Juhudi.

Juhudi was gathering some rich data from Echo Mobile SMS surveys. We knew from the thousands of responses to our annual customer satisfaction survey that our customers wanted short-term 'emergency' loans or 'top-up' loans to use for paying annual school fees or medical expenses that put temporary burdens on their cash flow. The only options for our clients were to borrow from friends or family or go to the local moneylender, who would charge as much as one hundred percent in interest and fees.

The process for developing, testing and rolling out a new loan product in microfinance can take years and can take significant investments. Most financial institutions in Kenya were not very successful at generating genuine game-changing products, based on my experience at KDA. Because of all this, many MFIs used the over-abundance of free grant money from donors for new product development. I witnessed first-hand at KDA how using grant money tends to pull the grant funded entity (KDA) away from the for-profit entity that should be receiving the new products (K-Rep Bank). The result is some wonderful loan products, like those which created Juhudi Kilimo, but that have limited commercial viability for banks or other financial institutions. If Juhudi were to create a new product development entity it would have to be housed in the business and ultimately answer to the needs of the business. However, I wanted to do something a little different.

Nairobi had such a vibrant startup community, especially for businesses focused on technology. The Growth Hub, M-Lab, iHub and 88Mph all supported entrepreneurs, in one way or another. Some of them, like the iHub, were well funded but had failed to deliver major businesses in the last few years of operation. I met with dozens of Kenyan tech start-ups who were developing apps or software for farmers. None of them seemed to grasp the idea that most of the rural Kenyan farmers did not have access to smartphones and had difficulty learning a complex SMS or USSD based content delivery systems, which was so popular at the time.

Nevertheless, our rural farmers at Juhudi had potentially so much to benefit from technology. We had already proven this with Echo Mobile and our new cloud systems. I thought about the experience we had testing the market for Echo Mobile with our clients and thought we could offer this same service to other Kenyan startup companies. We could leverage the brilliance of entrepreneurs in Kenya to help Juhudi provide innovative products and services to its farmers. In exchange, Juhudi would provide access to a captive market of thousands of rural smallholder farmers and connect the businesses with Juhudi's growing funding base. We thought we could also use Echo Mobile to gather real-time feedback from our farmers about a new product or service.

The example I used for this new concept was a solar-powered refrigeration system. Juhudi's rural smallholder farmers did not have access to electricity or cold storage, so there was no place for the farmers to store milk or excess produce before it spoiled. A small-scale solar-powered refrigeration system solved this problem. Juhudi could work with a start-up manufacturing these refrigeration systems and help them test the designs with select groups of farmers. Once a successful design was established, Juhudi could then finance the systems to the rest of its client base. We could also connect the startup company with funders like Kiva, who might provide early-stage working capital to the business to help it up-scale.

I worked with Mulago to create a concept note and then floated the idea to my board to start Juhudi Labs, which would develop new products for Juhudi and build partnerships with early stage businesses. The board was reluctant to invest in new product development at this stage of Juhudi's growth but said maybe I could find grant money to fund the idea.

The Acumen Fund had just started a technical assistance grant program for its investment companies and was asking for proposals. I spent weeks putting together a proposal for them, but ultimately it was rejected. I found a much better reception from other innovative donors such as the MasterCard Foundation, a Dutch organization called Finance For Agriculture (F4A) and, of course, Mulago Foundation. I estimated that we needed about $250,000 to run Juhudi Labs in the first two years, which would primarily fund technical staff and travel.

In the end I was able to secure almost $350,000, which meant we had enough to run the program for three years before we needed either to raise more money or roll the entity into Juhudi Kilimo business. The only caveat with taking the external grant money was that the products and services created needed to serve more than Juhudi Kilimo. The donors were not so eager to subsidize a research and development arm of a for-profit company. I did not have a problem with this, especially since our own investors had refused to fund the project.

I proceeded to learn as much as I could about incubators and accelerators, which worked with startup social businesses. I signed up to be a mentor with a few of the local incubators thinking that perhaps some of my experience with Juhudi would be helpful and to recruit some potential participants in Juhudi Labs. I even applied to be a participant in the GSBI incubator in Santa Clara University in the US, to better understand what it was like to actually go through a program.

All of this research was helpful, but one of the key takeaways I realized was that there was a real problem with the business model of using a 'cohort' of multiple participants at once from different industries and at different stages of development. It became difficult to provide valuable content or support to such a variety of participants. Plus, working with the participants individually (like a consultancy) was not cost-effective. If we were to make

Juhudi Labs work we would need to be very careful about how the participants were selected and make sure that enough potential shared value was created for both the participant and for Juhudi Kilimo. This was not an easy concept to estimate but became the crux of our selection process for Juhudi Labs.

We had the money to hire some great staff. I found Kulsoom Ally, who was working for Nokia at the time in Brazil. She was a Pakistani-Finn who had been raised in Southern Africa and turned out to be fabulous for the job. I picked up an energetic Mauritian named Fabrice to help with communications and from our Kenyan staff, I pulled in rock-star Elvin, to round out the team.

Our in-house incubator/entrepreneur in residence was up and running. We had a long list of potential start-ups and $100,000 in debt funding from Kiva to use to help them grow.

One of the more exciting companies to arise through the selection process was a credit sourcing and farmer advisory company called F3 Life. F3 provided training about environmental management and soil preservation on farms to improve yields and reduce costs for our clients. Later, famers who had demonstrated their abilities to incorporate these trainings were selected for a small loan to invest in their farms. With Juhudi Labs, we were able to raise $50,000 for F3 Life.

The other game-changer we started working with in Juhudi Labs was an advanced psychometric credit modeling initiative spun out of Harvard University, called the Entrepreneurial Finance Lab or EFL. EFL originally approached me in 2009 when they first started to get involved in Africa and were searching for partners. We were too small for them at the time and I was not interested in spending any money on un-proven concepts for Juhudi. Now, EFL boasted of major capabilities in boosting credit scoring with clients in South Africa who did not have any bank accounts or credit history. The system asked prospective clients over one-hundred bizarre questions on a tablet in thirty minutes on topics ranging from their opinions of bus drivers to memory picture games. The answers given to these questions and puzzles were calculated by the PhDs from Harvard and a score was produced. The score would tell the bank if the prospective client was likely to be credit-worthy. I did not immediately see the value of this science to Juhudi as our clients already were repaying their loans at rates of ninety-five percent and above. But for some reason Varick got excited about EFL. I had never seen Varick excited about new partners like this before. Varick's real talent was in credit modeling, so he understood the magnitude of EFL's initial success. Juhudi was already using tablets in the field and by combining M-Pesa for the loan disbursements we could appraise a client and send their loan that same day. We could get to the point where we empowered community leaders or youth to use the tablets and evaluate other potential clients in their communities, instead of relying on our expensive field staff who many times ended up stealing the company's money anyway. This model would allow us to scale up to hundreds of thousands of clients while dramatically reducing the price of our loans. If it actually worked, that is. We put EFL, F3 Life along with several others in the Juhudi Lab for testing and incubating.

Only time would tell if this Juhudi Labs concept was something worth continuing. I hoped it would.

Chapter 16 | The Longest Fall

2014 was starting off to be a spectacular year for Juhudi. We had finally converted all the debt to equity, K-Rep had exited and now all the new lenders and investors were eager to help Juhudi grow over the next two to three years. We also had a world-class IT system and an extremely disciplined support team thanks to the work of Varick. We ended 2013 with 14,461 clients, which was well short of our 25,000 target but still showed a solid forty-three percent growth from the year before. It was especially good, given that we had restricted growth until October, when the conversion had been completed. We were now sitting on a company with nearly $10 million in assets that had grown from $600,000 in assets in 2009. While that may be snail's-pace growth for an internet company, it was not too bad for a bricks-and-mortar financial services company based in Kenya. However, I knew that the company was capable of growing much more if we could finally have a year without any shareholder drama or any other external disasters.

The management team and I presented to our board an ambitious plan to reach 50,000 clients by the end of the year with assets of $30 million. Kenya had an estimated nine million rural smallholder farmers in need of financial services. The asset loans addressed both poverty and food security for the country. However Kenya was just a starting point in my mind. The problem we were solving in Kenya could also be found in Uganda, Rwanda, Tanzania and Zambia. Our new investors had a much grander perspective than K-Rep and were supportive of expanding Juhudi beyond the borders of Kenya.

To expand to the level I was thinking of, the HR department needed to hire an estimated ten new employees each month, which was something we had done on a regular basis in 2013. The marketing department needed to generate roughly 200,000 new leads, which was a big challenge but not impossible. Somehow, more investors continued to sprout up in Africa and I had a list of eager potential investors totaling more than $20 million, many of whom had already completed their due diligence. Nothing could stop us this year.

I told the board that even if we reached 30,000 clients, this would demonstrate significant growth. During this strategic planning process we also took the opportunity to refresh our mission statement, core values and rebrand, now that we had a professional brand manager working for the company. Once again I raised the issue of management shares in an executive session. Finally, I got the board to agree to a structure to my own share ownership plan. I was much more concerned with Aleke and the management team acquiring shares but perhaps this was a start. The shares at Juhudi did not seem particularly valuable to me as there were not many ways to sell my potential shares in Kenya for money. Also, if the shares were ever worth millions, I would seriously question how well the company was treating its rural smallholder clients. The shares in the company represented more than just the potential for future financial gains for me. I found appeal in the idea of being an owner of the company I worked so hard to create over the last few years. It was something to do with the underlying connection to the organization as a shareholder. I suppose this is the same kind of feeling many of our clients have as they near the end of their loan payments on their cows. Once the loan is fully repaid, the clients own the cows. They can tell their neighbors "this is my cow. It belongs to me. I have worked hard to own this cow." Perhaps I was wrong to have this desire, but I was still puzzled as to why the impact investors would not be interested in allocating equity for the founders and management team of their company.

Our next plan was to sell this new 50,000-client strategy and brand to the field offices and loan staff. I spent the following month driving out to each office in each region myself, to present our strategy. It was a nice way to interact with staff and they could also ask me questions directly. I also loved the opportunity to drive through the most beautiful parts of the country. We concluded the whole strategic process in March with an all-staff retreat on the shores of Lake Elementaita. The event also coincided with Juhudi's five-year birthday, which I considered a major milestone as many new companies do not survive past their third year.

In April of 2014, we had finally started to build the portfolio reports from the new system and were getting ready to make the transition from the legacy paper reports to the new MFI Flex reports.

One of the most important reports in microfinance is the portfolio at risk (PAR) report, which shows how well the clients are repaying. It is calculated by taking the total amount of money at risk – so if a client takes a loan for $500 and misses a loan payment, then the entire outstanding amount of $500 is considered at risk even though the client may still intend to pay. It is not a very good indicator for really understanding repayment quality and the likelihood of actual default but it is an industry standard metric that was included as a covenant in all our loan agreements.

Since 2009, Juhudi Kilimo's reported PAR had fluctuated between three and seven percent. This roughly equated to a client repayment rate of ninety-five percent leaving five percent of the portfolio delinquent. However, of that five percent we were usually able to collect (mostly from repossessing assets like the cows) around three percent each year, leaving us to write-off two percent of the portfolio.

This performance was astounding for a Kenyan microfinance institution, especially one engaged in one hundred percent agriculture lending. These portfolio numbers had been audited by Ernst and Young for the first four years of the company's operations, and by BDO (another audit firm) in 2013. This is not to mention the fifty international investment funds who had all conducted due diligence on the company. So it was a shock to the management team when Varick and his IT department were showing us PAR reports that showed thirty-five percent of the portfolio was actually at risk and not five percent as reported in the previous system. Of course everyone blamed the new IT system and its calculation methods. The reports could not possibly be real. If the PAR was that bad it would have shown up someplace else, such as in our cash management.

I shared the report with our board member Steve from Grameen and told him that we were still analyzing how the new system was calculating the PAR, because there must be some mistake. Varick and the IT team went through hundreds of sample loans and cross-referenced them with the clients and records in the field. They could not find much wrong with the way the system was calculating the PAR. Of course the team found some minor issues with the number of days used in a year to calculate the interest payments and when the loan start dates were being recorded, but both of these problems might account for a three to five percent change in the PAR, not a thirty percent discrepancy.

What was the most disheartening was seeing the reaction of the field staff to the new PAR reports. A loan officer's pride is attached to the quality and performance of their personal portfolios. In the past, the loan officers would fight vehemently to fix any data entry or accounting errors in their portfolio. When the loan officers and managers saw the reports they did not say a word to refute the numbers. It was a silent acceptance.

The other surprising reality was that the discrepancies seemed to be heavily concentrated in five offices and two regions across the company. Some offices only had a one to three percent discrepancy from the original reports. This finding suggested that a widespread system-based problem was not the cause of the high PAR. We clearly needed to investigate the problem more thoroughly, and I needed to inform the rest of our board right away.

The total amount of money at risk in bad loans topped KShs 160 million or about $1.8 million, which equated to about twenty percent of the entire company's assets. This was a "material adverse change" that had the potential to sink our young company. I thought all our major life-threatening disasters were behind us. This was a true crisis. If the PAR was accurate, it would mean we would automatically default on our $5.4 million in loans from our lenders which would bankrupt us. We would need to close the business. All the potential death spirals paled in comparison. Instead of a slow death from winding down, everything would just crash to a complete stop. Even if the lenders were merciful and did not decide to accelerate their loan payments we would still face the deeper question – did the business model of Juhudi Kilimo even work if over thirty percent of the clients were not paying on time?

I took the preliminary data and opinions that I had, and shared the news with our investors. The responses were solemn and mixed. Acumen and Grameen gravely accepted the news and started to prepare for the worst, which would be a potential $1,800,000 write-off and loss. Acumen and Grameen both had the hope that perhaps we could recover some of the bad loans from the clients or find a problem in the system that would improve the numbers. Soros, on the other hand, responded by threatening to sue me. They thought I had somehow concealed this information for years and wanted someone to blame. This response absolutely crushed me. To have my major supporters in the business turn against me like this was devastating. As equity investors in a company, the investors have the most to lose of anyone when bad news like this surfaces. The equity investors are also supposed to be the closest to management and offer the most support in times of crisis.

I prided myself on being brutally transparent with all our investors and I had absolutely nothing to hide. If the PAR was actually as high as the system was reporting then this was a problem that had been missed by all the auditors, investors and IT consultants, as well as our own internal auditor and operations team.

As a first step, we were able to correct many of the system problems and collect on the legitimately bad loans. This lowered the PAR to about twenty percent, though this was still enough to kill the company.

It was clear to all involved that if the company were to survive I would need to be to fully focused on developing and executing a plan. Acumen and Grameen talked to Soros and convinced them that dropping any potential court case was the best long-term solution. This would give me the breathing space to spend my time on crisis management.

I spent time conferring with our equity investors. On 25 June, I drafted an email for our lenders:

"Dear Lender,

Thank you again for your patience and support as we work on our portfolio-at-risk problem. I have an update after over a month of hard work on the system and reconciling with the field operations.

Unfortunately the PAR related to specific system issues seems to be much less than we had originally thought. A vast majority of the poorly performing portfolio is legitimate underpayments by clients that were either missed or deliberately under-reported by our field staff. We have corrected many of the system-related discrepancies, such as the disbursement date problem and interest accrual problem but it has only improved our PAR by a few percentage points.

Our field teams have been able to bring the PAR from over thirty percent in May to almost twenty percent today by working with our clients to make up old payments. Through this continuing process we expect to be below twenty percent by the end of this month and I personally have full confidence that my team and dedicated employees will be able to bring the PAR to ten percent by the end of July. This will, however, require a significant write-off of the older loans and cases of fraudulent client activities.

The current PAR 30 figure is roughly KES 124 and can be broken down as follows:

Potentially able to collect from clients (30-120 days) = 64m

Old non-collectable loans or client-related fraud (over 120 days)= KES 60m

Of the KES 124 million PAR 30 over fifty percent of the bad loans are concentrated in three of our twenty offices (Litein, Kericho and Nyamira). If we were to remove the

PAR 30 completely from these three offices the company's overall PAR 30 would come down to 11.8%.

Our Internal Auditor has visited every office and found no clear case of staff-related fraud or stolen funds from our current staff. However, the older loans and clients who cannot be located are more difficult cases to determine. We had a Regional Manager overseeing the Litein and Kericho offices who left the company in January and joined the local government, which makes it difficult to investigate or prosecute in Kenya. For the remaining funds, we are using all legal means available to get them returned from the clients. It may help to know that we have already collected over KES 60 million in the last month so another 60m should not be an unreasonable target.

Our board is prepared to write off KES 60 million to clear out the loans mentioned above. While this news is devastating to everyone involved in Juhudi Kilimo, there is plenty of hope that we will turn around the portfolio and return to growth to recover the losses for the year.

How this was missed

You may be wondering how the 35 due diligence visits, five years of external audits, a 2011 systems audit and various other internal controls in cash management and portfolio yield calculations have missed this PAR in the past.

This problem was very difficult for anyone to detect under the previous paper and IT systems. I personally visited several of our offices and spent time with each of our nineteen Branch Managers and three Regional Managers to verify the perspectives of our staff and clients on the PAR position. The reason cited by both staff and clients for the under-payments is due to laxity of the loan officers and limited follow up on bad loans by the field staff.

One of the challenges we had with a manual paper-based reporting system is that it is a slow way of moving data and easy to manipulate by the field staff. This was one of the main reasons why we started to roll out a new system in early 2013. Fortunately, now that we have a real-time web-based reporting system that can be viewed daily by all levels of management, it allows our loan officers to better manage their portfolio and provides visibility of poor performance as soon as it occurs.

Every field manager representing each office and region has provided us with targets to recover the outstanding portfolio and signed agreements to meet these targets by the end of July.

Changes to credit process going forward

The new system drastically cuts out all of the loopholes that could be exploited by clients and staff to hide arrears. However, this crisis has shown that Juhudi Kilimo also needs an urgent overhaul of its current credit process and risk management procedures. We have engaged an in-house team and external consultant to drive this process for the next six months to improve the appraisal process, group management, staff culture and train the cross-departmental team on credit management.

Equity raise and the future

We will not need additional capital after the potential write-off but I have already communicated to the prospective investors to be ready for an additional injection of $1-2 million once we get closer to reaching 50,000 clients.

Currently both of our front-runners for equity investments are aware of our PAR and still planning on closing an investment before the end of the year. As the PAR improves, we will also be continuing discussions with multiple lenders who are interested in providing subordinated debt to improve our solvency as needed. Additionally, all of our current investors are prepared to participate in an equity call if needed for a down round if the new investors delay or change their minds.

Juhudi Kilimo has been a beacon of hope for some of the poorest and most excluded communities in the world as well as signaling to larger financial institutions that providing finance to rural smallholder farmers can be a viable and profitable business. I still strongly believe in this business and ask that you allow us to recover the portfolio to its original level of performance. Each week I will be uploading our portfolio performance (like the one attached) into the 'Reports' folder on our DropBox site if you would like to track our performance. Alternatively I can also send more regular reports or provide you direct access to our new web-based system to view reports anytime you like.

Please let me know if you would like to discuss any of this over a call.

Thank you."

The conflicting responses from the lenders were puzzling. They ranged from the sympathetic and supportive responses from Kiva, ResponsAbility, and FEFISOL to the downright hostile reactions of Rockefeller and Ford, who wanted me to fire Shadrack immediately for missing this problem as CFO.

I could not understand the massively different responses to the same communication. I later pieced together that the funds with more experience of making direct investments in microfinance, such as Kiva and ResponsAbility had seen this same problem in previous investments. In fact, a large discrepancy in PAR of twenty-five percent or more was quite common in the microfinance industry after the institutions put new IT systems in place. KWFT, Vision Fund and MicroAfrica in Kenya had all gone through similar scenarios several years previously, and all of them had passed large write-offs to correct the PAR.

I was able to beg for two months from our lenders to allow us to correct the remaining software problems and collect on any legitimately bad loans. What terrified everyone was the high possibility of fraud or foul play by any of our staff. I immediately engaged our internal auditor to visit all the offices with the highest PAR discrepancy with the aim of finding any fraud and stolen funds. We also asked one of our IT consulting firms to run a quick diagnostics of MFI Flex to make sure the PAR was being reflected accurately.

The management team spent two more weeks analyzing the data and having conference calls with the software vendor to try and get a handle on the problem. We fixed a few of the software calculation bugs, which brought the PAR to thirty percent, but a massive number of loans were still reflecting as late.

I called in all the regional managers for a meeting and then a few days later I had a meeting with the branch managers along with Shadrack and Nancy. At each meeting, I showed them the large pie-chart of the real-time PAR over thirty days late, which was thirty percent of the pie, and asked them: "Is this right? Is this your work? Your portfolio? If not, tell me now so that we can fix this problem." The managers all hung their heads and unanimously said that the reason for the PAR was their sloppy portfolio management and dereliction of duty.

"Well, if we don't get the PAR from thirty percent to ten percent in the next two months – by the end of July – then we all go home. Juhudi will shut its doors and we can all look for another job," I told them.

It turned out that the managers all knew our old system had some gaps that could be exploited. With a monthly reporting system, it was easy for loan officers to give their clients extra time to repay their loan as long as the payment came in before the report was due the following month. Other, more devious, staff realized that they could collude with the manager and simply not report a small number of the bad loans each month to make their numbers look better. Since bank reconciliations were usually two to three months behind, it took a long time for the head office staff to discover any problems. This was clearly unacceptable and warranted immediate dismissal, but as we still needed the staff to manage the portfolios, we gave them two months to correct their wrong-doings. Now we were able to see which clients had not paid each day. I gave the same sobering speech to our branch managers the following week just to make sure everyone understood our predicament. All the managers agreed to work hard to get the portfolio back to normal. Each branch and region set their own PAR targets for the two months and then signed performance agreements against those targets.

What aided everyone tremendously were the beautiful web-based and real time reports now available from the new system. A loan officer could pull up loan repayment history of each client on their tablets in the field and physically show the clients their payments and where they still owed money. The managers and head office staff could monitor progress daily on the efforts.

Varick and the IT team put in more long hours to make sure the remaining software problems were addressed and to support the field teams in any of their technical questions about the new system. I expected the clients to be furious and not pay; especially those clients who may have been misinformed that their loans were on time, when in fact they were late. But the response from the clients was similar to that of our field staff. Many of the clients knew they were late, but since the loan officer was not asking them for money (or in many cases not even attending their monthly meetings) the clients were not paying. When confronted, a vast majority of the clients gladly paid their missing balances so they could be in good standing with the company. Juhudi was one of the few lenders in Kenya willing to provide uncollateralized loans directly to rural smallholder farmers. Local SACCOS and village savings and loans groups did exist in many parts of the country and would occasionally lend to farmers. Although these local groups were quite limited in the loan amounts available and did not bundle in the risk management components such as insurance and farmer training like Juhudi. Our farmers had a strong incentive to stay in good standing with Juhudi to access the larger loans and invest in their farms for the future. I believe Juhudi represented an opportunity to many farmers as a way to finally break their cycle of subsistence agriculture and dependence on uncertain seasonal income from crops. Fortunately, many of the loans were not late by large amounts so the clients did not need to pay much to be current on their loans. Each week I sent out a detailed portfolio report email by office and loan officer showing their progress week to week.

The emotional toll from this crisis was absolutely debilitating for me. I was not sleeping again and I had lost about ten pounds in the past month from the added stress. All 145 of our staff would need to find other jobs and all the investors I had spent the last five years cultivating would likely lose all their money. The thing that stung the most about the high PAR was that it put into question the entire validity of the business model itself. If the PAR had actually been at thirty percent for the past five years then there would have been no way for us to raise any money. It questioned whether rural smallholder farmers could actually repay loans or should be avoided by financial institutions.

This went against the entire premise I was trying to prove.

We had made so much progress in turning the heads of large investors, commercial banks, governments and aid agencies to see that rural smallholder farmers can take commercial credit to improve their farms and do not need to be dependent on aid and government subsidies.

One night while wide awake at 2am worrying about the future of Juhudi, I was startled to hear three very loud and quick gunshots seemingly right outside my bedroom window. I had heard enough of the rapid-fire AK-47s blasts in the night to know they usually belonged to the police and could differentiate their noise from the softer, single-shot handguns. However this shot was much louder than a handgun. Several people started shouting and arguing. My neighbor, Jen Cantwell, who probably still has some PTSD from the Westgate incident texted me if I had heard that. I told her that I believed it was the police and told her not to go near any windows. We heard a few more shots and yelling before a long period of silence.

The next morning I asked around and found an article buried on the 8th page of the Nairobi Standard paper about two men who were trying to steal a transformer off of a power line on my street. Police were celebrated for shooting and killing one of the thieves and capturing another. That pole with the transformer was twenty-seven feet from my bedroom window and my head. It was not too comforting knowing someone had been killed practically right next to me.

Turkana

In June, Steve Wardle was being transferred by Grameen back to the US. This was tough on Juhudi as Steve had become one of the most vocal and knowledgeable board members we had. Before his trip home Steve wanted one last adventure in Kenya.

One of the most wild and remote parts of the country is Lake Turkana in the northwestern corner of Kenya, near the border with Sudan and Ethiopia. This region is typically avoided, due to the high number of armed bandit attacks. It is nearly a two-day drive from Nairobi over rough, dry terrain. But the lake was said to be spectacular with its blue colors and amazing surrounding scenery.

Steve's father is a pastor and would visit Kenya regularly on mission trips. One of Steve's father's acquaintances ran the mission for a particular church in northern Kenya. Steve managed to work this connection for us to get a chartered flight from Nairobi to Turkana for up to five people and we only needed to pay the cost of fuel and the pilot's accommodation. I thought a trip like this might take my mind off things. Hopefully, Steve would not want to talk too much about Juhudi over the weekend. Besides, to get a private flight up to Turkana and around the lake was a fantastic opportunity.

Neeta, myself and Brian Dempsey – the one I played golf with and who worked for a rival micro-finance company – all joined Steve on the expedition. We loaded into the tiny prop plane and met the American pilot, named Joel, who briefed us on the flight. We were first to fly to Loiyangalani on the east side of the lake and refuel. Then we would fly over the lake and land on the west side to stay in a lodge for a night. The next day we would fly over the lake again and stay in Loiyangalani for a night before heading back to Nairobi. If at any time we saw something on the ground that was interesting we should let Joel know so he could make another pass. The flight path would take us over the Aberdares Mountains, if clouds did not get in the way. It turned out that the plane was not instrument rated, so was unable to fly safely through clouds.

We took off to the west and soared over the Ngong Hills and the Great Rift Valley. Then the clouds started to surround us and the pilot dropped very low to the ground to the point where I could see the drivers in the cars along the highway. We were trapped in dense clouds in the Rift Valley. Joel told us he would radio back to Wilson Airport to land and wait for the clouds to lift.

On our way back, Joel spotted a clearing in the cloud ceiling and quickly started to spiral the plane upwards in an ascent. Poor Neeta, who gets terribly airsick, was not enjoying the spins. We broke through the clouds into the sunshine above and, to the north, could see the bright green peaks of the Aberdares Mountains poking through. We drifted over the wide expanse of silvery wisps of clouds, which made it feel like we were on a ship at sea rather than a plane. Mount Kenya rose sharply to our right and we could make out herds of elephants below us grazing in the Aberdares.

The north side of the Aberdares gave way to the broad savannahs of the remote Laikipia region of Kenya. The clouds cleared but we ran into some wind shearing off the mountains, which tumbled the small plane around violently. In my dour mood I hardly noticed the heavy turbulence. A thought crept into my mind and I felt a strange sense of relief. If the plane went down and killed me, then at least I would not need to suffer any longer with the stress of running Juhudi.

I looked over at Neeta next to me and then young Brian who was sitting in the back and remembered that life was more valuable than that. At that moment I also realized that this company and its shareholders did not present a very healthy mental environment for me. It was time for me to start thinking about stepping aside before it all killed me. Of course, Juhudi still needed strong leadership during the PAR crisis but I told myself that I would get the company out of this crisis or honorably ride it to the bottom, but either way, I would leave.

The rest of the Turkana trip was nothing less than extraordinary. We made a quick refueling stop in Loiyangalani, where small children rolled the fuel barrels towards our plane and Steve, Brian and I all took turns manually pumping the fuel into the plane. Then we took off over the emerald green waters of Turkana to land in a remote field where a van picked us up to take us to our lakeside bungalow.

Turkana is home to a large wind farm, which generates electricity from the constant winds for the whole region. Those winds nearly blew down our thatched-roofed bungalows that night. In the morning Steve commandeered a motorboat to take us to an island in the lake not far from our lodge. Lake Turkana has the highest population of Nile crocodiles in the world. I had been in the water with the great white sharks in Cape Town that would leap out of the water to kill seals swimming on the surface. I wondered if the crocodiles could pull off the same move and leap into our boat. Luckily, they were all nesting on the island and none of them came near our boat.

The boat driver parked on a sandy beach and we took off, hiking up a steep incline towards a high ridge on the island. We were all expecting to see a grassy valley and maybe some more hills on the other side but were shocked and delighted to find a pristine blue lake and an island in the lake, with close to 10,000 pink flamingos. The island was formed from three volcanoes that had left large craters that filled with water. The high banks made it difficult for the crocodiles to reach the lake, which is why the flamingos flocked to the area.

We hiked down the ridge and went around the island to the next lake. This one was a deeper green in color, due to an abundance of plant life along the banks.

"This is the crocodile lake," the guide told us. Sure enough, a juvenile crocodile peeked out of the water to take a look at us. "The third lake on the other side is full of tilapia fish."

That island with the three colored lakes was one of the most bizarre and beautiful places I have ever seen. I hope to go back and fish for some of the tilapia next time.

In the afternoon, Joel whisked us away in his plane and we did a few laps around the top of the island, taking more pictures. The dirt runway had washed out so we needed to take two trips to carry all of us across the lake so that Joel could take off quicker with less weight. Joel actually paced the runway by foot to make sure he had enough distance to take off.

Fortunately, we had enough runway, and then all us took terrifying turns of co-flying the plane. We landed back again on the other coast in the town of Loiyangalani. It's the largest town on the massive lake and its mixed population was rich in culture from several local tribes from the surrounding communities. Young girls skipped along the dusty road adorned in brightly colored beadwork and wearing red and yellow dresses. They were on their way to a Samburu and Maasai wedding where young boys could be seen jumping in the distance, practicing their traditional dances. I could count the ribs on the cows, which made their way through the bleak landscape. Probably they were cows for the dowry payments at the wedding. Juhudi might not consider opening a branch in this town anytime soon because of the limited rainfall and agriculture. We were also at least a twelve-hour drive from the next town in any direction on bad roads full of bandits. But this community probably needed our loans more than any other place in Kenya. Astonishingly, several M-Pesa agents were in the town, marked out by their bright green Safaricom logo. Perhaps one day Juhudi Labs *would* find a way to provide asset loans to these remote communities via technology. That evening, we drove to a ridge to watch the sun melt away into the lake in the barren wasteland that looked more like the surface of a distant moon than Earth.

Turnaround

The trip to Turkana had helped clear my mind and pick up my spirits. We continued to monitor progress daily and I kept sending out my weekly performance email, highlighting the loan officers and branches that had shown the best improvement from the prior week.

Slowly the PAR started to drop. Some offices made massive improvements each week and by the end of June, the company had recovered KShs forty-six million. After the first week of July, an additional KShs ten million was collected, putting us on track to recover another KShs forty to fifty million in the month, which would bring the bad loans down to KShs seventy-four million. This was more than half of the original KShs 160 million. Shadrack's cool demeanor and relentless work ethic combined with Varick's brutal, data-driven directives pushed the field team's performance to levels not seen before. I was glad I had not listened to Rockefeller and fired Shadrack.

Miraculously, the company was not too far away from reaching the target of ten percent PAR by the end of July. I made a trip to New York that month to visit with our investors to reassure them and to try to convince them to put up another $1 million to float the company through the losses for the year.

I walked into the meeting with Acumen and sat down with one of the senior portfolio managers. The manager surprised me by how much he knew about Juhudi's current situation. He said he was interested in providing more equity but would only do it if Soros also committed. He added that he had a tight timeline and needed to get the money out the door in the next three to four months. This was difficult, especially given my experience with how slowly the legal process moves through Soros, Acumen and Grameen.

My next meeting was with Soros. I arrived early at the massive Soros building off Central Park and sat sweating in the July heat. I was surprised to have one of the most pleasant and positive meetings of my trip with their investment officer and in-house legal counsel. It turned out that Soros was still very supportive of Juhudi and quite interested in investing more money. The $1 million was a little small for them and they proposed to provide their share of an equity investment along with an additional $1 million in convertible debt if we needed it. This was great news.

With the two larger funds of Soros and Acumen on board for the investment, I thought Grameen would be easy. Not so. Grameen already had too many investments in Kenya and I deduced that they were not looking to make more investments for a while. However, Acumen and Soros eventually convinced Grameen to co-invest alongside them, although Grameen added the condition that Juhudi must first have a portfolio audit before anyone invested.

Back in Kenya, our field teams worked as if their jobs were on the line; which they were. Two regions in particular were becoming beacons of hope for the rest of the company. The largest region, the North Rift, had started off with one of the lowest discrepancies with a total PAR of sixteen percent in May and managed to bring that down to eight percent by the end of June. The Mount Kenya Region, which traditionally had had many problems with PAR and general compliance, was also in great shape with a PAR of eighteen percent down from twenty-six percent. The other two regions were continuing to struggle at twenty-three percent and thirty-three percent PAR.

Nancy and the Operations team were planning on enforcing the recent performance contracts, which would affect a large number of underperforming staff and branches. I held regular calls with our investors and lenders, updating them on the progress. We even had some fantastic new lenders such as Grameen Crédit Agricole from France who were still eager to provide us with a loan as soon as the PAR dropped below ten percent. Even the two new equity investors were holding on with interest as we continued to improve the portfolio quality.

The month of July came to a close with the PAR just above thirteen percent. While we did not quite reach our target, the massive improvement from over thirty-five percent in May to thirteen percent at the end of July was commendable. The board passed a write-off of KShs 35.9 million or $395,000, which was a fraction of the originally projected write-off. This write-off then brought the PAR down to 7.7% and back into compliance with many of our lender's contractual covenants.

The "turnaround" was one of the quickest our lenders had ever seen and spoke volumes about the committed team and drive of the field staff to perform. Of course, the crisis brought to light many problems with our internal controls, loan appraisals, staff training, oversight and general risk management.

After the write-off we were still not completely out of the woods, as several of the branch managers and one regional manager fell well short of their agreed targets. The regional manager for the Nyanza region was one of the oldest managers in the company and had worked with KDA when Juhudi was just a pilot program. His region had received an award for the best performing region in 2012 and the manager was a legend in the company. However the PAR for Nyanza was still at 16.5 percent before the write-off against a target of eight percent. There were some allegations of mismanagement and even fraud in the region, which our internal auditor was busy investigating. We called the manager in for a meeting along with five other branch managers from other branches that had not met their targets. Our intention was to hear from them about the challenges they were facing and what other measures the company could take to help improve the portfolio quality.

It is difficult to hire good quality managers and usually takes a minimum of six months to train a new manager, so we had no intention of immediately firing any of the managers. However, before we could even hold the meeting with the regional manager and the branch managers, they all resigned. We had seen this happen earlier in the year, when we implemented a quarterly performance appraisal system, and staff, who had received poor results, resigned before we could have the performance discussion with them. This self-selecting termination ultimately worked for the company, removing its low performing staff without legal logistics. The employment laws in Kenya make it extremely difficult for a company to terminate staff without significant documentation. A terminated employee can quickly become a major legal liability if their termination is not handled carefully. However if an employee resigns, that removes the question of liability for the company.

Our internal auditor fortunately had not turned up any major cases of fraud with staff taking money or creating fake clients. However, he did find numerous cases of dereliction of duty and gross mismanagement of clients. A vast number of the bad loans were provided legitimately to clients but little effort had been made by the loan officer or manager to appraise the loans adequately or provide any follow up services after those loans were made.

Juhudi badly needed an overhaul of its processes and better management oversight through stronger risk management. The company turned again to Varick Schwartz for help. Varick, who had had extensive experience in the risk department of a large bank in the US, was willing to establish a new risk management department and to improve the compliance of the field operations.

The company was battered by the massive turnaround and shaken up by the departure of five managers. It was not an easy time to put in place more changes. But we did not have a choice. All our investors were calling for a full investigation on the new IT system and the current portfolio to make sure our current numbers were accurate. The new equity investors were still moving forward with their due diligence and required this audit to be completed before they invested. We commissioned the international audit firm, BDO, to conduct a full portfolio audit and IT systems audit so everyone could sleep better at night. After a thorough and highly technical audit, BDO produced a 190-page report, outlining their findings on Juhudi's portfolio and new IT system. While they presented some very helpful findings, none of the problems uncovered were unknown to the Juhudi management. While BDO found that Juhudi fell short of global IT and banking process standards, the audit cleared the new IT system of any major problems and even hailed its functionality. This was all the news we needed to hear.

Rutundu Fire

My friend Andreas was turning thirty and planned a trip to Rutundu Lodge on a remote side of Mt. Kenya. This was the same lodge in which Prince William had proposed to Kate Middleton, which brought the location significantly more visitors each year. I had been up to the lodge twice before, for a quiet weekend away with friends. The lodge was also near two lakes full of large trout.

The nearly five-hour drive was held up by a massive ocean liner ship that was being transported by road from Mombasa to Lake Victoria. Something this large and dangerous would never be transported in the US or Europe, but there we were trying to pass the vessel which took up nearly two lanes of road. The road to Rutundu is not marked and Google Maps leads its faithful followers to a dead end nearly half way up Mt. Kenya. The occasional Kenyan farmer or pedestrian will know the way but, most of the time, they will just point in a random direction to be rid of us.

Once we finally made it to the lodge, we parked our cars in a lower lot and had our gear and supplies ferried across a large ravine while we walked around. There was no electricity and the lodges were self-catering so we needed to pack all of our food and drinks.

At nearly 12,000 feet the lodge can get quite cold at night. Fortunately, the designers had the foresight to build large fireplaces in each room. William and Kate certainly selected one of the most remote locations in the world to get engaged. The upper lake, called Lake Alice, was a solid two-hour climb up to an even higher altitude, but was well worth the effort. We were rewarded with crystal clear views of the rocky peaks of Mt. Kenya and the sprawling countryside below.

I noticed a plume of reddish grey smoke I could only think was a small forest fire in the distance. I had seen several clouds like this in Colorado during some of the major forest fires in that state. When the smoke blocks out the sun it bathes the ground in an eerie red hue. I did not think much about it, and we continued to climb up to one of the highest ridges in the hope of some more views.

Thick rainclouds rolled in and we were suddenly engulfed in fog. The temperature dropped noticeably and the rain started to trickle down on us. We put on our thin rain gear, which was effective against the rain but not so much against the wind and the freezing cold. The clouds made it difficult to navigate back to the primitive path that we had used on the way up to the lake. The five of us fanned out as we descended the mountainside in the hope of stumbling onto the trail. My hands started to go numb from the cold and the others around me were visibly shivering. We needed to get down quickly. It would be bad news if we could not find the trail back to the lodge as there was very little civilization for twenty miles in any direction. Hypothermia at that altitude was a serious threat and uncontrolled shivering was one of the first signs. I slipped and fell hard, spraining my left knee and right ankle. The combination made walking much more of a challenge for me. Finally, the rain started to subside and Andreas stumbled onto the trail and cheered for all of us to hear.

I limped back to the lodge where Neeta and some others were waiting with a fire and food. Water at the lodge was heated by wood furnaces and I used the scalding water to take one of the most enjoyable baths I have ever had in my life.

In the morning, the billowing clouds from the small forest fire had intensified and the air smelled of smoke. Small bits of white ash even drifted down on us from time to time. We did not have any mobile reception on the mountain so we asked the lodge caretaker (who had a two-way radio) if he had heard anything about the fire and if it was safe for us to drive back to Nairobi. The caretaker had not heard anything about a fire so we loaded up our two cars and started back down the rough mountain road.

We crested a hill where the smoke came into sight. All of us could see long tongues of flames lashing out at the brush below the smoke, less than a mile away. I followed the jagged line of fire along the horizon and noticed that it crossed the dirt road in the distance. There was only one road in and out of Rutundu, so we did not have much of a choice but to drive towards the fire. We rationalized that if a fire was burning up a mountain that it would eventually reach the Rutundu lodge at the higher elevation. So we continued on our way down towards the fire-line, hoping for the best.

The fire we found was a small brush fire only a few feet high but consuming everything in its path. We all jumped out to take some pictures and videos. The fire engulfed a taller bush and flames suddenly grew to well over twelve feet. We all jumped back into the cars and continued onward. We crossed into the burned section of the fire, which reminded me of a war zone or a post-apocalyptic landscape, with smoldering trees and everything covered in a grey ash. The road crossed the fire-line a few more times and we stopped to take pictures at each one. Then Andreas informed the group that his car was running out of gas.

Over the next hill, suddenly the smoke and flames intensified. An entire forest was ablaze in the distance, with flames reaching thirty to forty feet high. It was one of the most magnificent and terrifying fires I had ever seen. I was in the lead car and we stopped again to take more pictures and videos of the larger flames that were approaching us. But we were interrupted by Andreas honking his horn and waving his hands at us to move. Both cars pulled away just seconds before a long fireball rolled across the road, engulfing the bushes where we had just been taking pictures.

The inside of the cars started to get a little warmer and the road was difficult to see through all the smoke. I thought that things were getting a bit serious. I was worried that we could be engulfed by the flames, which would melt our tires or perhaps ignite the fuel tanks, or, we could die from the asphyxiating smoke all around us.

We came into a long flat section of road that lined by large flames on both sides. Only a few burning branches were in the middle of the road and it looked like the fire had lessened on the other side of the section, perhaps 300 feet away.

"Maybe if we drive fast we can make it," my friend, who was driving, suggested.

He revved the engine and we sped forward, bouncing through the rough road and fire. I was in the passenger seat and was shocked and horrified to realize that the left side of my face and my left arm were starting to heat up as if being burned by the sun. I shifted away from the hot door cursing the whole way as we hurtled through the flames. Andreas made it through with his car too. On the other side of the fire we came across two trucks full of park rangers and fire fighters. I half expected them to rush over to make sure we were all right and treat us for smoke inhalation. But then I remembered we were in Kenya. The rangers were sitting in their cars just watching the fire blaze away. With few resources to fight a major forest fire, there was not much that could be done.

The rangers, of course, asked us to provide our park entrance tickets, no doubt looking for bribes if we did not have our paperwork. Fortunately, we had all purchased entrance tickets days before and they let us pass while the flames continued their march up the mountain. The Kenyan newspapers did not mention a single thing about the fire that easily consumed tens of thousands of acres across one of the top tourist destinations. We have the pictures and videos to prove it and we were lucky to get out with our lives.

Chapter 17 | Road to Recovery

The new system was humming along and Varick and I were able to generate a beautiful analysis and report to share with management and our investors. At our next board meeting I thought the PAR fires had been dampened enough to ask the board again to consider equity shares for the management. This would be my fifth formal plea to the board and nothing had been done since the first meeting of the year. The management team had helped drive the recovery from certain destruction in 2014 and I thought that would justify recognition. The board spoke about needing to hire a consultant or lawyer to structure the plan and they were not ready. I offered to help them with this but it was decided that it might be a conflict of interest to structure my own employee share ownership plan. Something made me wonder if the board ever intended to make good on their promises for shares. I tried not to take this personally. I began to question if I was even wanted in the company any longer. While I had never once received a performance review as CEO, I had also never been given any negative feedback about how I was managing the company. What feedback there was from the board, had been positive.

However the feedback from the lenders and potential investors was quite different. In times of trouble, some of our lenders applauded me and my team for keeping the company alive, but others had laid into me. The two new equity investors were extremely critical of me and my style during their due diligence, yet they had emerged positive enough to want to invest in the company. Perhaps my sense of feeling unappreciated by the board is common to other entrepreneurs. I tried to put it behind me and to focus on the problems at hand, while looking to our clients during my road trips for my best source of feedback.

Looking back, if I were to start a rural microfinance institution again, I would have started by investing in a robust IT system before building the processes and hiring staff. Having a reliable and effective way to manage data was paramount to driving performance and combating fraud. Many of our offices were resisting the new changes and especially the presence of our new risk management department. Having now gone through multiple change processes, the management team was getting much better at communicating the changes and providing training to staff on the new processes or procedures. No change comes without resistance and communicating with our remote field offices was always a challenge. Patience and persistence had pulled us through the difficult times in the past and it would serve us well again.

We did have a few bright spots during this time. The global consulting company, Bain and Company, had recently conducted a major research study into Acumen Fund's portfolio companies to identify successful business models in the social enterprise sector. The consultants zeroed in on Juhudi and we became their poster child for a business model. The final report was called *Growing Prosperity* and Acumen wanted me to present it, along with the Bain consultants, in November at its annual Partner Gathering in New York. I was happy to participate and I planned to stay in the US the following week so I could spend Thanksgiving with my parents and brother for the first time in six years.

I continued to stay involved in the East Africa social business community by volunteering my time with start-up entrepreneurs through great programs such as Village Capital and the Unreasonable Institute, which select cohorts of entrepreneurs to incubate and accelerate them to improve their ideas or businesses by connecting them to resources and mentors.

I flew to Uganda for the inaugural Unreasonable Institute East Africa program and spent several days with social entrepreneurs. I connected with many of the participants as a like-minded colleague who had probably experienced some of the same challenges.

As well as my personal desire to save these entrepreneurs some of the headaches and hardships associated with starting a social business in the region, and especially all the drama I had faced with fundraising, there was also a professional reason for my engagement with these startup companies. The burgeoning Juhudi Labs Program was now gaining significant traction and funding.

HBS

The Harvard Business School invited me for an exclusive conference on access to finance at the Harvard campus in Boston in October. I was looking forward to the opportunity to pitch our new ideas from Juhudi Labs and especially some of the credit modeling work we were developing with Varick. Over the years I found myself flying to places like Jordan and Panama to present at various conferences about Juhudi's business model. Most of the conferences took a lot of my time away from running the company and did not result in many tangible benefits. In Panama, I was attending a VIP session along with forty other CEOs but the organizers confused me for one of the university volunteers and refused to let me in the room. I pleaded: "I am Nat Robinson and I am the CEO of Juhudi Kilimo in Kenya. I am scheduled to speak in five minutes in this session." Looking neither Kenyan nor old enough to be a CEO, they were not convinced. Although, one of the benefits from the trips was all the free airline miles. I had attained very high air miles status on Emirates Airlines from my multiple journeys so I used some miles for a cheap upgrade to first class on my trip to Harvard, which was just amazing. I had my own private mini bar and champagne in my seat.

I had always wondered what kind of people fly international first class on Emirates. A large group of men in dark suits with American accents arrived on the flight very late, clearly driven by a private car to the tarmac to board the plane. I thought perhaps they were all diplomats and started talking to the guy next to me. The group turned out to be from the World Bank and had just finished a meeting with the President of Kenya, Uhuru Kenyatta.

At the end of the flight, I was reaching for my bag in the overhead compartment when I accidentally knocked against another passenger, a short Asian man. I apologized politely and the man made a nice comment in a perfect American accent about still being asleep from the overnight flight. I noticed nearly everyone in the first-class cabin was staring at me in shock. Maybe because I was so tall and clearly did not look like I should be in first class, with my torn jeans and wrinkled shirt. Later that day I looked up news stories about the World Bank and what the visit to Kenya was all about. Sure enough, the short man I had bumped in the plane was none other than the President of the World Bank, Jim Yong Kim, who was negotiating a loan agreement with Kenya. So those are the people who fly first class on Emirates.

The Harvard conference was enlightening and I was able to spend some time with the world authorities on microfinance and credit. Amazingly, several of the professors and attendees had actually heard of Juhudi Kilimo, which made my little presentation even more engaging for them. The event was limited to fifty people so that regular dialogues and discussions could be conducted, like that of a business school class. One of the challenges that came up was the lack of adequate regulation of microfinance and the absence of client protection from predatory lending practices in countries where government and central banks were weak. I made a comment about utilizing more technology and social media for the clients to help in regulating the financial institutions, similar to the way TripAdvisor has changed the hospitality and restaurant industry. Thinking that the group might question the possibility of a rural Kenyan having access to the internet to post such feedback I referenced Juhudi Kilimo's own Facebook page, which was full of clients' comments and feedback.

Many of our younger clients were using internet cafes in rural Kenya to post their thoughts about the Juhudi Kilimo services. The other user group was made up of the relatives of our clients who lived in the cities and so had better access to computers to post on behalf of their parents or aunts, who were taking loans from Juhudi. I always thought it was healthy for a company to allow its customers to voice their comments, concerns and ideas for improving the company in a public and transparent way. We left any negative comments on our Facebook page at Juhudi and worked with the clients to try and resolve the issues or at least promote a dialogue. This was unheard of in Kenya at the time and shocked many of the people posting the comments. A vast majority of the issues were solved by a quick phone call to the loan officer or accounts team to reconcile a payment or loan application.

Time to go

Both Progression and I&P had received the green light to proceed with the negotiations for an equity investment of a combined $3 million with Juhudi Kilimo. Our board and investors were eager to get new equity into the company. Two other equity investors on my list also expressed interest but noted that it would take them a few more months to get their full offer together. This was nice since it put us in a position where we were not desperate and could choose the new investor. I pushed very hard for Progression and I&P because I strongly believed their experience in the region and sector would bring long-term value to Juhudi and complement our social investors in terms of their expertise.

Growth had started to return again, along with profitability. I thought this would be a good opportunity for me to tell the board that I was ready to leave. I believed I had reached my personal goal, where I could leave Juhudi in good hands to continue and thrive without me.

Both Progression and I&P were shocked that I did not have any shares in the business. They saw management equity as a way of retaining staff and aligning long-term incentives. Acumen, Grameen and Soros must have had their reasons for avoiding providing shares to the management of Juhudi. I certainly did not think the shares were worth anything and merely represented sentimental value. It would have been nice to have owned even a single piece of the company I helped start and worked so hard for over the years

I was also wrecked after the K-Rep drama and PAR crisis. My hair had started to go grey and I was perpetually tired from the previous months of exhaustion. I had sacrificed so much for Juhudi Kilimo.

But the pluses had dramatically outweighed these negative factors. Tens of thousands of farmers had benefited and I loved seeing the young Kenyan loan officers and interns grow into mature and professional managers. I thought of our many clients who had borrowed money from Juhudi to buy a cow, worked hard to raise the cow and produce milk, then repay their loan and went on to own that cow outright. The ownership of that income-generating asset is what brings sustaining and sustainable wealth to the rural poor. I hope that someday the shareholders of Juhudi will consider providing similar ownership of Juhudi to the employees and clients in the future. Regardless, even if I did have shares in Juhudi, it would not have changed the fact that I was burned out and ready for the next challenge in my life. It was time.

I decided to only talk to Aleke about my decision. Aleke certainly understood my position and was personally frustrated with the board and investors' positions on providing shares to management. I also thought that if I started talking to the board about my plans that they would try to convince me to stay longer, which I knew was not healthy for me. So I drafted my three-month notice and, at the end of one of our general board update conference calls, I dropped the bomb.

Nobody likes surprises, especially a board of investors. They were all shocked and asked for a few days to digest it all. The board sounded disappointed with me and begged that I at least extend my leave period from December until March so they could use the time to find a new CEO. I certainly did not want my departure to harm the company so I was happy to comply. I also offered to stay in touch remotely over email for several months after March to help with the transition.

I felt obligated also to inform the board of our two new potential investors, Progression and I&P. Over the last year I had developed a really good relationship with Progression and I&P and respected them deeply. I hoped that my news would not frighten them off and that they could see it as an opportunity to play a role in hiring the new CEO.

The responses from our investors to my imminent departure were varied. Grameen seemed indifferent; Soros was upset and genuinely sorry to see me moving on. But it was Acumen that really surprised me.

Ever since Acumen had been invested in 2011 I had gone out of my way to participate in their research, speak at their events, send my staff to their fellowship programs and generally promote their work and support as an investor at every opportunity. Juhudi was also important to Acumen. I had heard that Juhudi was one of the few companies in the Acumen portfolio that had a potential for a profitable exit, which would essentially prove Acumen's model of 'patient capital' after over fifteen years of trying. Jacqueline Novogratz had invited me for a one-on-one dinner several months earlier to show how much she cared about Juhudi and to thank me for the work that was put in over the years. I had met many important people before at my first job in Colorado with the El Pomar Foundation. While working at the 2004 G8 Summit I had met Tony Blair, Vladimir Putin and even shook hands a few times with President Bush and Laura Bush. However none of that prepared me for my meeting with Jacqueline. Jacqueline is one of those spectacular people who exude a 'reality distortion field', like Steve Jobs, which leaves people convinced they can do absolutely anything to change the world. We connected at dinner over being vegetarians and runners and I fell deeply under her spell. Jacqueline continued to send me encouraging emails and books to help light my way forward.

Overall, I thought Acumen was a fantastic investor. We had benefited significantly from their Fellows program and received considerable support from their TA grants. Acumen even convinced the international bestseller and business author, Seth Godin, to spend a day with our management team to share some of his wisdom about marketing. Of course, we also had tremendous challenges with Acumen due to the extremely high staff turnover in Nairobi, which churned out four Juhudi board members in four years. Acumen did not help us bring in any additional investors but that was no longer a priority for Juhudi. Our current board member from Acumen, Sapna Shah, was quickly becoming one of our greatest supporters and worked tirelessly to keep things moving at Acumen around Juhudi.

Two days after I informed the board of my decision I received a phone call from Sapna telling me that I was no longer invited to the Acumen Partner Gathering in New York, which was only a few weeks away. I told Sapna that I was still an employee of Juhudi and would be for many more months and

I was happy to represent the company at their conference. My family in the US was eagerly anticipating my visit for Thanksgiving that following week. It was too late to change or cancel my international flights without paying significant fees. Sapna was quite disappointed in Acumen's seemingly petty decision and I clearly understood it had nothing to do with her. I had thought I was special after having dinner with Jacqueline, but perhaps I was merely a pawn in the larger game. Maybe Acumen was more interested Juhudi's prospects in bringing them more donor money because of our story. As soon as they knew I was leaving Juhudi, Acumen had no further use for me. I suppose it was a good lesson for me not to think any of these investors or funds would actually care much about the CEO after receiving a resignation letter.

I held several meetings and calls with the Progression and I&P team who were getting concerned about all the major changes already going on with Juhudi, following the PAR crisis. Having a leadership change would not help anything. However, they eventually came around and continued to move forward with their investment. My board had told me to wait a few weeks before telling our lenders and staff, until the board could prepare a clear plan for the transition. Although, before I could personally inform our lenders, with whom I had spent years building relationships, I received an email from Rockefeller. Rockefeller had heard from an official at Acumen that I was leaving. The Rockefeller investment officers were quite hurt that the news did not come from me directly. I am not sure why Acumen did this. I quickly informed the rest of our lenders, management team and staff before the news could leak any further. It was not easy news to share on the heels of the PAR crisis. I wanted everyone to understand that I was not running away from a dying company, but that it was just the time in my life for a change. Acumen, Grameen and Soros offered to provide a very generous performance bonus for my hard work over the years. This was certainly a kind gesture and I appreciated the consideration. I again asked, one final time, if the company could provide me with shares of Juhudi instead for my bonus and save the cash for loans to farmers. The answer was no.

Most CEOs of microfinance institutions in Kenya last five to seven years, probably due to the elevated levels of stress in managing such difficult businesses with limited resources. I reiterated that Juhudi was in one of the strongest positions it had ever been in over the past few years and that this was a good time for me to transition. I followed the announcement with a round of visits to the field offices to quell any anxiety and have open discussions with the staff. This seemed to help somewhat, and I could reassure all of them that Juhudi would continue to survive after my departure. Nancy, Shadrack and I thought it might also be time for another all-staff retreat sometime in March to help with this transition.

Namibia

The long and terrible year of 2014 came to a close for Juhudi and the management team thought it would be a good idea to close the offices for a few weeks to let the staff recover from the brutal few months of recovery and change. With only three more months remaining for me at Juhudi, I wanted to get in a few more adventures in Africa before my next move took me away from Kenya. Neeta and I had always wanted to go to Namibia to see the picturesque deserts and vast shorelines of the Skeleton Coast. The only way to see Namibia properly is to rent a truck yourself and drive along its dusty country roads. Our friend Brian had moved to Botswana with his job and he was interested in coming along with us on a road trip through Namibia for Christmas and the New Year.

I very easily (and cheaply) rented a double cab pickup truck complete with two pop-up tents on the roof. These tents are fantastic and fold over to create spacious tents similar to that of a children's pop-up book. The tents allow you essentially to camp anyplace you can park the car. Since the tents are elevated, they provide slightly more security from the roving animals on the ground. However, if a determined lion or elephant really wanted to get at us they probably still could.

We rented the truck through a South African company, which impressed us at every step of the trip. The truck-turned camper came equipped with cooking equipment, pots, pans, camping chairs and a wonderful refrigerator/cooler, which hooked into the truck's battery to provide us with cold beer and fresh meat throughout the trip.

Namibia's small capital city of Windhoek did not offer much, other than a good place to relax and stock up for our journey. It seemed that all the major destinations were about a five-hour drive from one another, which meant we spent plenty of time in the truck together. Coming from Kenya, I could not help but be thoroughly impressed with the quality of the roads, especially the well-graded dirt roads that were wide and flat. However, the good roads also encouraged speeding. We certainly saw our share of cars that had slid or rolled off the roads.

We spent the first few days of the trip hiking and driving through the epic red sand dunes of Sossusvlei. We hiked to the top of the highest vlei, or dune, and tumbled down the other side getting covered in sand. The famous Deadvlei is known for its salt flat, which houses the eerie 400-year-old dead acacias that had once grown when the basin held water. The contrast of the flat white salt floor, black dead wood with branches reaching out like gnarled fingers all against the red backdrop of the rolling dunes makes for some fascinating pictures. After getting our truck stuck a few times in the sand we made our way across the desolate dry landscape towards the expansive Atlantic coast. We followed the pilgrimage of white pickup trucks along the coast to the quaint beach town of Swakopmund. The trucks were mostly owned by white South Africans and Namibians, who descended on the coast each Christmas to fish the productive shore for small sharks, bluefish and other game fish. The beaches were lined for hundreds of miles with groups of people fishing, barbecuing and camping.

Namibia was once a German colony. We found that several of the towns in Namibia still retained the German heritage and Swakopmund was no exception. The central square looked quite like that of Munich, with small beer halls and sausages hanging in the windows of German restaurants. The streets felt more like a town in Europe than any place in Africa. We spent New Year's Eve in Swakopmund dancing and singing with the Namibians and South Africans. I was most looking forward to driving through the remote Skeleton Coast, so named because of the high number of whale bones and shipwrecks on the beach that make the place look like a graveyard for giant beasts. But it could just as easily be the way the rippling sand dunes (running right into the ocean) look like the ribs of a skeleton.

We made our way up the long drive to the gates of the Skeleton Coast. Each gate was adorned with an ominous skull and crossbones. A few hours later we managed to find some great shipwrecks and huge whale bones still littering the coast. People told us that both the whales and ships sometimes get disoriented in the fog and crash into the rocky reefs just off the sandy desert beaches. We also found what looked like large hyena or lion tracks on the sand. Then we found dozens of dog-like skulls with bits of fur clinging to them. Only after we found the intact, curved vertebrae of one of the animals did we realize that they were fur seals.

We had stayed the night in a town called Cape Cross, which was near one of the largest fur seal colonies in the world. Over 200,000 seals flocked to this small jetty of land to breed and raise their young pups. I have never been more overwhelmed by the sheer crush of animals in my life. There were thousands of seals floating in the waves and covering every rock or piece of sand. All of them were barking, snorting and growling at each other. The young black pups were concentrated more on shore in the rocks and under the constructed boardwalk. They looked like black lab dog puppies, only with flippers and tails. The worst part of the colony was the putrid smell of wet seal, feces and decaying dead seals. The smell clung to certain types of clothes and Neeta had to hang her scarf out the window of our truck for several days to keep us all from passing out.

We continued to stay in campsites and cook dinners as we watched the sun set over the ocean or deserts. For our last few days we made a long drive inland to a more mountainous part of the country in search of a campsite and lodge that we had seen pictures of in a coffee table photobook at a restaurant in Cape Cross. The remote camp was set in a beautiful valley surrounded by rolling hills with large boulders scattered around. The owner was a middle aged German man born in rural Namibia, who had spent his whole life in the same small town. He was excited to have us as camping guests and proceeded to cook us a fabulous meal of several different kinds of grilled meat. We all enjoyed a peaceful sunset and evening of stories by the campfire that night before making our journey back home to Nairobi the next day.

The Mobius final tour

Nearly three years after providing the pre-order deposit of $500, the Mobius company had finally started rolling out its new vehicle. The founder and CEO, Joel Jackson, was brilliant at raising money and attracting all the fame needed to be successful at starting a car-manufacturing business. Joel had acquired some high-profile local investors and even convinced the Kenyan President, Uhuru Kenyatta, to purchase a Mobius, which dramatically helped local publicity. Joel was also recognized by Fortune Magazine's 30 under 30 of global entrepreneurs, all before he had even sold or produced his first commercial vehicle.

I was excited about the prospects of a low-cost vehicle specifically designed for operating in rural Kenya. Transportation in rural Kenya was a nightmare with the poor infrastructure. This type of new car could help our farmers move more of their farm produce to bigger markets and help them transport seeds, fertilizers and even livestock as needed.

I also saw an opportunity to use the Mobius vehicles for the Juhudi operations, especially with the branch offices. Our loan officers were spending between fifty percent and seventy percent of their day traveling to reach our rural clients by public transport, such as the matatus and motorcycle taxis. We had an experimental loan product for our staff to purchase motorcycles but it was not particularly popular. Riding a motorcycle was not only dangerous in Kenya but they were difficult to use, especially after the rains made the roads nearly impassable with mud.

The first model of the Mobius was extremely basic with no windows, manual steering and front-wheel drive, which did not make it particularly practical for the dusty mountainous roads in many parts of rural Kenya. Juhudi was provided with one of the first few models, along with President Kenyatta, Aleke and Benson from La Playa. The latter two were customers that I had introduced to Joel and Mobius.

We took the car for its inaugural drive by taking our head office staff to the go-karting track near the Wilson Airport in Nairobi. Every quarter I had taken our staff to the racecourse for an afternoon of racing and fun at the restaurant and bar that overlooked the track. The initiative was an idea of one of our young employees named Elvin (who also happened to be one of the best go-kart drivers at the company). We drove the Mobius through the Friday afternoon traffic and it received lots of attention. Other drivers were stopping to take pictures, pedestrians were pointing and I even had a group of people in a large SUV offer to buy the Mobius from me. I would answer all of their looks and questions by shouting "made in Kenya!" and slapping the side of the car. The Kenyans always beamed with pride at that comment.

The engineering team at Mobius requested that we first drive the vehicle for 75kms in Nairobi before taking it outside the city to make sure there were no problems. That weekend I took Andreas, his girlfriend Karis, and one of my other friends, who worked with Andreas, Mike Jelinske, out to Nairobi National Park for a game drive, to break in the Mobius. The vehicle performed beautifully, although it made a tremendous amount of noise, which made it difficult for us to stalk any animals. On our way out of the park, around dusk, we came headlong across a male lion standing in the middle of the road and blocking the way. The Mobius has an open cabin with no windows so my passengers were a little wary of the large predator coming our way. Fortunately, the lion veered off the road just fifteen feet in front of us and continued on his way around the vehicle before returning to the road and casually loping off into the sunset.

That next week I finished my last round of solo field office visits in the Mobius, making a grueling eleven-office tour over five days in Western Kenya. I am sure no guidebook would recommend any foreigner taking an open-air car with no locking doors on a week-long road trip by themselves through rural Kenya. But I had employees all over the country, I spoke Kiswahili and I had traveled to all of these areas many times before, so I was not worried. The only unknown variable was the Mobius.

I left Nairobi at 4am in the pitch black on my way to my first stop in Molo, about three hours away. I had a tight schedule in trying to reach our offices in Molo, Siongori, Kilgoris, Kenyenya and Kisii. A few hours in, I quickly realized that the phone charger connected to the cigarette lighter would not produce enough power to charge my phone. I was depending on Google Maps to guide me through the back roads of Kenya as it had done for so many years, so this could become a problem.

I was flagged down at the first police roadblock just outside of Nairobi. I had been harassed and threatened by so many police looking for bribes in Kenya that I knew the drill well. Just be polite and hit them with as much Kiswahili as possible in the first few minutes, then if they start asking for money or requesting documents just politely decline and wait them out with small talk. Most of the police will give up at this point and just let you go. However these police were more interested in the Mobius. From the front, the Mobius looked like a Land Rover Defender but had a bit of a utility or military look on the sides and back. One of the police officers thought I might be with Al-Shabaab until he looked closely at the driver. I had to tell them all the specifics of the Mobius and how it was made in Kenya as a low cost rural vehicle. They were all impressed and let me go on my way. I managed to get stopped three more times at various checkpoints and went through the same routine. One police officer even sat in the passenger seat with me to try out the seats.

The stops made me an hour late to the first office, where I quickly met with a stressed group of field officers worried about missing their first client meetings. I charged my dying phone and then made off down the dusty road to the next office. The day started to get a little warmer, so I opened up all the canvas flaps to get more ventilation into the Mobius. The problem with this was that when I was driving on the dirt roads, any oncoming vehicles would cover me and all my stuff in dust.

The Mobius excelled on the bumpy rural roads and I flew by all the slow moving taxis and motorcycles. I met with staff, showed them the Mobius, and answered questions about my departure as CEO or about the future of the company. Each small town I entered, I was greeted by whistles, shouts and chased by small children who all wanted to learn more about the strange looking Mobius.

Exhausted from the day of driving and meeting staff, I spent the night in a Kisii hotel and prepared for the next day of visiting three larger offices in the region. I believe my Kenyan staff loved these courtesy visits and the chance to speak with me about their problems or new ideas. At least this way none of the staff could give me a hard time for not coming to visit them at our retreat in March.

On my way to Molo I missed a turn, but Google re-routed me to another road that was still under construction but open. It had not rained in Kenya for many months. Opaque clouds of dust spewed up all around me as I plowed down the road. As long as I did not stop or come across another vehicle going the other way I would be fine. It was only a few miles to the town of Molo anyway. A few minutes later two massive trucks came down the other direction and coated me, and everything in the Mobius, with dust. I then came up to a small car kicking up a storm of dust which I passed as quickly as I could. When I pulled up to the Molo office, the Mobius had changed color, from black to brown. I stepped out of the door and the dust seemed to trail float from me in a mist at each step. The staff did not recognize me at first. Then they informed me that a pipe had broken in the office and there was not any water to wash the dust from my hands and face. I am sure they were wondering what kind of CEO takes an open-air vehicle along that road to Molo.

I drove onward through the rolling Nandi hills, which are covered in bright green tea estates that looked like freshly mown lawns. The sun started to set as I motored through a valley full of sugar cane fields, dotted with hills on both sides. I wondered if the Kenyans living in this divine valley appreciated the beauty of their landscape.

Earlier in the week I had been having some trouble with the door latches on the Mobius, which would not always lock properly when closed and occasionally opened when driving around a sharp corner. At one point I was driving up one of the steep inclines and passing a large cargo truck on a two-lane road. The Mobius had some decent power due to its light weight, which helped on these types of hills. A car appeared, coming down the hill in the other direction in my passing lane, so I accelerated around the corner to get past the truck quickly. The passenger door suddenly shot open, nearly clipping the truck as I passed. I lunged over to close the door and barely passed the truck before the other car barreled past me on the other side. I certainly hope Joel and the Mobius team have fixed that door problem.

I loved driving the Mobius throughout the rest of the trip around Kenya. The basic car has a way of connecting the driver to the road with the manual transmission and non-powered steering, which I think is lost in most modern cars.

I spent my last night in the middle of the peaceful Kakamega rainforest before returning to Nairobi, having driven over 1,000 kilometers on the solo trip. The trip was dangerous, something the US Embassy would have cringed about if they knew a US citizen was planning such a journey. My own Kenyan management team even objected to my going. The road trip was one of my last adventures in Kenya. I had learned Kiswahili, become an expert in navigating the country's deadly rural roads and built a network of offices full of friendly staff in some of the most remote towns and villages in rural Kenya. It was also my way of saying goodbye to a country I had come to love over the past six years.

Retreat and Bernard

Harold Rosen had heard the news that I was resigning and asked to meet for breakfast when he was in Nairobi. It was actually Harold's secretary who asked me and Harold was the last person I wanted to talk to. I still did not like the guy after he had left Aleke and me to fundraise all by ourselves. GBF had raised a ton more money after their 'success' with companies like Juhudi and I expected Harold to tell me all about how GBF had become the greatest fund known to man, much bigger than Juhudi could ever be. I remembered Aleke's wisdom about not holding grudges, sucked up my pride and agreed to meet with Harold. Besides, Harold's tough love approach to us worked and nearly all his general predictions about Juhudi turned out to be right.

I could not have anticipated a more pleasant and humbling breakfast with Harold. He was friendly, considerate and quite complimentary toward me. As it turned out, Harold had run into some difficulty raising his last round of money at GBF. His normally arrogant approach was muted by several high level rejections from big investors, including his own IFC. Getting told "no" hurts, as I certainly learned many times. Harold told me they were running out of money, and how painful it was to think he might not be able to pay his staff or the office rent after a few more months. This was something I had faced almost all the time at Juhudi. I remembered that Harold had spent basically his entire professional career at the World Bank and IFC. He said: "We had plenty of challenges working at the IFC but running out of money was certainly never one of them." Harold had a whole new level of respect for the realities faced by the entrepreneurs he was investing in at GBF.

I left our breakfast with much more admiration for Harold and his team. He was able to overcome his cash problems at GBF and raise tens of millions of dollars for the organization. The GBF is still one of the few impact investors transparent enough to post their internal rate of returns from their investment on their website. My guess is that the rest of the impact investors are losing money but, hopefully, that will change over time.

The idea behind me staying on at Juhudi through to March of 2015, even though I had handed in my official resignation the previous October, was to give the board more time to find my replacement. Over the last few years I had been grooming Shadrack to be my clear number two and regularly exposed him to our investors and board so that he could be a strong candidate for the CEO position. In the scenario where an outside candidate was not found, Shadrack would make a fine CEO. He had already served in this position with an MFI in Burundi. He was also well liked and respected among the Juhudi employees.

In typical impact investor style, our board and investors did not even start the recruitment process until January of 2015. An external executive search firm was engaged and both Progression and I&P provided multiple resumés of potential candidates for everyone to consider. As a member of the board, I was asked to participate in the final shortlisting and even sat in on the interviews.

Fortunately, by February we had established an impressive short-list of six candidates, half of whom were current CEOs of microfinance institutions, and all of them had significant leadership experience in banking or microfinance in East Africa. All of them were Kenyan too, which was a significant advantage. Over the last six years I had intentionally tried not to rely on the abundance of cheap high-quality talent coming to Kenya from the US and Europe, so that we could build a strong Kenyan management team. Most of the social enterprises at the time, such as One Acre Fund, Bridge International, Sanergy, M-Kopa and nearly all the numerous cookstove and solar companies, had senior management positions held by expatriates. In their defense, it is difficult to find management talent and especially any technical skills in Kenya for a reasonable price that a young social enterprise could afford.

In my opinion, most of this was due to the NGO and multinational wage inflation in Kenya, but it is also just supply and demand in the local market for talent. However, the greatest long-term risk I saw with having expatriates in critical management positions was the likelihood that those staff could leave the country at any time if Kenya experienced more election violence, an Ebola outbreak or even if Kenya continued to tighten the already restrictive immigration policies. Other than a few exceptions, most of the expats I had met in Kenya did not last more than two or three years, causing the organizations to have to re-hire and train new staff constantly.

Shadrack was included among the finalists, but I think the board wanted to compare him with the other candidates. I personally wanted a candidate who could take Juhudi from 20,000 clients and an asset base of $10 million to a company with 100,000 and $50 million in assets. These types of managerial skills seemed to be easier to find in the market than someone with successful early-stage startup experience. I was looking for a manager who had demonstrated a strong ability to organize a team and improve performance. All of Juhudi Kilimo's current problems were people-related. We had the finances, systems, processes, market and products but we needed a lot of help in driving the senior management team in one direction and building our young middle managers, who found themselves now running offices after all the departures in the previous year.

A good manager will see the need both to bolster growth and control risk, without letting either area take too much priority over the other. Most importantly, Juhudi needed someone with experience of running a larger commercial microfinance institution, which was ideally regulated by a central bank. While commercial banking shared some similarities with microfinance, anyone in the industry will tell you that the business models are quite different and it is a mistake to assume that 'lending is lending' and 'money is money'. The unsecured, group-based lending model requires much more focus on people and processes than traditional bank lending, which requires efficient use of collateral. On a deeper, more cultural level, it is a difficult psychological leap for a commercial banker, who is used to juicy profit margins on their loans, to want to lend to rural low-income clients with no asset base and who barely makes any money in the transaction.

As each candidate came through the interviews I tried to imagine how they would do when facing Shadrack or Nancy in a meeting. I asked tough questions about specific staff conflicts we have had in the past at Juhudi and how they might approach them. At the board's suggestion, I even put together a case study with a hypothetical management problem and artificial data so the candidates could show the board how they would approach a challenge and communicate their solutions.

After the interviews, one candidate, in my mind, stood well above the rest. His name was Bernard and he was a current CEO for a midsized, regulated, commercial microfinance institution in Rwanda, which was larger than Juhudi. Bernard answered all of the management questions brilliantly and had a spotless track record of balancing both growth and quality control, which are the two most important things in microfinance (or most growing businesses for that matter). He was gruff, slightly arrogant, had limited charisma and very limited understanding of some of the innovations taking place in the microfinance sector at the time. But he was perfect for what Juhudi needed at the time. This was not easy for me to admit, after I had spent so much time developing Shadrack for the position. Shadrack was too much like me. He was kind and understanding to the staff, with a subtle management style that encouraged collaboration. The problem to this approach is that kindness can be taken advantage of by insincere staff looking to defraud the company. Juhudi had let too many of these employees chip away at the company for many years. Juhudi needed someone new who would change this company culture. We needed a tough manager who knew how to get results.

I made a strong case for hiring Bernard to the board, stating that this was exactly the type of person I would have wanted as my replacement. It was not a hard sell, given Bernard's track record and resumé. We made an offer in early March and were hoping to get Bernard to attend our all-staff retreat at the end of at that month, where I could officially introduce him to the staff. The board wanted the rest of our staff to know that I was not being kicked out by the board and was truly leaving on my own accord.

Bernard accepted our offer, to the dismay of those running the parent company of the Rwanda institution

I flew out to Kigali on my way back from a trip to the Democratic Republic of Congo. I met up with Bernard for dinner to answer any questions and clear up any rumors or perceived drama surrounding Juhudi. We were not going to get any time to overlap before I left Juhudi, so this was a good opportunity to build a relationship with him. I was committed to seeing Juhudi succeed after investing so much of my life in the organization over the past six years and I thought I could be a reference in the future.

DRC and the Volcano

Neeta left Kenya in January of 2015 for the US, to look for a job in public health. We would likely be apart until one of us landed a new job someplace. The last few months I had at Juhudi were sad and busy with work. Andreas wanted to have one last big adventure with me so he started planning a trip to climb an active volcano called Nyiragongo, which was in the Democratic Republic of the Congo (DRC).

The DRC had known armed conflict for longer than nearly any other country in Africa. Especially recently in eastern DRC near Lake Kivu, where an ethnic rebel group named FDLR had been carrying out attacks and human rights abuses in the nearby villages since 2002, with the most recent attacks in 2010. Another militant group called M23, which was made up of former DRC government military troops had started the 2012 M23 rebellion against the DRC government in the same Kivu area. The conflict displaced thousands of people and ultimately took control of the city of Goma for a short period. Then the UN had stepped in to aid government troops in disarming the group and initiating peace talks. In March of 2013, the head of the M23 group, Bosco Ntaganda, handed himself in to the US Embassy in Kigali, Rwanda, thus ending the conflict. However, the FDLR was still active along with a few others and there were rumors of the M23 gaining strength again.

Our planned route to the summit of the active volcano was now mostly clear of fighting. Groups of hikers could climb to the 11,382 foot peak and peer into the depths of the crater to the fiery lake of lava below. The volcano had erupted in 2002, pouring lava into the town of Goma before halting at the cool banks of Lake Kivu. Nearly forty percent of the city had been destroyed, killing 147 and forcing 400,000 people to evacuate. So between the threat of the remaining armed paramilitary groups in the jungle and the lava, I think Andreas had picked a perfect trip for me. This was also on the heels of the Ebola outbreak in Western Africa, where some of the cases had turned up in the DRC, just to add to the adventure.

The best way to get to Goma from Nairobi was to fly to Kigali and then travel overland for several hours to the DRC border. Our group had by now grown to twelve people. I had always loved the green rolling hills of Rwanda as well as the clean, well-maintained city of Kigali. The roads were so much better than anything we had in Kenya and all of us were admiring the effectiveness of a benevolent dictator like Rwanda's President Kagame. Once a month, the citizens of Rwanda would spend a day cleaning up their neighborhood of trash, or in some way improving the country. The results were quite clear for anyone visiting to see.

The border crossing into the DRC was about as shady and disorganized as we had expected. It reminded me more of the entrance to a seedy nightclub, with one burly man standing at a gate who acted like the bouncer letting in people he knew (or gave him money) and making the rest stand in line. Large trucks carrying unknown goods passed in and out of the single gate, which only had a metal bar across it, like that of a toll booth.

We handed all our paperwork and passports over to our 'handler' who disappeared into the back room of the immigration building while we all sat on the steps watching the myriad of people cross the border in both directions. While a majority of the crowd were Congolese and Rwandese, carrying live chickens or bags of maize on their daily errands a few who fit the stereotypical image of a Russian mafia figures came through in black SUVs. What was immediately different from Kenya was the heavy UN military presence. Nearly one in four of the vehicles passing through the crossing were white UN vehicles bearing flags from countries as far off as Uruguay, driven by personnel in fatigues. One of our drivers later told us that many of the UN officials live in the beautiful resort town of Gisenyi, next door in Rwanda, and then drive to work on the other side of the border in Goma every morning. This way if things got bad with the rebels they had a safe place to go to in Rwanda.

I managed to slice open a long gash across my right knuckle against the bus window as I was reaching for a pen in my bag to fill out the immigration form. Blood from my hand was gushing all over the form. The Ebola signs were everywhere warning the public about the symptoms and requesting everyone to stay away from sick or bleeding people. Panicking that I might be quarantined, I fished out some toilet paper from my bag and wrapped my hand, then completed the form with my left hand. My writing was barely legible, but since our group seemed legitimate and we were using an official DRC travel agency they let us through. The Congolese in Goma spoke a mix of French, and the Bantu-based Kikongo, but I was amazed to hear many of them understand Kiswahili.

Expecting a lava-covered war zone, I was surprised and thoroughly impressed by Goma. We watched a beautiful sunset along banks of Lake Kivu surrounded by lush, green volcanoes. We had a very nice dinner and then drove through the bustling town. People, dressed in colorful shirts and dresses, flowed in and out of the various buildings, which were blasting music. The volcano we were to climb the next day was called Mt. Nyamuragira, which loomed over us in the distance. Our group made a few references to it as Mt. Doom, from the fiery mountain in the Lord of the Rings.

The next morning we drove along the lava flow, which cut a wide swath through the town, burying everything in its wake under black rubble of lava rock. Our drivers told us in French and Kiswahili about the recent rebel news and how they thought two of the more minor groups might form an alliance to bring more trouble to the government and to UN forces in the region. We bounced along the muddy road out of town towards the volcano, which was covered in dense jungle. A pickup truck loaded with men carrying AK-47s passed us. I had grown accustomed to seeing groups of armed police and military in Nairobi. But this group was not wearing any uniform and two of the men held long rocket-propelled grenade launchers. I asked our driver if they were rebels and he said something about the M23 coming back. Then he muttered something I could not understand in Kikongo along with a scowl, so I did not push him.

Our expedition group had now swelled to twenty-five, with five armed guards, seven porters, two guides and a cook. It looked like we were on a week-long expedition through the wild jungles of the Congo. I was still not sure what we should do if the volcano erupted again and started spewing lava. The guide told me that the lava does not travel too fast and most people can run fast enough to get out of its way. Also, the lava usually erupts out of the side of the volcano from several large vents about halfway to the summit. Once we were past that section we would be safe. A few of my group members wanted to try and roast a marshmallow over lava.

What I had learned about climbing volcanoes like Mt. Kenya, Kilimanjaro, Cotopaxi in Ecuador and Sajama in Bolivia, was that they are steeper than they look. Most of the mountains I grew up with in Colorado held collapsed slopes and ridgelines, which made the ascents easier. Volcanoes usually form a cone of equal pitch on all sides to the summit, however, and there are no other ways to the top.

The climb up Nyamuragira was long and brutal. Several basic cabins were built near the summit for tourists to stay in overnight as shelter against the cold and ferocious winds. One of the women on our trip was a hilarious Canadian, called Claire Markham. She had replaced Mac Parish at Kiva in Nairobi. Claire had contracted altitude sickness along with a few others on the hike but seemed to be able to push through the vomiting and dizziness to make it to the summit.

We were rewarded with some incredible views of Lake Kivu and the towns far below. Billowing puffs of steam and sulfur came from the volcano, which would obscure the views when the wind shifted directions. We climbed the final stretch to the lip of the volcano and peered down. The lava was far below, roughly 800 feet, but we could make out a huge lake of bubbling and cracking lava. It would be hard to roast a marshmallow but the occasional explosion and spray of molten red lava was exciting enough to watch. I found a vent in the rocks where the heated air blew out like a hot hairdryer and we all took turns warming our hands. The sunset was rapid and nightfall brought spectacular stars and a bright moon. The lava was even more pronounced at night with the explosions lighting up the entire crater basin.

We avoided any rebel attacks, eruptions or Ebola outbreaks and safely returned to Nairobi. The trip made me wonder if the DRC might be my next destination to start another social business. There was so much potential in the pockets of civilization in that war-torn country. I would probably need to learn some French, but it was those kinds of places that presented the most opportunity to build a successful business while helping people in dire need.

Finale

Nearly all of the 175 staff attended the company retreat on the shores of Lake Elementaita. I drove the Mobius from Nairobi and parked it in the front of the hotel so all our staff could walk by and see Kenya's first commercially-built car. Our fabulous Mauritian, Fabrice, was full of energy and busy developing the company's internal and external communication practices. This role put him on center stage for the retreat. Fabrice had set up a 'JET on the Bench' event which required the senior management team to sit at the front of the conference hall while our staff asked tough questions. The forum was something unconventional for Kenya and our staff was certainly intimidated. Topics ranged from increasing the travel allowances for branch managers to helping loan officers to better understand their legal rights when making an asset recovery on a loan. Questions were written down and then handed to Fabrice who read them to the management team. It turned out to be a great way to get in the open some heated questions, which helped build trust among the staff and bring more awareness to management of some of the problems in the company.

Bernard had agreed to come by the retreat for a few hours on the last afternoon to greet staff and be formally introduced. He gave a perfect speech, outlining how he wanted to improve the 'people pillar' through training, which calmed fears that he would be making any major changes to staff. The rest of the retreat was a big success and we ended the night with a huge ceremony to recognize our high performing staff. I closed the night with a speech, thanking everyone for the six years and telling the young Kenyan staff that their country needed them to become hard working and just leaders, given the decades of corruption that has held Kenya back in so many ways.

"Since its inception in 2009, Juhudi has provided 52,480 loans worth $30 million and raised over $20 million in investment capital," I reminded them. "We have over 21,000 active clients across its twenty offices and is one of the more respected microfinance institutions in East Africa with global recognition. What is breathtaking to me is knowing that this company has financed a total of 23,100 cows which have produced, on average, 77.5 million liters of milk each year (which we know from our tens of thousands of Echo Mobile survey responses from farmers) valued at over $22 million in the equivalent local Kenyan markets, which is added to the economy each year. We can be proud of ourselves. Juhudi has become the new 'cash cow' of Kenya. This milk not only brings badly needed income to poor families but is also a valuable source of nutrition for the children of our farmers, which is much harder for us to quantify." The roomed cheered in support.

"These outcomes have all derived from a small company that a majority of the investors I spoke to said would never make it and was 'a terrible idea'. Well, we proved them wrong. I think that's a cause for celebration. I'm proud of your achievement, and of mine." Cheers all round.

Sometimes I wonder if we would have been able to help more rural low-income Kenyan farmers simply by giving out the $20 million as donations. We could have purchased close to 50,000 cows with that money. But I still believe the best way to improve the lives of the billion people living in poverty is through well-directed private enterprise and access to the capital markets. It empowers people to be pro-active about their own success. To repay borrowed money, instead of simply receiving a donation, makes them work harder and value their assets more. If Juhudi continues to grow and keep its clients' needs at the forefront of its strategy, then I have no doubt that this model can easily mobilize hundreds of millions of dollars in commercial capital to deploy to millions of rural smallholder farmers living in poverty across East Africa. I just hope the greed and private interest that plagued the growth of Juhudi in its first six years will not continue to hold it back in the next sixty years.

I said goodbye to my good friends, sold my car and moved out of my apartment. My plan was to spend the next three months traveling around South America before making my next move. I somehow managed to fit everything else I owned into four small bags for my flight back to Colorado. I boarded the Emirates Flight 720 and soared off, looking down at Nairobi National Park for the giraffes and wondering what I would do next, after this adventure in Kenya.

Epilogue	Eight Lessons for the Social Entrepreneur

To help those entrepreneurs who do not have time to sit down and read an entire book, I have outlined some of the key lessons I thought might be helpful especially to a social entrepreneur looking to fund a company from impact investors.

1. Fundraising

- Get organized. Build a list of potential investors and keep all of them warm. We had several high-potential investors drop out in the final negotiations and other long-shot investors who suddenly wanted to invest. I found I could keep about ten potential investors well informed during the fundraising process.
- Do not be afraid to talk to investors too early. When I started I had no idea what I was doing but stumbled along to raise $20 million for Juhudi Kilimo. I found that many of the impact investors are quite helpful in asking thought provoking questions or highlighting weaknesses in a business plan. After each meeting take the criticism and incorporate it back into the business plan.
- Win the hearts of the gatekeepers. Convince them of an investment's value and they will do the work for you. It was the junior staff that put together the initial investment memos for their committees and

participated in the due diligence visits. They were the people to fight for our investment later in the process.

- Brutal honesty and transparency never hurt us. It is tempting to only talk about the good things during an investor meeting but I was extremely open with our problems, weaknesses and challenges. Apparently this was a rare asset in Africa and all the European and American investors appreciated the approach.

- Nobody wants to be first to the party. We had an extremely difficult time getting our first major investor since nobody wanted to make a bad investment and be blamed. Several investors expressed interested but none were making a move. We invited all the local investors to a lunch event to generate a buzz and spark competition. It worked. After Kiva first invested the rest were much more eager to invest.

- It is not all about the money. It is nice to focus on funds with deeper pockets that can participate in future investment rounds. However, do not let this aspect outweigh other considerations, such as how the investor will bring value to the board or how quickly decisions can be made. With an equity investor, the relationship is like that of a marriage. Do not jump into a long-term relationship with an equity investor without first being very comfortable.

- Have a few back-ups. Emergency back-up financing or bridge financing to call on quickly is invaluable. Investors will always delay disbursements and nothing is more frustrating than to run out of cash while waiting for an approved investment to hit the bank account. We had an overdraft facility from a local bank, which we used frequently during our early days. Deutsche Bank was also wonderful in quickly approving small amounts of financing to keep us afloat for several months at a time.

- Crowdsourcing is a fantastic source of early-stage financing. Juhudi would not have survived past its first year without the crowd-sourced funding from Kiva. The money was cheap and it put us on the map for other investors. There are several websites out there, all of which can be useful for setting up crowdsourcing campaigns. If you are fortunate enough to work with Kiva make sure to take their process seriously and embed the Kiva process into everyday operations.

2. Impact Investors

- Beware of the structure risks. Impact investors are usually structured as non-profit funds and are willing to take a lower return over a longer investment period, if the investment is providing additional social or environmental benefits. While the structure sounds great the industry is still in its early stages of development but has come a very long way since I started working with them in 2009. One of the main challenges I faced with impact investors is inherent to the structure of the fund. Funds, which were created as nonprofits and funded through donations, tended to lack the profit alignment needed to make critical decisions quickly. Since non-profit funds receive their income through donations and not necessarily from their investments, this focuses the fund's attention on raising the donor money versus responding to the needs of the investment. I had times when we needed to get a critical resolution passed for opening a bank account or accepting a new loan yet the impact investor's staff were all deposed for two weeks since some of the fund's donors were visiting Kenya on a field trip.

- Decision making is extremely slow. Some of this is due to the limited staffing and reliance on pro-bono legal services, but any entrepreneur needs to consider the extended time required of impact investors to make decisions. The pro-bono lawyers tend only to work on legal documents when they have some free time away from their normal jobs and tend to over-engineer the legal agreements since they are quite removed from the business transactions of the investment funds.

- Limited staff experience and high turnover leads to poor governance. Because the salaries and operating expenses of non-profit funds are closely scrutinized, there is a tendency to hire junior staff to represent the funds on boards of their investment companies. While most impact investors have brilliant and hardworking staff, it was difficult for us to have a properly functioning board of directors when the average age was 32 and very few providing any business operational experience. This is also a reason some of the funds experienced higher turnover of investment staff. The staff who could make several multiples of their salary for their skill sets in commercial funds would leave the impact investor after several years to get an MBA.

- Lack of focus on profitability or social impact creates ambiguity. Since many impact investors do not have a specific target return on their fund or investors of their own to repay, this leads to confusion of targets for the investment companies. Social performance goals are also extremely difficult to evaluate for most companies. When a fund has a five-year time frame that it needs to exit its investment then it will help drive the performance of the investment company towards that goal. While it is nice to have flexibility, too much ambiguity on the targets was detrimental to us at Juhudi.

- Pay attention to who funds the investor. I would steer clear of investors who are funded by donations. Of course not all of them are bad. Low interest loans from these sources can be better, but inviting them onto the board can lead to many governance problems such as those we had at Juhudi. Just because an investor is a for-profit does not mean they are not social. A growing number of impact funds are financed through semi-commercial means so they can still have lower return expectations and longer investment periods.

- Technical assistance grants can be wonderful but also do damage in the long run. Many impact investors also provide grants alongside their debt or equity, which can be a tremendous help for building IT systems, training staff or hiring consultants. Juhudi benefited tremendously from these generous grants. I focused these subsidies on activities like training staff and building processes that I did not see as core operations but long-term investments. However we began to depend on these grants to train our staff and improve our operations so did not invest in creating in-house training programs or in-house operational improvement capabilities. I think over the long run this will continue to hurt the company.

3. Partnerships

- Leverage partners, but know what is required. Juhudi could not have survived without the partnerships with local insurance companies for our livestock insurance or the government technical assistance providers who trained many of our farmers just to name two. Partners can bring new markets, products or other assistance at a scale otherwise unattainable to an early-stage company. However keep in mind the different priorities and organizational cultures driving partners as well as the work required to maintain a strong partnership.

- Evaluate partnerships before jumping in too deeply. Juhudi failed to make any partnerships work with any major corporations or government entities but made numerous attempts. Setting up a separate team or dedicated employee to evaluate and manage a partnership can be helpful. I was famous for agreeing to partnerships before adequately evaluating the costs and benefits involved to both parties. This sometimes resulted in frustration after money and time were spent attempting to make a partnership work, which was doomed from the start. Cut off bad partnerships quickly to avoid wasting time and damaging relationships.

4. Social Performance and Impact Measurement

- Great if you can afford it or someone else has offered to do it for you. We used a volunteer to complete our GIIRS assessment, which allowed us to become a certified B-Corporation.
- Align impact metrics with business metrics. By capturing client feedback and basic PPI data we were able to develop better loan products for our farmers. The primary function of the data was to improve the business but we could also generate some nice social impact reports and analysis.
- Leveraging cheap yet effective data collection technologies like Echo Mobile was a game changer. We did not need to spend tens of thousands of dollars on focus groups and paper surveys.

- Do not do it simply to please investors or in the hope of raising money. Shockingly, none of our initial impact investors required any significant social impact studies before investing. Perhaps this has changed now but the social performance work we did had no impact on the amount of funds we were able to raise. This does not mean impact measurement should not be done.

5. Fraud

- Build culture and systems. I always felt that the best protection against fraud is good systems with checks and balances along with a strong anti-fraud company culture. This is easier said than done. Especially in a country that has enormous social pressure to provide economic support to even distant relatives. When our staff is faced with providing health care payments for a dying uncle or school fees for young children who lost a father to HIV, it is tempting to steal money from a rich company.
- Manage the eighty percent. I was continually shocked by the people I had hired, trained, trusted and become friends with, who would later defraud the company. Aleke once told me that about ten percent of people will steal from you no matter what and another ten percent will never steal from you. The remaining eighty percent will only steal if there is a low likelihood of being caught. Our goals were to remove as much of the temptation as possible from the eighty percent through strong systems and company culture. Screen out the bad ten percent of characters before hiring them and have a zero tolerance policy for fraud and make examples out of them if caught.

Then with the remaining ten percent who would never steal, put them in the risk management or audit departments.

6. Technology

- System is king. I said earlier that if I were to start with Juhudi again I would start with a robust system and then build the people and processes around it. The ability to track and use real-time reliable data is essential in decision-making. A process that is well supported or automated through technology tends to be much easier to scale quickly. A workforce takes time to mature and learn which can be difficult when the clock is running on reaching profitability.

- Field test first but not for too long. Before we launched our flexible Salesforce.com cloud system, we first tested using tablets in rural Kenya with a smaller leads management system. From that experience we were able to determine that our loan officers could use the tablets to connect to the internet, not have the tablets stolen and the battery life could get through most of the day. Of course we did not address all of our concerns from the initial testing but the testing could have gone on forever. We needed to establish a timeline to make a decision to adopt the new technology.

- Technology will not solve all problems. It is easy to think technology can solve all of a company's problems but new technology can also disrupt a well-functioning existing process. Someone once told me "more mobile, more problems" which certainly was true in many of our challenges of implementing mobile technology in rural Kenya. Many of the local application developers in Nairobi developed mobile solutions for farmers without actually consulting farmers about user interfaces or applicability. That all being said, Juhudi benefited tremendously overall from some of the technology implemented but only after it was well field tested and evaluated.

- Hire an expert to help pick a new system. Perhaps this is a later step in a company's life cycle but I was happy we used competent IT consultants to help us develop our requirements for a new system and then evaluate the bids from vendors. However when implementing the new system, it is best to be driven by the company.

7. People

- Use the volunteers to fill gaps but build a workforce of full-time committed local employees. The social enterprise community is full of fabulous volunteers with MBAs, JDs or other technical skills. Juhudi benefited significantly from our volunteers from McKinsey, Google, SAP, Accenture and others. In Kenya, I found that we could hire an experienced expatriate volunteer for a fraction of the cost of a Kenyan manager with slightly less experience. The temptation is to then build the organization around expat management but this creates long-term risks for the company if (and when) the expats leave. Some of our most effective and loyal staff were junior Kenyan staff who we trained with the expatriates and then promoted into management. Of course there is a risk that these junior staff will then be poached away, as happened to us with the Acumen Fellows program. We were fortunate to have an extremely low turnover at Juhudi over the first six years of operations. I think a lot of it was related to our mission to help farmers and the culture of growth and innovation which attracted the younger workforce.

- Make key management hires slowly, after serious consideration. Hiring the "almost-right" person quickly is much more detrimental than not hiring anyone. A three-month evaluation period can be helpful but the best is to try and simulate a work situation or problem during the interview.
- When hiring for a technical role you do not understand, bring in an objective expert to evaluate the candidates. Then listen to those experts.

8. The lonely entrepreneur

- Find a group of other entrepreneurs. It is tough as a lone entrepreneur to deal with all the stress and chaos of starting a business. Fortunately, I had Aleke to work with for the first few years. A co-founder is a nice thing to have. I also loved the opportunities to vent to other entrepreneurs in Nairobi, like Joel and Andreas, who were sharing many of the same challenges. One of the greatest outcomes of some of the incubators like Mulago Foundation and GSBI was the opportunity to meet similar minded entrepreneurs around the world. I would highly recommend building a network of peers before starting a company.
- Read The *Hard Thing About Hard Things*, by Ben Horowitz. I found this book very helpful when I was going through some of our stressful death spirals at Juhudi. The "struggle" outlined in the book is something that all entrepreneurs endure. It made me quite glad Juhudi was not a publicly traded company with the entire world watching in the news. I found another story in Inc. Magazine

comparing being an entrepreneur to riding a lion. Everyone around is saying how amazing that person is to be riding a lion. But the person riding the lion is wondering how they got on the lion in the first place and how to get off without being eaten.[xii]

[xii] Jessica Bruder "The Psychological Price of Entrepreneurship," Inc. Magazine, September 2013.

About the Author

Nat Robinson was recently the Chief Executive Officer and founder of Juhudi Kilimo Company Limited which provides micro-asset financing to rural smallholder farmers in Kenya. Nat is originally from the U.S. but has traveled, worked or studied in over 60 countries across six continents in the areas of business, nonprofit and government. After working as a financial consultant in China and then in the U.S. for Accenture, he accepted a short-term project in Kenya with the K-Rep Development Agency (KDA) and the Grassroots Business Fund in 2008. After the project, Nat decided to stay in Kenya and helped launch what is now Juhudi Kilimo. He received a sponsorship from the UNDP and IFC African Management Services Company (AMSCO) to be the company's CFO and in 2010 he was appointed to the CEO. Juhudi Kilimo was recognized in 2011 at the World Economic Forum with the Social Entrepreneur of the Year Award and then in 2013 by CIO Magazine's

CIO 100 list of companies using innovative technology to deliver business value. Juhudi Kilimo is supported by investors such as the Acumen Fund, Ford Foundation, Rockefeller Foundation, Grameen Foundation and the Soros Economic Development Fund. Nat is a Rainer Arnhold Fellow with the Mulago Foundation, served on the board of the Kenyan Association of Microfinance Institutions, and has an MBA from Vanderbilt University in Tennessee.

Made in the USA
Middletown, DE
02 May 2016